THE BRITISH CAMPAIGN
IN FRANCE AND FLANDERS
1914

BOOKS BY A. CONAN DOYLE

THE FIRM OF GIRDLESTONE.
THE WHITE COMPANY.
THE MYSTERY OF CLOOMBER.
MICAH CLARKE.
THE REFUGEES.
THE CAPTAIN OF THE POLESTAR.
THE DOINGS OF RAFFLES HAW.
THE GREAT SHADOW.
THE PARASITE.
A STUDY IN SCARLET.
THE SIGN OF FOUR.
THE ADVENTURES OF SHERLOCK HOLMES.
THE MEMOIRS OF SHERLOCK HOLMES.
THE RETURN OF SHERLOCK HOLMES.
ROUND THE RED LAMP.
THE EXPLOITS OF BRIGADIER GERARD.
THE STARK-MUNRO LETTERS.
RODNEY STONE.
THE TRAGEDY OF THE KOROSKO.
UNCLE BERNAC.
THE GREEN FLAG.
SONGS OF ACTION.
SONGS OF THE ROAD.
THE GREAT BOER WAR.
A DUET, WITH AN OCCASIONAL CHORUS.
THE HOUND OF THE BASKERVILLES.
THE ADVENTURES OF GERARD.
SIR NIGEL.
THE VALLEY OF FEAR.
THE LAST GALLEY.

THE BRITISH CAMPAIGN

IN FRANCE AND FLANDERS

1914

BY

ARTHUR CONAN DOYLE

AUTHOR OF
'THE GREAT BOER WAR,' ETC.

THIRD EDITION

The Naval & Military Press Ltd

Published by

The Naval & Military Press Ltd
Unit 10 Ridgewood Industrial Park,
Uckfield, East Sussex,
TN22 5QE England

Tel: +44 (0) 1825 749494
Fax: +44 (0) 1825 765701

www.naval-military-press.com
www.military-genealogy.com

In reprinting in facsimile from the original, any imperfections are inevitably reproduced and the quality may fall short of modern type and cartographic standards.

TO

GENERAL SIR WILLIAM ROBERTSON

THIS CHRONICLE OF THE GREAT WAR

IN WHICH HE RENDERED

SUCH INVALUABLE SERVICE TO HIS COUNTRY

IS

DEDICATED

PREFACE

It is continually stated that it is impossible to bring out at the present time any accurate history of the war. No doubt this is true so far as some points of the larger strategy are concerned, for the motives at the back of them have not yet been cleared up. It is true also as regards many incidents which have exercised the minds of statesmen and of many possibilities which have worried the soldiers. But so far as the actual early events of our own campaign upon the Continent are concerned there is no reason why the approximate truth should not now be collected and set forth. I believe that the narrative in this volume will in the main stand the test of time, and that the changes of the future will consist of additions rather than of alterations or subtractions.

The present volume deals only with the events of 1914 in the British fighting-line in France and Belgium. A second volume dealing with 1915 will be published within a few months. It is intended that a third volume, covering the current year, shall carry on this contemporary narrative of a tremendous episode.

From the first days of the war I have devoted much of my time to the accumulation of evidence from first-hand sources as to the various happenings of these great days. I have built up my narrative from letters, diaries, and interviews from the hand or lips of men who have been soldiers in our armies, the deeds of which it was my ambition to understand and to chronicle. In many cases I have been privileged to submit my descriptions of the principal incidents to prominent actors in them, and to receive their corrections or endorsement. I can say with certainty, therefore, that a great deal of this work is not only accurate, but that it is very precisely correct in its detail. The necessary restrictions which forbade the mention of numbered units have now been removed, a change made possible by the very general re-arrangements which have recently taken place. I am able, therefore, to deal freely with my material. As that material is not always equally full, it may have occasionally led to a want of proportion, where the brigade occupies a line and the battalion a paragraph. In extenuation of such faults, and of the omissions which are unavoidable, I can only plead the difficulty of the task and throw myself upon the reader's good nature. Some compensation for such shortcoming may be found in the fact that a narrative written at the time reflects the warm emotions which these events aroused amongst us more clearly than the more measured story of the future historian can do.

It may seem that the political chapters are somewhat long for a military work, but the reader will

PREFACE

find that in subsequent volumes there are no further politics, so that this survey of the European conditions of 1914 is a lead up to the whole long narrative of the actual contest.

I would thank my innumerable correspondents (whom I may not name) for their very great help. I would also admit the profit which I have derived from reading Coleman's *Mons to Ypres,* and especially Lord Ernest Hamilton's *The First Seven Divisions.* These books added some new facts, and enabled me to check many old ones. Finally, I desire to thank my friend Mr. P. L. Forbes for his kind and intelligent assistance in arranging my material.

ARTHUR CONAN DOYLE.

WINDLESHAM, CROWBOROUGH,
October 1916.

CONTENTS

CHAPTER I
THE BREAKING OF THE PEACE . . PAGE 1

CHAPTER II
THE OPENING OF THE WAR . . 31

CHAPTER III
THE BATTLE OF MONS

The landing of the British in France—The British leaders—The advance to Mons—The defence of the bridges of Nimy—The holding of the canal—The fateful telegram—The rearguard actions of Frameries, Wasmes, and Dour—The charge of the Lancers—The fate of the Cheshires—The 7th Brigade at Solesmes—The Guards in action—The Germans' rude awakening —The Connaughts at Pont-sur-Sambre 50

CHAPTER IV
THE BATTLE OF LE CATEAU

The order of battle at Le Cateau—The stand of the 2nd Suffolks— Major Yate's V.C.—The fight for the quarries—The splendid work of the British guns—Difficult retirement of the Fourth Division —The fate of the 1st Gordons—Results of the battle—Exhaustion of the Army—The destruction of the 2nd Munsters—A cavalry fight—The news in Great Britain—The views of General Joffre— Battery L—The action of Villars-Cotteret—Reunion of the Army 96

CHAPTER V

THE BATTLE OF THE MARNE

The general situation—" Die grosse Zeit "—The turn of the tide—The Battle of the Ourcq—The British advance—Cavalry fighting—The 1st Lincolns and the guns—6th Brigade's action at Hautvesnes—9th Brigade's capture of Germans at Vinly—The problem of the Aisne—Why the Marne is one of the great battles of all time 138

CHAPTER VI

THE BATTLE OF THE AISNE

The hazardous crossing of the Aisne—Wonderful work of the sappers—The fight for the sugar factory—General advance of the Army—The 4th (Guards) Brigade's difficult task—Cavalry as a mobile reserve—The Sixth Division—Hardships of the Army—German breach of faith—*Tâtez toujours*—The general position—Attack upon the West Yorks—Counter-attack by Congreve's 18th Brigade—Rheims Cathedral—Spies—The siege and fall of Antwerp . 162

CHAPTER VII

THE LA BASSÉE—ARMENTIÈRES OPERATIONS

The great battle line—Advance of Second Corps—Death of General Hamilton—The farthest point—Fate of the 2nd Royal Irish—The Third Corps—Exhausted troops—First fight of Neuve Chapelle—The Indians take over—The Lancers at Warneton—Pulteney's operations—Action of Le Gheir 200

CHAPTER VIII

THE FIRST BATTLE OF YPRES

The Seventh Division—Its peculiar excellence—Its difficult position—A deadly ordeal—Desperate attacks on Seventh Division—Destruction of 2nd Wilts—Hard fight of 20th Brigade—Arrival of First Corps—Advance of Haig's Corps—Fight of Pilken Inn—Bravery of enemy—Advance of Second Division—Fight of

CONTENTS xiii

PAGE

Kruiseik cross-roads—Fight of Zandvoorde—Fight of Gheluvelt
—Advance of Worcesters—German recoil—General result—A
great crisis 232

CHAPTER IX

THE FIRST BATTLE OF YPRES (*continued*)

Attack upon the cavalry—The struggle at Messines—The London Scots
in action—Rally to the north—Terrible losses—Action of Zillebeke—Record of the Seventh Division—Situation at Ypres—
Attack of the Prussian Guard—Confused fighting—End of the first
Battle of Ypres—Death of Lord Roberts—The Eighth Division . 278

CHAPTER X

A RETROSPECT AND GENERAL SUMMARY

Position of Italy—Fall of German colonies—Sea affairs—Our Allies . 311

CHAPTER XI

THE WINTER LULL OF 1914

Increase of the Army—Formation of the Fifth Corps—The visit of
the King—Third Division at Petit Bois—The fight at Givenchy
—Heavy losses of the Indians—Fine advance of Manchesters—
Advance of the First Division—Singular scenes at Christmas . 318

INDEX 337

MAPS AND PLANS

Map to illustrate the British Campaign in France and Flanders, 1914	*face p.* 1

	PAGE
Position of Second Army Corps at Mons, August 23	59
First Morning of Retreat of Second Army Corps, August 24	81
Sketch of Battle of Le Cateau, August 26	101
Line of Retreat from Mons	125
L Battery Action, September 1, 1914	129
British Advance during the Battle of the Marne	147
British Advance at the Aisne	165
Diagram to illustrate Operations of Smith-Dorrien's Second Corps and Pulteney's Third Corps from October 11 to October 19, 1914	205
Southern End of British Line	213
General View of Seat of Operations	223
Line of Seventh Division (Capper) and Third Cavalry Division (Byng) from October 16 onwards	235
General Scene of Operations	257
Sketch of Battle of Gheluvelt, October 31	267

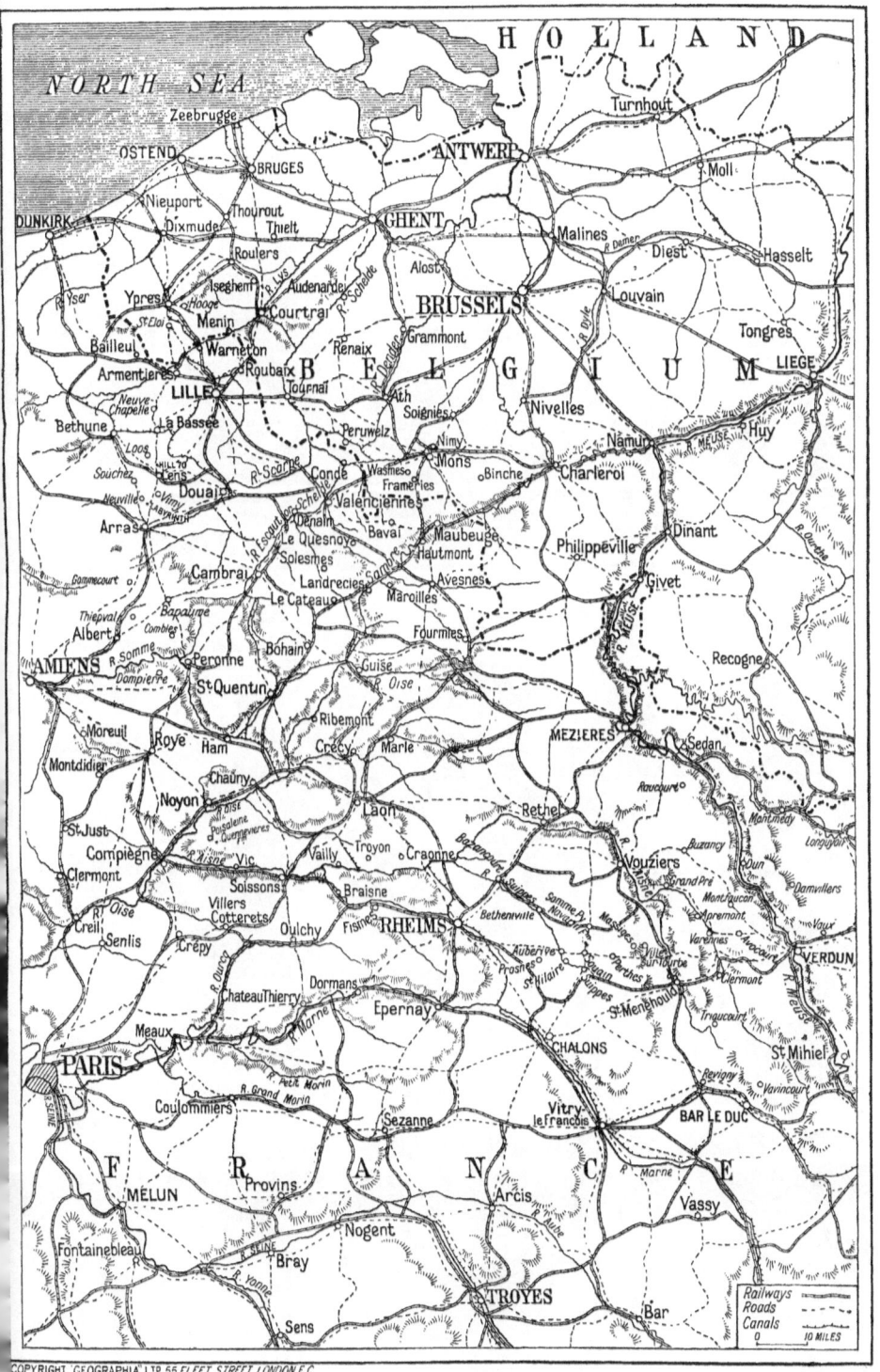

CHAPTER I

THE BREAKING OF THE PEACE

IN the frank, cynical, and powerful book of General Bernhardi which has been so often quoted in connection with the war there is one statement which is both true and important. It is, that no one in Great Britain thought seriously of a war with Germany before the year 1902. As a German observer he has fixed this date, and a British commentator who cast back through the history of the past would surely endorse it. Here, then, is a point of common agreement from which one can construct a scheme of thought.

Why then should the British people in the year 1902 begin to seriously contemplate the possibility of a war with Germany? It might be argued by a German apologist that this date marks an appreciation by Great Britain that Germany was a great trade rival who might with advantage be crushed. But the facts would not sustain such a conclusion. The growth of German trade and of German wealth was a phenomenon with which the British were familiar. It had been constant since the days when Bismarck changed the policy of his country from free trade to protection, and it had competed for twenty years without the idea of war having entered British

CHAPTER I.
The breaking of the peace.

minds. On the contrary, the prevailing economic philosophy in Great Britain was, that trade reacts upon trade, and that the successful rival becomes always the best customer. It is true that manufacturers expressed occasional irritation at the methods of German commerce, such as the imitation of British trade-marks and shoddy reproductions of British products. The Fatherland can produce both the best and the worst, and the latter either undersold us or forced down our own standards. But apart from this natural annoyance, the growing trade of Germany produced no hostility in Great Britain which could conceivably have led to an armed conflict. Up to the year 1896 there was a great deal of sympathy and of respect in Great Britain for the German Empire. It was felt that of all Continental Powers she was the one which was most nearly allied to Britain in blood, religion, and character. The fact that in 1890 Lord Salisbury deliberately handed over to Germany Heligoland—an island which blockaded her chief commercial port and the harbour of her warships—must show once for all how entirely Germany lay outside of any possible world-struggle which could at that time be foreseen. France has always had its warm partisans in this country, but none the less it can most truthfully be said that during all the years that Britain remained in political isolation she would, had she been forced to take sides, have assuredly chosen to stand by the Triple Alliance. It is hard now to recall those days of French pinpricks and of the evil effects which they produced. Germany's foreign policy is her own affair, and the German people are the judges of those who control it, but to us it must appear absolutely demented in taking a line which has driven this great world-power away from her side—or, putting it at its lowest, away from an absolute neutrality, and into the ranks of her enemies.

In 1896 there came the first serious chill in the relations between the two countries. It arose from the famous telegram to Kruger at the time of the Jameson Raid—a telegram which bore the name of the Kaiser, but which is understood to have been drafted by Baron Marschall von Bieberstein. Whoever was responsible for it did his country a poor service, for British feelings were deeply hurt at such an intrusion into a matter which bore no direct relation to Germany. Britons had put themselves thoroughly in the wrong. Britain admitted and deplored it. Public opinion was the more sensitive to outside interference, and the telegram of congratulation from the Emperor to Kruger was felt to be an uncalled-for impertinence. The matter passed, however, and would have been forgiven and forgotten but for the virulent agitation conducted against us in Germany during the Boer War—an agitation which, it is only fair to say, appeared to receive no support from the Kaiser himself, who twice visited England during the course of the struggle. It could not be forgotten, however, that Von Bülow, the Chancellor, assumed an offensive attitude in some of his speeches, that the very idea of an Anglo-German Alliance put forward by Chamberlain in 1900 was scouted by the German Press, and that in the whole country there was hardly a paper which did not join in a chorus of unreasoned hatred and calumny against ourselves, our policy, and our arms. The incident was a perfectly astounding revelation to the British,

CHAPTER I.

The breaking of the peace.

who looked back at the alliance between the two countries, and had imagined that the traditions of such battles as Minden or Dettingen, where British blood had been freely shed in Prussia's quarrel, really stood for something in their present relations. Britons were absolutely unconscious of anything which had occurred to alter the bonds which history had formed. It was clear, once for all, that this was mere self-deception, and as the British are a practical race, who are more concerned with what is than why it is, they resigned themselves to the situation and adjusted their thoughts to this new phase of their relations.

But soon a new phenomenon engaged their attention. They had already realised that the Germans, for some motive which appeared to them to be entirely inadequate, were filled with hatred, and would do the British Empire an injury if they had the power. Hitherto, they had never had the power. But now it was evident that they were forging a weapon which might enable them to gratify their malevolence. In 1900 was passed the famous German law regulating the increase of their navy. The British, preoccupied by their South African War, took no great notice of it at the time, but from 1902 onwards it engaged their attention to an ever-increasing degree. The original law was ambitious and far-reaching, but it was subjected to several modifications, each of which made it more formidable. By a system as inexorable as Fate, year after year added to the force which was being prepared at Wilhelmshaven and at Kiel—a force entirely out of proportion to the amount of German commerce to be defended or of German coast-line to be protected. The greatest army in the world was rapidly being supplemented by a fleet which would be dangerously near, both in numbers and quality, to our own. The British Admiralty, more influenced by party politics than the German, showed at times commendable activity, and at other periods inexcusable indifference. On the whole, it was well ahead in its building programmes, for a wide circle of the public had become thoroughly awakened to the danger, and kept up a continual and most justifiable agitation for a broader margin of safety. Fortunately, the two final rulers of the Navy—McKenna and Churchill—rose to their responsibilities, and, in spite of a clamour from a section of their own party, insisted upon an adequate preponderance of naval construction. A deep debt of gratitude is owed also to the action of Lord Fisher, who saw the danger afar off and used all his remarkable powers of organisation and initiative to ensure that his country should be ready for the approaching struggle.

Great Britain, being much exercised in mind by the menacing tone of Germany, expressed not only in her great and rapid naval preparations, but in an astonishing outburst of minatory speeches and literature from professors, journalists, and other leaders of the people, began from 1902 onwards to look round her for allies. Had she continued to remain isolated, some turn of the political wheel might have exposed her to a Continental coalition under the leadership and inspiration of this bitter enemy. But for the threats of Germany, Britain would in all probability have been able to keep aloof from entanglements, but as it was, the enemies of her enemy became of necessity her friends. In an attempt to preserve her independence of action so far as was still possible, she refused to form an alliance, and only committed

6 THE BRITISH CAMPAIGN, 1914

CHAPTER I.

The breaking of the peace.

herself in a vague fashion to an ill-defined *entente*. By settling several outstanding causes of friction with France, an agreement was come to in the year 1903 which was extended to Russia in 1907. The general purport of such an arrangement was, that the sympathies of Great Britain were with the Dual Alliance, and that these sympathies would be translated into action if events seemed to warrant it. An aggressive policy on the part of France or Russia would be absolutely discountenanced by Britain, but if France were attacked Britain would pledge herself to do her utmost to prevent her from being overwhelmed. It was recognised that a victorious Germany would constitute a serious menace to the British Empire—a fact which neither the Pan-German fanatics nor the German national Press would ever permit us to forget. In this policy of insuring against a German attack King Edward VII. took a deep interest, and the policy is itself attributed to him in Germany, but as a matter of fact it represented the only sane course of action which was open to the nation. Germans are fond of representing King Edward's action as the cause of subsequent events, whereas a wider knowledge would show them that it was really the effect of five years of German irritation and menace.

This, then, was the political situation up to the time of the actual outbreak of war. Upon the one side were the German and Austrian Empires in a solid alliance, while Italy was nominally allied, but obviously moved upon an orbit of her own. On the other hand, Russia and France were solidly allied, with Britain moving upon an independent orbit which had more relation with that of her friends than Italy's with that of Central Europe. It might clearly

THE BREAKING OF THE PEACE

have been foreseen that Britain's fate would be that of France, while Italy would break away under any severe test, for a number of open questions divided her vitally from her secular enemy to the north-east. The whole story of the campaign of Tripoli in 1911 showed very clearly how independent, and even antagonistic, were the interests and actions of Italy.

Germany, in the meanwhile, viewed with considerable annoyance the formation of the elastic but very real ties which united France and Britain, while she did not cease to continue the course of action which had encouraged them. It had been one of the axioms of Wilhelmstrasse that whilst the British occupied Egypt, no friendship was possible between them and the French. Even now they were incredulous that such a thing could be, and they subjected it to a succession of tests. They desired to see whether the friendship was a reality, or whether it was only for fair-weather use and would fly to pieces before the stress of storm. Twice they tried it, once in 1905 when they drove France into a conference at Algeciras, and again in 1911, when in a time of profound peace they stirred up trouble by sending a gunboat to Agadir in south-western Morocco, an event which brought Europe to the very edge of war. In each case the *entente* remained so close and firm that it is difficult to imagine that they were really surprised by our actions in 1914, when the enormous provocation of the breach of the Belgian treaty was added to our promise to stand by France in any trouble not of her own making.

Allusion has been made to the campaign of threats and abuse which had been going on for many years in Germany, but the matter is of such importance in its

CHAPTER I.

The breaking of the peace.

bearing upon the outbreak of war that it requires some fuller discussion. For a long period before matters became acute between the two countries, a number of writers, of whom Nietzsche and Treitschke are the best known, had inoculated the German spirit with a most mischievous philosophy, which grew the more rapidly as it was dropped into the favourable soil of Prussian militarism. Nietzsche's doctrines were a mere general defence of might as against right, and of violent brutality against everything which we associate with Christianity and Civilisation. The whooping savage bulked larger in this perverted philosophy than the saint or the martyr. His views, however, though congenial to a certain class of the German people, had no special international significance. The typical brute whom he exalted was blonde, but a brute of any other tint would presumably suffice. It was different in the case of Treitschke. He was a historian, not a philosopher, with nothing indefinite or abstract about his teaching. He used his high position as Professor in the Berlin University to preach the most ardent Chauvinism, and above all to teach the rising generation of Germans that their special task was to have a reckoning with England and to destroy the British Empire, which for some reason he imagined to be degenerate and corrupt. He has passed away before he could see the ruin which he helped to bring about, for there is no doubt that his deeds lived after him, and that he is one of half a dozen men who were prominent in guiding their country along the path which has ended in the abyss. Scores of other lesser writers repeated and exaggerated his message. Prominent among these was General von Bernhardi, a man of high standing and a very great authority upon theoretical warfare. In the volume on *Germany and the Next War*, which has been already quoted, he declared in the year 1911 that Germany should and would do exactly what it has done in 1914. Her antagonists, her allies, and her general strategy are all set forth with a precision which shows that German thinkers had entirely made up their minds as to the course of events, and that the particular pretext upon which war would be waged was a matter of secondary importance. These and similar sentiments naturally increased the uneasiness and resentment in Great Britain, where the taxation had risen constantly in the endeavour to keep pace with German preparations, until it was generally felt that such a state of things could not continue without some crisis being reached. The cloud was so heavy that it must either pass or burst.

The situation had been aggravated by the fact that in order to win popular assent to the various increases of the naval estimates in Germany, constantly recurring anti-British agitations were deliberately raised with alarms of an impending attack. As Britain had never thought of attacking Germany during the long years when she had been almost defenceless at sea, it was difficult to perceive why she should do so now; but none the less the public and the politicians were gulled again and again by this device, which, while it achieved its purpose of obtaining the money, produced a corresponding resentment in Great Britain. Sometimes these manœuvres to excite public opinion in favour of an increased navy went to extreme lengths which might well have justified an official remonstrance from England. A flagrant example was the arrest, trial, and condemnation of Captain Stewart for espionage upon the evidence of a suborned and perjured criminal. It is a story which is little to the credit of the Imperial Government, of the High Court at Leipzig, or of the British authorities who failed to protect their fellow-countryman from most outrageous treatment.

So much for the causes which helped to produce an evil atmosphere between the two countries. Looking at the matter from the German point of view, there were some root-causes out of which this monstrous growth had come, and it is only fair that these should be acknowledged and recorded. These causes can all be traced to the fact that Britain stood between Germany and that world-empire of which she dreamed. This depended upon circumstances over which this country had no control, and which she could not modify if she had wished to do so. Britain, through her maritime power and through the energy of her merchants, had become a great world-power when Germany was still a collection of petty States. When Germany became a powerful Empire with a rising population and an immense commerce, she found that the choice places of the world, and those most fitted for the spread of a transplanted European race, were already filled up. It was not a matter which Britain could help, nor could she alter it, since Canada, Australasia, and South Africa would not, even if she had desired it, be transferred to German rule. And yet it formed a national grievance, and if we can put ourselves in the place of the Germans we may admit that it was galling that the surplus of their manhood should go to build up the strength of an alien and possibly a hostile State. To this point we could fully see that grievance—or rather that misfortune, since no one was in truth to blame in the matter. It was forgotten by their people that the Colonial Empire of the British and of the French had been built up by much outlay of blood and treasure, extending over three centuries. Germany had existed as a united State for less than half a century, and already during that time had built up a very considerable oversea dominion. It was unreasonable to suppose that she could at once attain the same position as her fully grown rivals.

CHAPTER I.

The breaking of the peace.

Thus this German discontent was based upon fixed factors which could no more be changed by Britain than the geographical position which has laid her right across the German exit to the oceans of the world. That this deeply rooted national sentiment, which for ever regarded Britain as the Carthage to which they were destined to play the part of Rome, would sooner or later have brought about war, is beyond all doubt. There are a score of considerations which show that a European war had long been planned, and that finally the very date, determined by the completion of the broadened Kiel Canal, had been approximately fixed. The importations of corn, the secret preparations of giant guns, the formations of concrete gun-platforms, the early distribution of mobilisation papers, the sending out of guns for auxiliary cruisers, the arming of the German colonies, all point to a predetermined rupture. If it could not be effected on one pretext, it certainly would on another. As a matter of fact, an occasion was furnished by means which have not yet been fully cleared up. It was one which admirably suited the German book, since it enabled her to make her ally the apparent protagonist and so secure her fidelity to the bond. At the same time, by making the cause of quarrel one which affected only the Slavonic races, she hoped to discourage and detach the more liberal Western Powers and so divide the ranks of the Allies from the outset. It is possible, though not certain, that she might have effected this in the case of Great Britain, but for her own stupendous blunder in the infraction of Belgian neutrality, which left us a united nation in our agreement as to the necessity of war.

The political balance of the Great Powers of Europe is so delicately adjusted that any weakening of one means a general oscillation of all. The losses of Russia in a sterile campaign in East Asia in 1904 disturbed the whole peace of the world. Germany took advantage of it at once to bully France over Morocco; and in 1908, judging correctly that Russia was still unfit for war, Austria, with the connivance and help of Germany, tore up the Treaty of Berlin without reference to its other signatories, and annexed the provinces of Bosnia and Herzegovina. Russia immediately issued a futile protest, as did Great Britain, but the latter had no material interest at stake. It was otherwise with Russia. She was the hereditary guardian of Slav interests which were directly attacked by this incorporation of an unwilling Slav population into the Austrian Empire. Unable for the moment to prevent it, she waited in silent wrath for the chance of the future, humiliated and exasperated by the knowledge that she had been bullied at the moment of her temporary weakness. So great had been the indignity that it was evident that were she to tolerate a second one it would mean the complete abandonment of her leadership of the race.

On June 28, 1914, the Archduke Francis Ferdinand,

THE BREAKING OF THE PEACE

heir to the throne of the Austrian Empire, made a state visit to Sarajevo in the newly annexed provinces. Here he was assassinated, together with his wife. The immediate criminals were two youths named Princip and Cabrinovic, but what exact forces were at the back of them, or whether they merely represented local discontent, have never yet been clearly shown. Austria was, however, naturally incensed against Serbia, which was looked upon as the centre of all aggressive Slavonic action. Politics take fantastic shapes in this south-eastern corner of Europe, and murder, abduction, forgery, and perjury are weapons which in the past have been freely used by all parties. The provocation in this instance was so immense and the crime so monstrous that had it been established after trustworthy examination that Serbia had indeed been directly connected with it, there is no doubt that the whole of Europe, including Russia, would have acquiesced in any reasonable punishment which could be inflicted. Certainly the public opinion of Great Britain would have been unanimous in keeping clear of any quarrel which seemed to uphold the criminals.

Austria seems to have instantly made up her mind to push the matter to an extreme conclusion, as is shown by the fact that mobilisation papers were received by Austrians abroad, bearing the date June 30, so that they were issued within two days of the crime. An inquiry was held in connection with the trial of the assassins, which was reported to have implicated individual Serbians in the murder plot, but no charge was made against the Serbian Government. Had Austria now demanded the immediate trial and punishment of these accomplices, she would

Chapter I.
The breaking of the peace.

once again have had the sympathy of the civilised world. Her actual action was far more drastic, and gave impartial observers the conviction that she was endeavouring not to obtain reparation but to ensure war. It is inconceivable that so important a document as her ultimatum was launched without the approval of Berlin, and we have already seen that Germany was in a mood for war. The German newspapers, even before the Austrian demands were made, had begun to insist that in view of the distracted domestic politics of Great Britain, and of the declaration by M. Humbert in the French Senate that the army was unprepared, the hour for definite settlements had arrived.

The Austrian ultimatum was such a demand as one nation has never yet addressed to another. Indeed, it could hardly be said that Serbia would remain a nation if she submitted to it. Some clauses, though severe, were within the bounds of reason. That papers should not be allowed to incite hatred, and that secret societies which were supposed to be connected with the crime should be forcibly suppressed, were not unfair demands. So, too, that all accessories to the plot, some of whom are mentioned by name, should be tried, and that certain measures to prevent a possible recurrence of such plots should be adopted. All these demands might be justified, and each of them was, as a matter of fact, accepted by Serbia. The impossible conditions were that Austrian judges should sit in Serbia upon political cases and that delegates of Austria should have partial administrative control in the neighbouring kingdom. Even these outrageous demands were not rejected absolutely by the Serbian Government, though it proclaimed itself to be unable to accept them in the crude form in which they were presented. A humble and conciliatory reply concluded with an expression of the desire to submit any point still open to impartial arbitration. The Austrian Government—or the forces behind it—appeared, however, to have no desire at all to find a peaceful solution. So precipitate were they in their action, that on the receipt of the Serbian reply, in less than an hour the Austrian Minister had left Belgrade, and a diplomatic rupture, the immediate prelude to war, had taken place between the two countries. So far only two figures were on the stage, but already vast shadows were looming in the wings, and all the world was hushed at the presentiment of coming tragedy.

It has been shown that Russia, the elder brother of the Slav races, had once already been humiliated over Austrian policy and could not be indifferent to this new attempt to coerce a Slavonic people. The King of Serbia in his sore need appealed to the Czar and received a sympathetic reply. A moderate castigation of Serbia might have been condoned by Russia, but she could not contemplate unmoved a course of action which would practically destroy a kindred State. The Austrian army was already mobilising, so Russia also began to mobilise in the south. Events crowded rapidly upon each other. On July 28 came the declaration of war from Austria to Serbia. Three days later—days which were employed by Great Britain in making every possible effort to prevent the extension of the mischief— Germany as Austria's ally declared war upon Russia. Two days later Germany declared war upon France. The current ran swiftly as it drew nearer to Niagara.

Chapter I.

The breaking of the peace.

The scope of this chronicle is more immediately concerned with the doings of Great Britain in this sudden and frightful misfortune which had fallen upon Europe. Her peaceful efforts were thrust aside, for she was dealing with those who had predetermined that there should be no peace. Even Austria, the prime mover in discord, had shown herself inclined to treat at the last moment, but Germany had hastened her onwards by a sudden ultimatum to Russia. From that instant the die was cast. The attitude of France was never in doubt. She was taken at a disadvantage, for her President was abroad when the crisis broke out, but the most chivalrous of nations could be relied upon to fulfil her obligations. She took her stand at once by the side of her ally. The one all-important question upon which the history of the world would depend, as so often before, was the action of Great Britain.

Sir Edward Grey had proposed a conference of ambassadors to deal with the situation, a suggestion which was set aside by Germany. So long as the matter was purely Balkan it was outside the sphere of special British interests, but day by day it was becoming more clear that France would be involved, and a large party in Great Britain held that it would be impossible for us to stand by and witness any further dismembering of our neighbour. Thus the shadow which had settled so heavily upon the south-east of Europe was creeping across from east to west until it was already darkening the future of Britain. It was obviously the German game, whatever her ultimate designs might be upon the British Empire, to endeavour to keep it peaceful until she had disposed of her Continental opponents. For this reason a strong bid was made for British neutrality upon July 29, through the Ambassador at Berlin, Sir Edward Goschen. In an official conversation the German Chancellor, Bethmann-Hollweg, declared that Germany was ready to pledge herself to take no territory from France in case of victory. He would make no promise as regards the French colonies, nor was anything said as to the French Fleet, nor as to the gigantic indemnity which was already discussed in some of the German papers. In a word, the proposition was that Great Britain was to abandon her friend at the hour of her need on condition that she should be robbed but not mutilated. Subsequent experience of German promises may lead us to doubt, however, whether they would really have insured France against the worst that the victor could inflict.

Sir Edward Grey answered with as much warmth as the iced language of diplomacy will permit. His dispatch of July 30 begins as follows :

" His Majesty's Government cannot for a moment entertain the Chancellor's proposal that they should bind themselves to neutrality on such terms.

" What he asks us in effect is, to engage to stand by while French colonies are taken and France is beaten so long as Germany does not take French territory as distinct from the colonies.

" From the material point of view such a proposal is unacceptable, for France, without further territory in Europe being taken from her, could be so crushed as to lose her position as a great Power, and become subordinate to German policy.

" Altogether apart from that, it would be a disgrace for us to make this bargain with Germany at the expense of France, a disgrace from which the good name of this country would never recover."

At a subsequent period the Premier, Mr. Asquith, voiced the sentiment of the whole nation when he declared that the proposal was infamous.

The immediate concern of the British Government was to ascertain the views of the rival Powers upon the question of Belgian neutrality, which had been solemnly guaranteed by France, Prussia, and ourselves. How faithfully this guarantee had been observed by France in the past is shown by the fact that even when an infraction of the frontier at Sedan in 1870 would have saved the French Army from total destruction, it had not been attempted. There were signs in advance, however, that Germany proposed to turn the French defences by marching through Belgium. The arrangement of the new German strategic railways upon the frontier all pointed to such a plan. It was evident that such an action must at once bring Britain into the struggle, since it is difficult to see how she could ever hold up her head again if, after promising protection to a smaller nation, she broke her bond at the moment of danger. The French, too, who had left their northern frontier comparatively unfortified in reliance upon the integrity of Belgium, would have rightly felt that they had been betrayed by Britain if they suffered now through their confidence in the British guarantee. The Balkans were nothing to Great Britain, but she had more than her interests, she had her national honour at stake upon the Belgian frontier.

On July 31 the British Government asked France and Germany whether they were still prepared to stand by their pledge. France answered promptly that she was, and added that she had withdrawn her armies ten kilometres from the frontier, so as to prove to the world that her position was defensive only. From Germany there came an ominous silence. Meanwhile, in Brussels the German representative, Herr von Below-Saleske, was assuring the Belgian Government that nothing was further from the intention of Germany than an infraction of the frontier. These assurances were continued almost to the moment of the arrival of German troops in Belgium, and give one more instance of the absolute want of truth and honour which from the days of Frederick the Great has been the outstanding characteristic of German diplomacy. Just as the Seven Years' War was begun by an attack upon an ally in times of peace, so her last two campaigns have been opened, the one by the doctored telegram of Ems, and the other by the perfidy to Belgium, which is none the less shameful because it has been publicly admitted by the Chancellor.

Another incident of these crowded days deserves some record, as it has been quoted in Germany as an instance of Great Britain having stood in the way of a localisation of the war. This impression is produced by suppressing a telegram in which it is shown that the whole episode arose from a mistake upon the part of Prince Lichnowsky, the German Ambassador. On August 1 Sir Edward Grey, still feeling round for some way in which the evil might be minimised, suggested through the telephone to Prince Lichnowsky that if both Germany and France could see their way to stand out, the conflict would then be limited to Austria and Russia. This practical and possible suggestion was transmitted to Berlin in the absurd form that Britain would hold France out of the war, while Russia would be abandoned to Germany and Austria. The Kaiser lost no time in assenting to so delightful a proposal. It was at once pointed out to Prince Lichnowsky that he had made a mistake, and the Prince telegraphed to Berlin a correction of his previous message. This second telegram was suppressed by the German Government, while, some weeks afterwards, they published the inaccurate dispatch in order to give the world the impression that Britain had actually made a move towards peace which had been withdrawn when it was found that it was eagerly welcomed by Germany. The very idea that Britain could in any way pledge the actions of France is grotesque upon the face of it. Whilst making this false suggestion as to the action of Britain, the German Government carefully concealed the fact that Sir Edward Grey had actually gone the extreme length in the interests of peace, of promising that we should detach ourselves from our Allies if a conference were held and their unreasonable attitude was an obstacle to an agreement.

Whether, if Belgian neutrality had been honoured, Great Britain would or would not have come into the war is an academic question which can never be decided. Certainly she would never have come in as a united nation, for public opinion was deeply divided upon the point, and the Cabinet is understood to have been at variance. Only one thing could have closed the ranks and sent the British Empire with absolute unanimity into the fight. This was the one thing which Germany did. However great her military power may be, it seems certain that her diplomatic affairs were grievously mismanaged, and that, in spite of that cloud of spies who have been the precursors of her Uhlans in each of her campaigns, she was singularly ill-informed as to the sentiments of foreign nations. The columns of a single honest British paper would have told her more of the true views and spirit of the nation than all the eavesdroppers of her famous secret service.

We now come to the critical instant as regards Britain, leading to a succession of incidents in Berlin so admirably described in Sir Edward Goschen's classical report that it seems a profanation to condense it. Having received no reply to their request for a definite assurance about Belgium, the British Government instructed their Ambassador to ask for an immediate answer upon August 4. The startling reply from Von Jagow, Secretary of Foreign Affairs, was that the German troops had actually crossed the frontier. With a cynical frankness the German statesman explained that it was a matter of life or death to the Imperial Army to get their blow in quickly by the undefended route. In answer to the shocked remonstrance of the British Ambassador, he could only assert that it was now too late to reconsider the matter. About seven in the evening Sir Edward Goschen conveyed an ultimatum upon the subject to the German Government, declaring war unless by midnight a more satisfactory answer could be given.

From Herr von Jagow the Ambassador passed to the Chancellor, whom he found much agitated. He broke into a harangue in which he used the phrase, now become historic, that he could not understand the British Government making such a fuss about a mere scrap of paper, and declared that a breach of territorial neutrality was a matter of no great consequence. A recollection of the history of his own country would none the less have reminded him that it was precisely on account of an infringement of their frontier by the troops of Napoleon that Prussia had entered upon the ill-fated war of 1806. He continued by saying that he held Great Britain responsible for all the terrible events which might happen. Sir Edward pointed out that it was a matter of necessity that Great Britain should keep her engagements, and added with dignity that fear of the consequences could hardly be accepted as a valid reason for breaking them.

Such in brief was the momentous interview which determined the question of peace or war between these two great Empires. Sir Edward immediately forwarded a telegraphic summary of what had occurred to London, but this telegram was never forwarded by the Berlin authorities—one more of those actions for which the word "caddish" is the most appropriate British adjective. Throughout all our German experiences both before the war and during it, we have always found our rivals to be formidable; they have usually proved themselves to be both brave and energetic; but hardly ever have we recognised them as gentlemen. Three centuries ago the leading nations of Europe had attained something subtle and gracious which is still denied to the Germans.

The populace of Berlin hastened to show these same unamiable characteristics. Whereas the retiring Ambassadors in London, Paris, and also in Vienna, met with courteous treatment, the German mob surrounded the British Embassy and hurled vituperations, and finally stones, at its occupants. Defenceless people were hustled, assaulted, and arrested in the streets. A day or two previously the Russian Embassy had been brutally insulted by the populace upon its departure—a fact which produced some regrettable, but very natural, reprisals in Petrograd, to use the new name for the Russian capital. The French Ambassador and his suite had also been very badly treated in their journey to the Dutch frontier. Thus it was shocking, but not surprising, to find that the Berlin mob indulged in excesses towards the British representatives, and that shameful scenes marked the final hours of Sir Edward Goschen's official duties. Truly, as Herr von Jagow admitted, such incidents leave an indelible stain upon the reputation of Berlin. It is pleasant to be able to add that Von Jagow himself behaved with propriety, and did what he could to mitigate the violence of the populace.

It is difficult for us to imagine how any German could possibly for an instant have imagined that Great Britain would stand by in silent acquiescence while the little country which she had sworn to protect was overrun by German troops; but that such a delusion existed is shown not only by the consternation of the Chancellor at Sir Edward's message, but also by the extreme irritation of the Emperor. What part Emperor William had played in the events which led up to the war may possibly remain for ever the subject of debate. There are those who argue that the Crown Prince and the military party had taken advantage of his absence on one of his Norwegian tours, and had hurried matters into such an *impasse* that he was unable to get them back to more peaceful lines. One would wish to think that this were true, and there is evidence that on previous occasions his influence has been exerted upon the side of peace to an extent which was unwelcome to many of his own subjects. On the other hand, it is very difficult to believe that such a situation, led up to by many preparatory steps which included the *fons et origo mali*, the provocative and impossible Austrian ultimatum, could have been arranged without the assent of a man who has notoriously continually interfered directly in all large, and many small, transactions of state. However this may be, it is beyond dispute that the action of Great Britain deprived him for the instant of his usual dignity and courtesy, and he dispatched a verbal message by one of his aides-de-camp in the following terms:

"The Emperor has charged me to express to your Excellency his regret for the occurrences of last night, but to tell you at the same time that you will gather from those occurrences an idea of the feelings of his people respecting the action of Great Britain in joining with other nations against her old allies of Waterloo. His Majesty also begs that you will tell the King that he has been proud of the titles of British Field-Marshal and British Admiral, but that in consequence of what has occurred he must now at once divest himself of those titles."

The Ambassador adds feelingly that this message lost nothing of its acerbity by the manner of its delivery. Some artist of the future will do justice to the scene where the benign and dignified old diplomatist sat listening to the rasping utterances of the insolent young Prussian soldier. The actual departure of the Embassy was effected without molestation, thanks once more to the good offices of Herr von Jagow. On the same day, in the presence of a large but silent crowd, the German Ambassador left London and embarked for home in a vessel placed at his disposal by the British Government. His voyage back, via Flushing, was safely accomplished, but it is worth recording that it was only the warning from a British warship which prevented him and his staff from being blown up by the mines which had already, within a few hours of the outbreak of hostilities, been strewn thickly by his countrymen in the path of neutral shipping across the highway of commerce in the North Sea. Should our kinsmen of America ever find themselves in our place, let them remember that it is "all in" from the beginning with the Germans.

Let America also remember our experience that no pupil can go to a German school, no scholar to a German university, and no invalid to a German health-resort, without the chance of some sudden turn of politics leaving them as prisoners in the country. Even the elderly heart patients at Nauheim were detained by the German authorities. An old admiral among them, Admiral Neeld, made a direct appeal as sailor to sailor to Prince Henry of Prussia, and was answered by the proverb that "War is war." Our contention is that such actions are *not* war, and that their perpetration will never be forgotten or forgiven by the nations of the world, who can have no security that when their subjects pass the German frontier they will ever get clear again. Such practices are, of course, entirely distinct from that of interning reservists or males of fighting age, which was freely done by the Allies. It is only fair to say that after a long delay there was a release of schoolgirls, and afterwards one of doctors, by the Germans, but many harmless travellers, students, and others were held for a long period of the war at a time when tens of thousands of Germans were free in Great Britain.

By a gross perversion of facts German publicists have endeavoured to show that Great Britain was to blame for the final rupture. The pretence is too absurd to deceive any one, and one can hardly think that they believe it themselves. One has only to ask what had Great Britain to do with the death of the Heir Apparent of Austria, with the sending of the fatal ultimatum, with the declaration of war against Russia and France, or, finally, with the infraction of the Belgian frontier? She had nothing to do with any one of these things, which all, save the first, emanated from Vienna or Berlin, and were the obvious causes of the war. Britain was only involved because she remained true to her solemn contract, a breach of which would have left her dishonoured. It is mere effrontery to pretend that she desired war, or that she left anything undone which could have prevented it. We lay our record with confidence before foreign nations and posterity. We have nothing to conceal and nothing to regret.

On the other hand, supposing that one were to grant the whole of the German contention, suppose one were to admit that Germany did not know of the terms of the Austrian ultimatum or foresee its effect upon the other nations of Europe, that she took her stand by the side of Austria purely out of motives of chivalrous loyalty to an ally, and that she was forced, by so doing, to find herself at variance with Russia and France—suppose so inconceivable a hypothesis as this, even then it cannot in any way condone the admitted wrong which Germany did in invading Belgium, nor does it show any possible cause why, because Germany was false to her word in this matter, Britain should be so also. This point is so unanswerable that the only defence, if it can be called a defence, which Germany has ever put forward is, that if she had not infringed Belgian neutrality, somebody else would have done so. Not one shadow of evidence has ever been put forward to justify so monstrous an assertion, which is certainly not endorsed by the Belgians themselves.

In this connection one may allude to the so-called secret military engagements which were found and published by the Germans at Brussels and which were supposed to show that Great Britain herself contemplated the infraction of Belgian neutrality. One can only realise how bankrupt is Germany of all reason and argument when one considers such a contention as this. For years the German threats had been obvious to all the world. They had brought their strategic railways to the frontier of Belgium, and erected their standing camps there. Naturally Belgium was alarmed at such preparations and took counsel with Great Britain how her pledge should be redeemed and how her soil could be defended in case Germany proved perfidious. It was a simple military precaution which involved not the breach of a treaty but the fulfilment of one—not the invasion of Belgium but its protection after it was invaded. Each successive so-called " revelation " about the actions of Great Britain has only proved once more that—

> " Whatever record leaps to light
> She never shall be shamed."

These attempts to confuse the issue irresistibly recall the message of Frederic to Podowils when he was about to seize Silesia even as William seized Belgium. "The question of right," he said, "is the affair of ministers. It is your affair. It is time to work at it in secret, for the orders to the troops are given." March first and find some justification later.

Germany would have stood higher in the world's esteem and in the estimate of history if, instead of playing in most grotesque fashion the wolf to the lamb, and accusing her unprepared and distracted neighbours of making a surprise attack upon her at the moment when she was at the height of her preparations, she had boldly stated her true position. Her dignity and frankness would have been undeniable if she had said, " I am a great power. I believe I am the greatest. I am willing to put it to the test of war. I am not satisfied with my geographical position. I desire a greater seaboard. You must give it to me or I shall take it. I justify my action by the fact that the position of every state rests ultimately upon its strength in war, and that I am willing to undergo that test."

Such a contention would have commanded respect, however much we might resent it. But these repeated declarations from the Emperor himself, the Chancellor, and so many others that they were deliberately attacked, coupled with appeals to the Almighty, make up the most nauseous mixture of falsehood and blasphemy which the world has ever known. The whole conception of religion became grotesque, and the Almighty, instead of a universal Father of the human race, was suddenly transformed into " our good old God," a bloodthirsty tribal deity worthy of those Prussian pagans who as late as the fourteenth century offered human sacrifices to their idols in the Eastern Mark. The phenomenon was part of that general national madness to which, it is to be hoped, the German of the future will look back with bewilderment and shame.

One contention put forward by certain German apologists in connection with the war would hardly be worth referring to, were it not for the singular light which it casts upon the mental and moral position of a large number of the German public. It was that some special culture had been evolved by Germany which was of such value that it should be imposed by force upon the rest of the world. Since culture must in its nature be an international thing, the joint product of human development, such a claim can only be regarded as a conspicuous sign of its absence. In spiritual and intellectual matters it could not be asserted that Germany since 1870 had shown any superiority over France or England. In many matters she was conspicuously behind. It might fairly be claimed that in chemistry, in music, and in some forms of criticism, notably biblical exegesis, she was supreme. But in how many fields was she inferior to Great Britain? What name had she in poetry to put against Tennyson and Browning, in zoology to compare with Darwin, in scientific surgery to excel that of Lister, in travel to balance Stanley, or in the higher human qualities to equal such a man as Gordon? The fruits of German culture do not bear out the claim that it should forcibly supplant that of either of the great Western nations.

We have now seen how the great cloud which had

hung so long over Europe burst at last, and the blast of war swept the land from end to end. We have passed through the years of hopes and alarms, of the *ententes* of optimists and the *détentes* of politicians, of skirmishes between journals and wrestles of finance, until we reach the end of it all—open primitive warfare between the two great branches of the Germanic family. In a purple passage Professor Cramb spoke of the days when the high gods of virility would smile as they looked down upon the chosen children of Odin, the English and the Germans, locked in the joy of battle. The hour had struck, and it is a partial record of those crowded and heroic days which is here set forth with such accuracy of detail as diligence may command and circumstances allow.

CHAPTER II

THE OPENING OF THE WAR

THERE can be no doubt that if Germany had confined her operations to an attack upon France without any infraction of Belgian neutrality, the situation in Great Britain would have been extraordinarily difficult. The Government was the most democratic that has ever been known in our political history, and it owed its power to an electorate, many of whom were passionate advocates for peace at almost any conceivable price. The preparations for naval war, necessitated by the ever-growing German power, had been accompanied and occasionally retarded by a constant murmur of remonstrance which swelled periodically into a menacing expostulation. McKenna and Churchill found their only opponents in the members of their own party, who persistently refused to look obvious facts in the face, and impatiently swept aside the figures of the German armaments while they indulged in vague and amiable aspirations towards international friendship. This large and energetic party would certainly have most strenuously resisted British interference in a Continental war. The statesmen who foresaw that the conquest of France would surely lead to the conquest of Britain might have carried the country with them, but none the less they would have gone to war with such an incubus upon them as the traitorous Charles James Fox and his party had been in the days of Napoleon. A disunited British against a united German Empire would have been a grievous disadvantage, be our allies who they might, for, as Shakespeare sang, "If England to herself be true," it is then only that she is formidable.

This great misfortune, however, was obviated by the policy of Germany. The most peace-loving Briton could not face the national dishonour which would have been eternally branded upon him had his country without an effort allowed its guarantee to be treated as waste paper by a great military nation. The whole people were welded into one, and save for a few freakish individuals who obeyed their own perversity of mind or passion for notoriety, the country was united as it has never been in history. A just war seemed to touch the land with some magic wand, which healed all dissensions and merged into one national whole those vivid controversies which are, in fact, a sign rather of intense vitality than of degeneration. In a moment the faddist forgot his fad, the capitalist his grievance against taxation, the Labour man his feud against Capital, the Tory his hatred of the Government, even the woman her craving for the vote. A political millennium seemed to have dawned. Best and most important of all was the evident sign that the work done of late years to win the friendship of Ireland had not been in vain. If the mere promise of domestic institutions has ranged all responsible Irishmen upon one side on the day of battle, what may we not hope for ourselves and for the Empire when they have been fully established and Time has alleviated the last lingering memories of an evil past? It is true that at a later period of the war this fair prospect was somewhat overcast by an insane rebellion, in which the wrongs of Ireland, once formidable and now trivial, were allowed by a colossal selfishness to outweigh the martyrdom of Belgium and the mutilation of France. Still the fact remains (and it must sustain us in our future efforts for conciliation) that never before have we had the representative nationalists of Ireland as our allies in a great struggle.

The leaders of the Unionist party, Lord Lansdowne and Mr. Bonar Law, had already, on August 2, signified to the Government that they considered Britain to be honour-bound to France, and would support without hesitation every practical step to give effect to the alliance. Fortified by this assurance, the Government could go strongly forward. But after the Belgian infraction, its position was that of the executive of a united nation. Sir Edward Grey's analysis in Parliament of the causes which had brought us to war convinced the reason and claimed the sympathy of every political party, and even the most fervent advocates of peace found themselves silenced in the presence of the huge German aggression which could never admit of a peace founded upon mutual respect and equality, but only of that which comes from ascendancy on the one side and helplessness upon the other.

Should Britain ever be led into an unjust war, she will soon learn it from the fearless voices of her children. The independent young nations which are rising under the red-crossed flag will not be dragged, in the train of the Mother-Country, into any enterprise of which their conscience does not approve. But now their assent was whole-hearted. They were vehement in their approval of the firm stand made for the pledged word of the nation. From every quarter of the world deep answered deep in its assurance that the sword should not be sheathed until the wrong was righted and avenged.

Strong, earnest Canada sent her 30,000 men, with her promise of more. Fiery Australia and New Zealand prepared as many, Maori vying with white man in his loyalty to the flag. South Africa, under the splendid leadership of Botha, began to arm, to speak with the foe in her own gates. India poured forth money and men with a lavish generosity which can never be forgotten in this country. The throb of loyalty to the old land passed through every smallest Dependency, and then beyond the frontier to those further lands which had known us as a just and kindly neighbour. Newfoundland voted a contingent. Ceylon sent of her best. Little Fiji mustered her company of fighting men, and even the mountains of Nepaul and the inaccessible plateaux of Thibet were desirous of swelling that great host, gathered from many races, but all under the one banner which meant to each a just and liberal rule.

On the very eve of the outbreak of hostilities one man was added to the home establishment whose presence was worth many army corps. This was Lord Kitchener, whose boat was actually lying with steam up to bear him away upon a foreign mission, when, at the last instant, either the universal public demand or the good sense of the Government recalled him to take supreme charge of the war. It was a strange and a novel situation that a soldier who was no party politician should assume the rôle of War Minister in a political Cabinet, but the times called for decided measures, and this was among them. From that day onwards until the dark hour which called him from his uncompleted task the passer-by who looked up at the massive front of the War Office was gladdened by the thought that somewhere in the heart of it those stern, immutable eyes were looking out at Britain's enemies, and that clear, calculating brain was working for their downfall. Slow, safe, methodical, remorseless, carefully preparing the means at every stage that led him to the distant but preordained end, he had shown, both in the Soudan and South Africa, that the race of great British generals was not yet extinct. He knew and trusted his instrument even as it knew and trusted him.

That instrument was an army which was remarkably well prepared for its work. It cannot be said that the Boer War had increased the prestige of the British forces, though only those who have studied the subject can realise how difficult was the task with which they were then faced, or how considerable an achievement it was to bring it to a success. But the campaign had left behind it a valuable legacy, all the richer because so great a proportion of the land forces had been drawn into the struggle. In 1914 a large proportion of senior officers and a considerable number of non-commissioned officers and reservists had passed through that ordeal, and learned by experience what can be done, and, even more important, what cannot be done, in face of modern rifles in skilful hands.

The lesson had been well pressed home after the

CHAPTER II.

The opening of the war.

war, and every general, from Lord Roberts downwards, had laid emphasis upon the importance of cover and of accuracy of fire. Apart from the sound technical training of the soldiers, the administration of the Army had, after an experimental period, fallen into the hands of Lord Haldane, who has left his mark more deeply than any one since Cardwell upon the formation of the land forces. A debt of gratitude is owing to him for his clear thought and his masterful dispositions. Had he been a prophet as well as organiser, he would no doubt have held his hand before he made the smallest decrease of our regular forces; but, on the other hand, by turning our haphazard, amateurish volunteers into the workmanlike Territorials, in forming the invaluable Officers' Training Corps which tapped our public schools for something better than athletic talent, and in rigidly defining our expeditionary corps and providing the special reserves for its reinforcements, he did work for which he can never adequately be thanked. The weapon which he had fashioned was now thrust into the strong right hand of the new Minister of War.

It is well to survey this weapon before we show how it was used. The total personnel of the Army with its reserves called up was about 370,000 men. Of this 160,000 were set aside as an expeditionary force, but only a portion of this number could be counted as immediately available on the outbreak of war, though the system of mobilisation had been brought to a fine point. It was hoped that three army corps numbering about 110,000 men, with two divisions of cavalry, about 10,000 horsemen, would be immediately available, petty numbers as compared with the millions of the Continent, but highly trained

THE OPENING OF THE WAR

professional soldiers, capable, perhaps, of turning the balance in the clash of equal hosts. The rest of the Regular Army had to provide garrisons for India, Egypt, Gibraltar, and other dependencies, but it was hoped that in time nearly all of it would be available for service.

Behind these first-line troops was the special reserve, something under 100,000 in number, who were the immediate reinforcements to fill the gaps of battle. Next in order came the Territorials, whose full complement was 340,000 men. Unhappily at this time they were nearly 100,000 under strength, and there are many who think that if the National Service League in their earnest campaign, which was inspired by a clear vision of the coming danger, had insisted upon a great enlargement of this constitutional force, instead of agitating for a complete change which presented practical and political difficulties, their efforts would have been more fruitful. These troops were raw, inexperienced, and only enlisted for home service, but with a fine spirit they set to work at once to make themselves efficient, and the great majority signified their readiness to go anywhere at the country's call. Many brigades were sent abroad at once to relieve the regulars in Egypt and India, while others were ready to join the fighting line on the Continent after a few months, where, as will be shown, they acquitted themselves remarkably well. The enthusiasm for the war rapidly sent the numbers of the Territorials up to nearly half a million. In addition to these troops there was the promise of 70,000 highly trained men (one quarter of whom were British regulars) from India. Canada, Australia, and New Zealand came forward to offer some 60,000 men between them, with the promise of as many more as should be called for. Brave and hardy, these were splendid raw material, though their actual technical training was not, save in some special corps, more advanced than that of the British Territorials. Altogether, the British War Lord could see, at the very beginning of hostilities, nearly 1,000,000 of men ready to his hand, though in very different stages of efficiency.

But already he had conceived the idea of a campaign of attrition, and, looking forward into the years, he was convinced that these forces were insufficient. Some entirely new *cadres* must be organised, which should have no limitations, but be as reliable an instrument as the regular forces of the Crown. With a prescience which found no counterpart either among our friends or our foes he fixed three years as a probable term for the war, and he made preparation accordingly. Early in August he called for half a million fresh volunteers for the war, and early in October he had got them. Still unsatisfied, he called for yet another half-million, and before Christmas his numbers were again complete. It was a wonderful autumn and winter in Britain. Every common and green was loud with the cries of the instructors, and bare with the tramp of the men. Nothing has ever been seen in the world's history which can compare in patriotic effort with that rally to the flag, for no bounty was offered, and no compulsion used. The spirit of the men was extraordinarily high. Regiments were filled with gentlemen who gave up every amenity of life in order to face an arduous and dangerous campaign, while even greater patriotism was shown by the countless thousands of miners, artisans, and other well-paid workmen who sacrificed high wages and a home life in order to serve for an indefinite time upon the humble pay of the soldier, leaving, very often, a wife and children in straitened circumstances behind them. It is at such times that a democratic country reaps the rich fruits of its democracy, for if you make the land such that it is good to live in, so also does it become good to die for. These forces could not be ready, even with the best of wills, and the most intensive culture, before the summer of 1915, but at that date, including her sea forces, Great Britain had not less than 2,000,000 volunteers under arms and ready for immediate use, a number which had risen to 4,000,000 by the end of that year, and 5,000,000 by the spring of 1916.

So much for the wise provisions of Lord Kitchener, which would have been useless had they not been supported by a stern and self-sacrificing national spirit. The crisis was met with a cold determination which gave some superficial observers the impression that the nation was listless, when it was, in truth, far too earnest for mere shoutings or flag-waving. "Wakened at last!" cried some foreign cartoon when a German outrage aroused the country for an instant to some visible gleam of wrath. A deeper observer might have known that a country which finds 5,000,000 volunteer fighters, and which, instead of putting the expenses of the war upon future generations, as was done by Germany, elects to meet a considerable proportion of them by present taxation, is in grim earnest from the start. The income tax was doubled without a remonstrance by a unanimous vote of the Commons, thus finding an extra £40,000,000 a year for the prosecution of the war. Other taxes were levied by which the working classes bore their fair share of the burden, and they also elicited no complaints. Before Christmas no less than £450,000,000 had been raised by a loan, a gigantic financial effort which was easily borne at a charge of 4 per cent.

But if Britain was able to face the future with confidence, both in finance and in her military preparation, it was entirely to her silent, invisible, but most efficient Navy that she owed it. By wise foresight the Grand Fleet, numbering some 400 vessels, had been assembled for Royal inspection before the storm broke and when it was but a rising cloud-bank upon the horizon. This all-important move has been attributed to Prince Louis of Battenberg, First Sea Lord of the Admiralty, but it could not have been done without the hearty concurrence and co-operation of Mr. Winston Churchill, who should share the honour, even as he would have shared the blame had we been caught unawares. The so-called inspection had hardly been completed at Spithead before war was upon us, and the Fleet, ready manned, provisioned, and armed, moved straight away to take up its war stations. The main fighting squadrons vanished into a strategic mist from which they did not emerge for very many months, but it was understood that they were assembled at centres like Scapa Flow and Cromarty Firth which were outside the radius of the German torpedo-boats and smaller submarines, while they were near enough to the enemy's ports to be able to bring him to action should he emerge.

Numerous patrols of small vessels were let loose in the North Sea to keep in touch with our opponents, who were well known to be both daring and active. It is said that no less than 3000 ships, large and small, were flying the white ensign of St. George. A portion of these were told off for the protection of the great commercial sea-routes, and for the hunting down of some score of German cruisers which were known to be at sea. Some of these gave a very good account of themselves and others were innocuous; but the net result in loss, which had been discounted in advance as 5 per cent of the merchant fleet at sea, worked out at less than half that figure, and, by the new year, the marauders had been practically exterminated.

CHAPTER II.

The opening of the war.

Now as always—but now more than ever in the past—it was absolutely vital to hold the seas. Who wins the sea wins Britain. Of every five loaves in the country four come to us from abroad, and our position in meat is no better. It is victory or starvation when we fight upon the sea. It is ill to play for such stakes, however safe the game—worse still when it is a game where the value of some of the cards is unknown. We have little to fear from a raid, nothing from invasion, everything from interference with our commerce. It is one of the points in which our party politics, which blind so many people to reason, might well have brought absolute ruin upon the country. The cultivation of British food supplies should never have been a question of free trade or protection, but rather of vital national insurance.

Had the war come ten years later we might have been in deadly danger, owing to the rapidly growing power of the submarine. These engines turned upon our food-carriers might well have starved us out, especially if we had continued our national folly in being scared by bogeys from building a Channel tunnel. But by a merciful Providence the struggle came at a moment when the submarine was half developed, and had not yet reached either the speed or the range of action which would make it the determining factor in a war. As it was, the fruits of submarine warfare, in spite of a wise and timely warning on the eve of hostilities by Admiral Sir Percy Scott, astonished the public, but the mischief done was a very small thing compared to the possibilities which have to be most carefully guarded against in the future.

In their present stage of development, the submarine could only annoy. With the great fleet in existence and with the shipbuilding facilities of Great Britain, nothing could vitally harm her save the loss of a pitched battle. The British superiority was rather in her small craft than in her large ones, but in capital ships she was able to place in line at the beginning of the war enough to give a sufficient margin of insurance. There was never any tendency to underrate the excellence of the hostile ships, nor the courage and efficiency of the men. It was well understood that when they came out they would give a good account of themselves, and also that they would not come out until the circumstances seemed propitious. They were under a disadvantage in that the Russian fleet, though small, was not negligible, and therefore some portion of the German force on sea as well as on land had always to face eastwards. Also the British had the French for their allies, and, though the great ships of the latter were nearly all in the Mediterranean, a swarm of small craft was ready to buzz out of her western ports should the war come down-channel.

Yet another advantage lay with the British in that their geographical position put a six-hundred-mile-long breakwater right across the entrance to Germany, leaving only two sally-ports north and south by which commerce could enter or raiders escape. The result was the immediate utter annihilation of Germany's sea-borne commerce. Altogether it must be admitted that Germany was grievously handicapped at sea, and that she deserves the more credit for whatever she accomplished, save when, as on land, she transgressed and degraded the recognised laws of civilised warfare. It is time now to turn to those military events upon the Continent which were the precursors of that British campaign which is the subject of this volume.

Want of space and accurate material make it impossible to do justice here to the deeds of our Allies, but an attempt must be made to indicate briefly the main phases of the struggle abroad, since its course reacted continually upon the British operations. It may be shortly stated, then, that so far as the western theatre of war was concerned, hostilities commenced by two movements, one an attack by the French upon the occupants of those lost provinces for which they had mourned during forty-four years, and the other the advance of the Germans over the Belgian frontier.

The former was a matter of no great importance. It took two distinct lines, the one from the Belfort region into Alsace, and the other from Nancy as a centre into Lorraine. The Alsatian venture gained some ground which was never wholly lost, and was adorned by one small victory near Mülhausen before it was checked by the German defence. The Lorraine advance had also some initial success, but was finally thrown back on August 20 in a severe action in which the French were defeated. Luneville, across the French frontier, was occupied by the Germans, but they made no headway, and their subsequent attempts upon Nancy were repulsed by the army of General Castelnau. General Pau, a fiery, one-armed septuagenarian, was the French leader in the Alsatian invasion, but it was soon realised by General Joffre that he and the bulk of his men would be more useful at the vital point upon the northern frontier, to which early in September they were transferred.

The main drama, however, quickly unfolded upon the Belgian frontier. Speed and secrecy were vital to the German plans. On July 31, before any declaration of war, and while the German representative at Brussels was perjuring his soul in his country's service by representing that no infringement was possible, three German army corps, the seventh, ninth, and tenth, fully mobilised and highly equipped, were moving up from their quarters so as to be ready for a treacherous pounce upon their little neighbour whom they were pledged to defend. Von Emmich was in command. On the night of Saturday, August 1, the vanguard of the German armies, using motor traffic followed by trains, burst through the neutral Duchy of Luxemburg, and on August 3 they were over the Belgian line at Verviers. The long-meditated crime had been done, and, with loud appeals to God, Germany began her fatal campaign by deliberate perjury and arrogant disdain for treaties. God accepted the appeal, and swiftly showed how the weakest State with absolute right upon its side may bring to naught all the crafty plottings of the strong.

THE OPENING OF THE WAR

For time was the essence of the situation. For this the innumerable motors, for this the light equipment and the lack of transport. It was on, on, at top speed, that there be no hindrance in the path of the great hosts that soon would be closing up behind. But time was life and death for the French also, with their slower mobilisation, their backward preparation, and their expectations from Great Britain. Time was the precious gift which little Belgium gave to the Allies. She gave them days and days, and every day worth an army corps. The Germans had crossed the Meuse, had taken Visé, and then had rushed at Liége, even as the Japanese had rushed at Port Arthur. With all their military lore, they had not learned the lesson which was taught so clearly in 1904—that a fortress is taken by skill and not by violence alone.

Leman, a great soldier, defended the forts built by Brialmont. Both defender and designer were justified of their work. On August 5 the seventh German Corps attempted to rush the gaps between the forts. These gaps were three miles wide, but were filled with entrenched infantry. The attack was boldly pressed home, but it completely failed. The German loss was considerable. Two other corps were called up, and again on August 7 the attack was renewed, but with no better result. The defenders fought as befitted the descendants of those Belgae whom Caesar pronounced to be the bravest of the Gauls, or of that Walloon Guard which had so great a mediaeval reputation. There were 25,000 in the town and 120,000 outside, but they were still outside at the end of the assault.

Liége, however, had one fatal weakness. Its

CHAPTER II.

The opening of the war.

garrison was far too small to cover the ground. With twelve forts three miles apart it is clear that there were intervals of, roughly, thirty-six miles to be covered, and that a garrison of 25,000 men, when you had deducted the gunners for the forts, hardly left the thinnest skirmish line to cover the ground. So long as the Germans attacked upon a narrow front they could be held. The instant that they spread out there were bound to be places where they could march almost unopposed into the town. This was what occurred. The town was penetrated, but the forts were intact. General Leman, meanwhile, seeing that the town itself was indefensible, had sent the garrison out before the place was surrounded. Many a Belgian soldier fought upon the Yser and helped to turn the tide of that crowning conflict who would have been a prisoner in Germany had it not been for the foresight and the decision of General Leman.

The Germans were in the town upon the 8th, but the forts still held out and the general advance was grievously impeded. Day followed day, and each beyond price to the Allies. Germany had secretly prepared certain monstrous engines of war—one more proof, if proof were needed, that the conflict had been prearranged and deliberately provoked. These were huge cannon of a dimension never before cast—42 centimetres in bore. More mobile and hardly less effective were some smaller howitzers of 28-centimetre calibre said to have come from the Austrian foundries at Skoda. Brialmont, when he erected his concrete and iron cupolas, had not foreseen the Thor's hammer which would be brought to crush them. One after another they were smashed like eggs. The heroic Leman was dug out from under the débris of the last fort and lived to tell of his miraculous escape. Liége was at last in the hands of the invaders. But already the second week of August was at an end—the British were crowding into France, the French line was thickening along the frontier—all was well with the Allies. Little David had left a grievous mark upon Goliath.

The German mobilisation was now complete, and the whole vast host, over a million strong, poured over the frontier. Never was seen such an army, so accurate and scientific in its general conception, so perfect in its detail. Nothing had been omitted from its equipment which the most thorough of nations, after years of careful preparation, could devise. In motor transport, artillery, machine guns, and all the technique of war they were unrivalled. The men themselves were of high heart and grand physique. By some twisted process of reasoning founded upon false information they had been persuaded that this most aggressive and unnecessary of wars was in some way a war of self-defence, for it was put to them that unless they attacked their neighbours now, their neighbours would certainly some day or other attack them. Hence, they were filled with patriotic ardour and a real conviction that they were protecting their beloved Fatherland. One could not but admire their self-sacrificing devotion, though in the dry light of truth and reason they stood forth as the tools of tyranny, the champions of barbarous political reaction and the bullies of Europe. It was an ominous fact that the troops were provided in advance with incendiary discs for the firing of dwellings, which shows that the orgy of destruction and cruelty which disgraced the name of the German Army in Belgium and in the north of France was prearranged by some central force, whose responsibility in this matter can only be described as terrific. They brought the world of Christ back to the days of Odin, and changed a civilised campaign to an inroad of pagan Danes. This wicked central force could only be the Chief Staff of the Army, and in the last instance the Emperor himself. Had Napoleon conducted his campaigns with as little scruple as William II., it can safely be said that Europe as we know it would hardly exist to-day, and the monuments of antiquity and learning would have been wiped from the face of the globe. It is an evil precedent to be expunged from the records for ever—all the more evil because it was practised by a strong nation on a weak one and on a defenceless people by one which had pledged themselves to defend them. That it was in no wise caused by any actions upon the part of the Belgians is clearly proved by the fact that similar atrocities were committed by the German Army the moment they crossed the frontiers both of France and of Poland.

The Allies had more than they expected from Liége. They had less from Namur. The grey-green tide of German invasion had swept the Belgian resistance before it, had flooded into Brussels, and had been dammed for only a very few days by the great frontier fortress, though it was counted as stronger than Liége. The fact was that the Germans had now learned their lesson. Never again would they imagine that the *Furor Teutonicus* alone could carry a walled city. The fatal guns were brought up again and the forts were crushed with mechanical precision, while the defenders between the forts, after enduring for ten hours a severe shelling, withdrew from their trenches. On August 22 the fortress surrendered, some of General Michel's garrison being taken, but a considerable proportion effecting its retreat with the French Army which had come up to support the town. By the third week of August the remains of the Belgian forces had taken refuge in Antwerp, and the Germans, having made a wide sweep with their right wing through Brussels, were descending in a two-hundred-mile line upon Northern France.

The French plans had in truth been somewhat disarranged by the Belgian resistance, for the chivalrous spirit of the nation would not permit that their gallant friends be unsupported. Fresh dispositions had been made, but the sudden fall of Namur brought them to naught. Before that untoward event the French had won a small but indubitable victory at Dinant, and had advanced their line from Namur on the right to Charleroi on the left. With the fall of Namur their long wall had lost its corner bastion, and they were at once vigorously attacked by all the German armies, who forced the Sambre on August 22, carried Charleroi, and pushed the French back with considerable loss of guns and prisoners along the whole line. There was defeat, but there was nothing in the nature of a rout or of an envelopment. The line fell back fighting tooth and nail, but none the less Northern France was thrown open to the invaders. In this general movement the British forces were involved, and we now turn to a more particular and detailed account of what befell them during these most momentous days.

CHAPTER III

THE BATTLE OF MONS

The landing of the British in France—The British leaders—The advance to Mons—The defence of the bridges of Nimy—The holding of the canal—The fateful telegram—The rearguard actions of Frameries, Wasmes, and Dour—The charge of the Lancers—The fate of the Cheshires—The 7th Brigade at Solesmes—The Guards in action—The Germans' rude awakening—The Connaughts at Pont-sur-Sambre.

<small>Chapter III.
The Battle of Mons.

The landing of the British in France.</small>

THE bulk of the British Expeditionary Force passed over to France under cover of darkness on the nights of August 12 and 13, 1914. The movement, which included four infantry divisions and a cavalry division, necessitated the transportation of approximately 90,000 men, 15,000 horses, and 400 guns. It is doubtful if so large a host has ever been moved by water in so short a time in all the annals of military history. There was drama in the secrecy and celerity of the affair. Two canvas walls converging into a funnel screened the approaches to Southampton Dock. All beyond was darkness and mystery. Down this fatal funnel passed the flower of the youth of Britain, and their folk saw them no more. They had embarked upon the great adventure of the German War. The crowds in the streets saw the last serried files vanish into the darkness of the docks, heard the measured tramp upon the stone quays dying farther away in the silence of the night, until at last all was still and the great steamers were pushing out into the darkness.

No finer force for technical efficiency, and no body of men more hot-hearted in their keen desire to serve their country, have ever left the shores of Britain. It is a conservative estimate to say that within four months a half of their number were either dead or in the hospitals. They were destined for great glory, and for that great loss which is the measure of their glory.

Belated pedestrians upon the beach of the southern towns have recorded their impression of that amazing spectacle. In the clear summer night the wall of transports seemed to stretch from horizon to horizon. Guardian warships flanked the mighty column, while swift shadows shooting across the surface of the sea showed where the torpedo-boats and scouts were nosing and ferreting for any possible enemy. But far away, hundreds of miles to the north, lay the real protection of the flotilla, where the smooth waters of the Heligoland Bight were broken by the sudden rise and dip of the blockading periscopes.

It is well to state, once for all, the composition of this force, so that in the succeeding pages, when a brigade or division is under discussion, the diligent reader may ascertain its composition. This, then, is the First Army which set forth to France. Others will be chronicled as they appeared upon the scene of action. It may be remarked that the formation of units was greatly altered with the progress of the campaign, so that it has been possible without indiscretion to raise the veil of secrecy which was once so essential.

THE FIRST ARMY CORPS—GENERAL HAIG

DIVISION I.
General LOMAX.

1st Infantry Brigade—
General Maxse.
1st Coldstream Guards.
1st Scots Guards.
1st Black Watch.
2nd Munster Fusiliers.

2nd Infantry Brigade—
General Bulfin.
2nd Sussex.
1st N. Lancs.
1st Northampton.
2nd K.R. Rifles.

3rd Infantry Brigade—
General Landon.
1st West Surrey (Queen's).
1st S. Wales Borderers.
1st Gloucester.
2nd Welsh.

Artillery—
Colonel Findlay.
25th Brig. R.F.A. 113, 114, 115.

26th Brig. R.F.A. 116, 117, 118.
39th Brig. R.F.A. 46, 51, 54.
43rd (How.) Brig. R.F.A. 30, 40, 57.

Engineers—
Colonel Schreiber.
23 F. Co.
26 F. Co.
1 Signal Co.

DIVISION II.
General MUNRO.

4th Infantry Brigade—
General Scott-Kerr.
2nd Grenadier Guards.
2nd Coldstream Guards.
3rd Coldstream Guards.
1st Irish.

5th Infantry Brigade—
General Haking.
2nd Worcester.
2nd Ox. and Bucks L.I.
2nd Highland L.I.
2nd Connaught Rangers.

6th Infantry Brigade—
General Davies.
1st Liverpool (King's).
2nd S. Stafford.
1st Berks.
1st K.R. Rifles.

Artillery—
General Perceval.
34th Brig. R.F.A. 22, 50, 70.
36th Brig. R.F.A. 15, 48, 71.
41st Brig. R.F.A. 9, 16, 17.
How. Brig. R.F.A. 47, 56, 60.
35th Batt. R.G.A.
R.E. 5, 11, Field Cos.

THE SECOND ARMY CORPS—GENERAL SMITH-DORRIEN

DIVISION III.
General HAMILTON.

7th Infantry Brigade—
General McCracken.
3rd Worcester.
2nd S. Lancs.
1st Wilts.
2nd Irish Rifles.

8th Infantry Brigade—
General B. Doran.
2nd Royal Scots.
2nd Royal Irish.
4th Middlesex.
1st Gordon Highlanders.

9th Infantry Brigade—
General Shaw.
1st North. Fusiliers.
4th Royal Fusiliers.
1st Lincoln.
1st Scots Fusiliers.

Artillery—
General Wing.
23rd Brigade 107, 108, 109.
30th Brigade (How.) 128, 129, 130.
40th Brigade 6, 23, 49.
42nd Brigade 29, 41, 45.
48th Batt. R.G.A.

R.E.—Colonel Wilson.
56, 57 F. Corps.
3 Signal Co.

DIVISION V.
General FERGUSON.

13th Infantry Brigade—
General Cuthbert.
2nd K.O. Scot. Bord.
2nd West Riding.
1st West Kent.
2nd Yorks. Light Infantry.

14th Infantry Brigade—
General Rolt.
2nd Suffolk.
1st East Surrey.
1st D. of Cornwall's L.I.
2nd Manchester.

15th Infantry Brigade—
General Gleichen.
1st Norfolk.
1st Bedford.
1st Cheshire.
1st Dorset.

Artillery—
General Headlam.
15th Brig. R.F.A. 11, 52, 80.
27th Brig.   „   119, 120, 121.
28th Brig.   „   122, 123, 124.
8 How. Brig. 37, 61, 65.
Heavy G.A. 108 Battery.

R.E.—Colonel Tulloch.
17th and 59th Field Cos.
5 Signal Co.

The Cavalry consisted of four Brigades forming the first cavalry division, and of one extra Brigade. They were made up thus:

1st Cavalry Brigade (Briggs).—2nd and 5th Dragoon Guards; 11th Hussars.
2nd Cavalry Brigade (De Lisle).—4th Dragoon Guards; 9th Lancers; 18th Hussars.
3rd Cavalry Brigade (Gough).—4th Hussars; 5th Lancers; 16th Lancers.
4th Cavalry Brigade (Bingham).—3rd Hussars; 6th Dragoon Guards; Comp. Guards Regt.
5th Cavalry Brigade (Chetwode).—Scots Greys; 12th Lancers; 20th Hussars.

D, E, I, J, and L batteries of Horse Artillery were attached to these Brigades.

The Battle of Mons

Such was the Army which first set forth to measure itself against the soldiers of Germany. Prussian bravery, capacity, and organising power had a high reputation among us, and yet we awaited the result with every confidence, if the odds of numbers were not overwhelming. It was generally known that during the period since the last war the training of the troops had greatly progressed, and many of the men, with nearly all the senior officers, had had experience in the arduous campaign of South Africa. They could also claim those advantages which volunteer troops may hope to have over conscripts. At the same time there was no tendency to underrate the earnest patriotism of our opponents, and we were well aware that even the numerous Socialists who filled their ranks were persuaded, incredible as it may seem, that the Fatherland was really attacked, and were whole-hearted in its defence.

The crossing was safely effected. It has always been the traditional privilege of the British public to grumble at their public servants and to speak of "muddling through" to victory. No doubt the criticism has often been deserved. But on this occasion the supervising General in command, the British War Office, and the Naval Transport Department all rose to a supreme degree of excellence in their arrangements. So too did the Railway Companies concerned. The details were meticulously correct. Without the loss of man, horse, or gun, the soldiers who had seen the sun set in Hampshire saw it rise in Picardy or in Normandy. Boulogne and Havre were the chief ports of disembarkation, but many, including the cavalry, went up the Seine and came ashore at Rouen. The soldiers everywhere received a rapturous welcome from the populace, which they returned by a cheerful sobriety of behaviour. The admirable precepts as to wine and women set forth in Lord Kitchener's parting orders to the Army seem to have been most scrupulously observed. It is no slight upon the gallantry of France—the very home of gallantry—if it be said that she profited greatly at this strained, over-anxious time by the arrival of these boisterous over-sea Allies. The tradition of British solemnity has been for ever killed by these jovial invaders. It is probable that the beautiful tune, and even the paltry words of "Tipperary," will pass into history as the marching song, and often the death-dirge, of that gallant host. The dusty, poplar-lined roads resounded with their choruses, and the quiet Picardy villages re-echoed their thunderous and superfluous assurances as to the state of their hearts. All France broke into a smile at the sight of them, and it was at a moment when a smile meant much to France.

Whilst the various brigades were with some deliberation preparing for an advance up-country, there arrived at the Gare du Nord in Paris a single traveller who may be said to have been the most welcome British visitor who ever set foot in the city. He was a short, thick man, tanned by an outdoor life, a solid, impassive personality with a strong, good-humoured face, the forehead of a thinker above it, and the jaw of an obstinate fighter below. Overhung brows shaded a pair of keen grey eyes, while the strong, set mouth was partly concealed by a grizzled moustache. Such was John French, leader of cavalry in Africa and now Field-Marshal commanding the Expeditionary Forces of Britain. His defence of Colesberg at

THE BATTLE OF MONS

a critical period when he bluffed the superior Boer forces, his dashing relief of Kimberley, and especially the gallant way in which he had thrown his exhausted cavalry across the path of Cronje's army in order to hold it while Roberts pinned it down at Paardeberg, were all exploits which were fresh in the public mind, and gave the soldiers confidence in their leader.

French might well appreciate the qualities of his immediate subordinates. Both of his army corps and his cavalry division were in good hands. Haig, like his leader, was a cavalry man by education, though now entrusted with the command of the First Army Corps, and destined for an ever-increasing European reputation. Fifty-four years of age, he still preserved all his natural energies, whilst he had behind him long years of varied military experience, including both the Soudanese and the South African campaigns, in both of which he had gained high distinction. He had the advantage of thoroughly understanding the mind of his commander, as he had worked under him as Chief of the Staff in his remarkable operations round Colesberg in those gloomy days which opened the Boer War.

The Second Army Corps sustained a severe loss before ever it reached the field of action, for its commander, General Grierson, died suddenly of heart failure in the train between Havre and Rouen upon August 18. Grierson had been for many years Military Attaché in Berlin, and one can well imagine how often he had longed to measure British soldiers against the self-sufficient critics around him. At the very last moment the ambition of his lifetime was denied him. His place, however, was worthily filled by General Smith-Dorrien, another South African veteran whose brigade in that difficult campaign had been recognised as one of the very best. Smith-Dorrien was a typical Imperial soldier in the world-wide character of his service, for he had followed the flag, and occasionally preceded it, in Zululand, Egypt, the Soudan, Chitral, and the Tirah before the campaign against the Boers. A sportsman as well as a soldier, he had very particularly won the affections of the Aldershot division by his system of trusting to their honour rather than to compulsion in matters of discipline. It was seldom indeed that his confidence was abused.

Haig and Smith-Dorrien were the two generals upon whom the immediate operations were to devolve, for the Third Army Corps was late, through no fault of its own, in coming into line. There remained the Cavalry Division commanded by General Allenby, who was a column leader in that great class for mounted tactics held in South Africa a dozen years before. It is remarkable that of the four leaders in the initial operations of the German War—French, Smith-Dorrien, Haig, and Allenby—three belonged to the cavalry, an arm which has usually been regarded as active and ornamental rather than intellectual. Pulteney, the commander of the Third Army Corps, was a product of the Guards, a veteran of much service and a well-known heavy-game shot. Thus, neither of the more learned corps were represented among the higher commanders upon the actual field of battle, but brooding over the whole operations was the steadfast, untiring brain of Joffre, whilst across the water the silent Kitchener, remorseless as Destiny, moved the forces of the Empire to the front. The last word in each case lay with the sappers.

THE BATTLE OF MONS

The general plan of campaign was naturally in the hands of General Joffre, since he was in command of far the greater portion of the Allied Force. It has been admitted in France that the original dispositions might be open to criticism, since a number of the French troops had engaged themselves in Alsace and Lorraine, to the weakening of the line of battle in the north, where the fate of Paris was to be decided. It is small profit to a nation to injure its rival ever so grievously in the toe when it is itself in imminent danger of being stabbed to the heart. A further change in plan had been caused by the intense sympathy felt both by the French and the British for the gallant Belgians, who had done so much and gained so many valuable days for the Allies. It was felt that it would be unchivalrous not to advance and do what was possible to relieve the intolerable pressure which was crushing them. It was resolved, therefore, to abandon the plan which had been formed, by which the Germans should be led as far as possible from their base, and to attack them at once. For this purpose the French Army changed its whole dispositions, which had been formed on the idea of an attack from the east, and advanced over the Belgian frontier, getting into touch with the enemy at Namur and Charleroi, so as to secure the passages of the Sambre. It was in fulfilling its part as the left of the Allied line that on August 18 and 19 the British troops began to move northwards into Belgium. The First Army Corps advanced through Le Nouvion, St. Remy, and Maubeuge to Rouveroy, which is a village upon the Mons-Chimay road. There it linked on to the right of the Second Corps, which had moved up to the line of

58   THE BRITISH CAMPAIGN, 1914

CHAPTER III.
The Battle of Mons.

the Condé-Mons Canal. On the morning of Sunday, August 23, all these troops were in position. The 5th Brigade of Cavalry (Chetwode's) lay out upon the right front at Binche, but the remainder of the cavalry was brought to a point about five miles behind the centre of the line, so as to be able to reinforce either flank. The first blood of the land campaign had been drawn upon August 22 outside Soignies, when a reconnoitring squadron of the 4th Dragoon Guards under Captain Hornby charged and overthrew a body of the 4th German Cuirassiers, bringing back some prisoners. The 20th Hussars had enjoyed a similar experience. It was a small but happy omen.

The advance to Mons.

The forces which now awaited the German attack numbered about 86,000 men, who may be roughly divided into 76,000 infantry, 10,000 cavalry, and 312 guns. The general alignment was as follows: The First Army Corps held the space between Mons and Binche, which was soon contracted to Bray as the eastward limit. Close to Mons, where the attack was expected to break, since the town is a point of considerable strategic importance, there was a thickening of the line of defence. From that point the Third Division and the Fifth, in the order named, carried on the British formation down the length of the Mons-Condé Canal. The front of the Army covered nearly twenty miles, an excessive strain upon so small a force in the presence of a compact enemy.

If one looks at the general dispositions, it becomes clear that Sir John French was preparing for an attack upon his right flank. From all his information the enemy was to the north and to the east of him, so that if they set about turning his position it must be from the Charleroi direction. Hence, his right

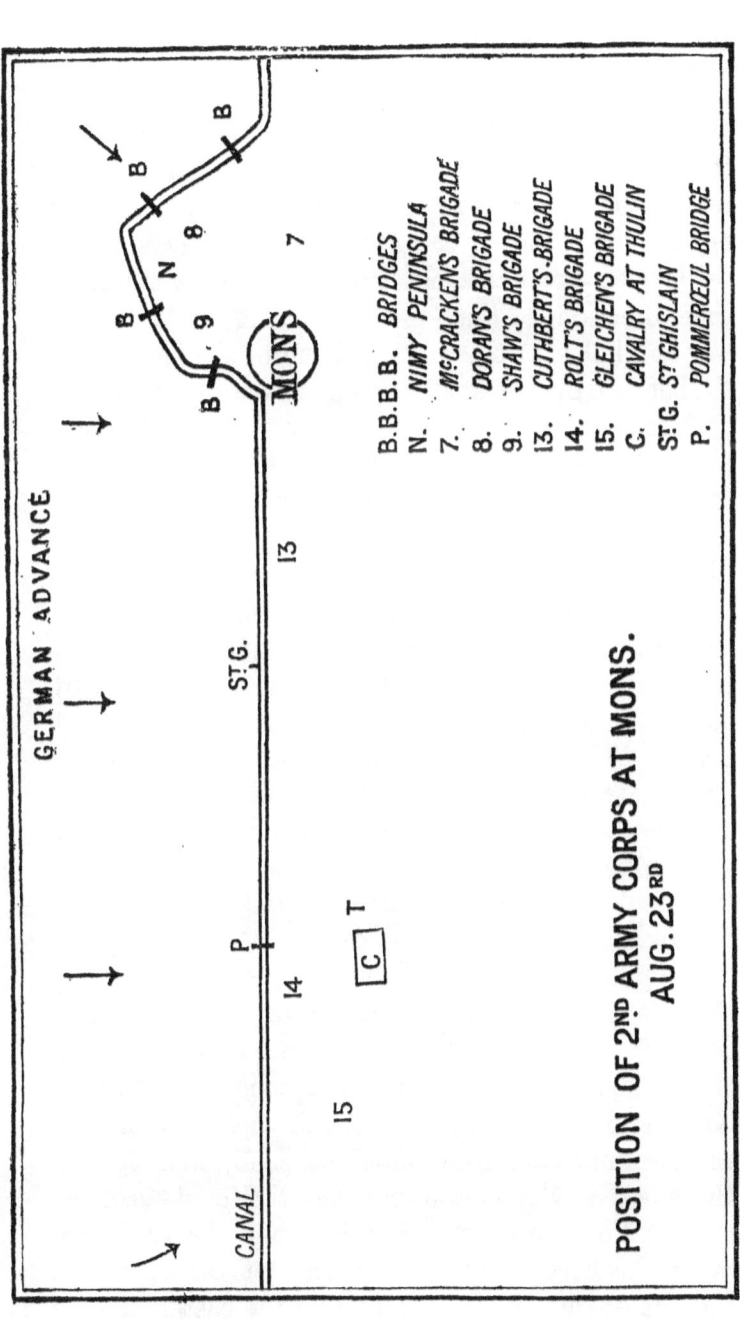

wing was laid back at an angle to the rest of his line, and the only cavalry which he kept in advance was thrown out to Binche in front of this flank. The rest of the cavalry was on the day of battle drawn in behind the centre of the Army, but as danger began to develop upon the left flank it was sent across in that direction, so that on the morning of the 24th it was at Thulin, at the westward end of the line.

The line of the canal was a most tempting position to defend from Condé to Mons, for it ran as straight as a Roman road across the path of an invader. But it was very different at Mons itself. Here it formed a most awkward loop. A glance at the diagram will show this formation. It was impossible to leave it undefended, and yet troops who held it were evidently subjected to a flanking artillery fire from each side. The canal here was also crossed by at least three substantial road bridges and one railway bridge. This section of the defence was under the immediate direction of General Smith-Dorrien, who at once took steps to prepare a second line of defence, thrown back to the right rear of the town, so that if the canal were forced the British array would remain unbroken. The immediate care of this weak point in the position was committed to General Beauchamp Doran's 8th Brigade, consisting of the 2nd Royal Scots, 2nd Royal Irish, 4th Middlesex, and 1st Gordon Highlanders. On their left, occupying the village of Nimy and the western side of the peninsula, as well as the immediate front of Mons itself, was the 9th Brigade (Shaw's), containing the 4th Royal Fusiliers, the 1st Northumberland Fusiliers, and the 1st Royal Scots Fusiliers, together with the 1st Lincolns. To the left of this brigade, occupying the eastern end of

THE BATTLE OF MONS

the Mons-Condé line of canal, was Cuthbert's 13th Brigade, containing the 2nd Scottish Borderers, 2nd West Ridings, 1st West Kents, and 2nd Yorkshire Light Infantry. It was on these three brigades, and especially on the 8th and 9th, that the impact of the German army was destined to fall. Beyond them, scattered somewhat thinly along the line of the Mons-Condé Canal from the railway bridge west of St. Ghislain, were the two remaining brigades of the Fifth Division, the 14th (Rolt's) and the 15th (Gleichen's), the latter being in divisional reserve. Still farther to the west the head of the newly arrived 19th Brigade just touched the canal, and was itself in touch with French cavalry at Condé. Sundry units of artillery and field hospitals had not yet come up, but otherwise the two corps were complete.

Having reached their ground, the troops, with no realisation of immediate danger, proceeded to make shallow trenches. Their bands had not been brought to the front, but the universal singing from one end of the line to the other showed that the men were in excellent spirits. Cheering news had come in from the cavalry, detachments of which, as already stated, had ridden out as far as Soignies, meeting advance patrols of the enemy and coming back with prisoners and trophies. The guns were drawn up in concealed positions within half a mile of the line of battle. All was now ready, and officers could be seen on every elevation peering northwards through their glasses for the first sign of the enemy. It was a broken country, with large patches of woodland and green spaces between. There were numerous slag-heaps from old mines, with here and there a factory and here and there a private dwelling, but the sappers

CHAPTER III.

The Battle of Mons.

had endeavoured in the short time to clear a field of fire for the infantry. In order to get this field of fire in so closely built a neighbourhood, several of the regiments, such as the West Kents of the 13th and the Cornwalls of the 14th Brigades, had to take their positions across the canal with bridges in their rear. Thrilling with anticipation, the men waited for their own first entrance upon the stupendous drama. They were already weary and footsore, for they had all done at least two days of forced marching, and the burden of the pack, the rifle, and the hundred and fifty rounds per man was no light one. They lay snugly in their trenches under the warm August sun and waited. It was a Sunday, and more than one have recorded in their letters how in that hour of tension their thoughts turned to the old home church and the mellow call of the village bells.

A hovering aeroplane had just slid down with the news that the roads from the north were alive with the advancing Germans, but the estimate of the aviator placed them at two corps and a division of cavalry. This coincided roughly with the accounts brought in by the scouts and, what was more important, with the forecast of General Joffre. Secure in the belief that he was flanked upon one side by the 5th French Army, and on the other by a screen of French cavalry, whilst his front was approached by a force not appreciably larger than his own, General French had no cause for uneasiness. Had his airmen taken a wider sweep to the north and west,[1] or had the French commander among his many pressing

---

[1] An American correspondent, Mr. Harding Davis, actually saw a shattered British aeroplane upon the ground in this region. Its destruction may have been of great strategic importance. This aviator was probably the first British soldier to fall in the Continental War.

THE BATTLE OF MONS 63

preoccupations been able to give an earlier warning to his British colleague, the trenches would, no doubt, have been abandoned before a grey coat had appeared, and the whole Army brought swiftly to a position of strategical safety. Even now, as they waited expectantly for the enemy, a vast steel trap was closing up for their destruction.

Let us take a glance at what was going on over that northern horizon. The American Powell had seen something of the mighty right swing which was to end the combat. Invited to a conference with a German general who was pursuing the national policy of soothing the United States until her own turn should come round, Mr. Powell left Brussels and chanced to meet Von Kluck's legions upon their western and southerly trek. He describes with great force the effect upon his mind of those endless grey columns, all flowing in the same direction, double files of infantry on either side of the road, and endless guns, motor-cars, cavalry, and transport between. The men, as he describes them, were all in the prime of life, and equipped with everything which years of forethought could devise. He was dazed and awed by the tremendous procession, its majesty and its self-evident efficiency. It is no wonder, for he was looking at the chosen legions of the most wonderful army that the world had ever seen—an army which represented the last possible word on the material and mechanical side of war. High in the van a Taube aeroplane, like an embodiment of that black eagle which is the fitting emblem of a warlike and rapacious race, pointed the path for the German hordes.

A day or two before, two American correspondents,

CHAPTER III.

The Battle of Mons.

Mr. Irvin Cobb and Mr. Harding Davis, had seen the same great army as it streamed westwards through Louvain and Brussels. They graphically describe how for three consecutive days and the greater part of three nights they poured past, giving the impression of unconquerable energy and efficiency, young, enthusiastic, wonderfully equipped. "Either we shall go forward or we die. We do not expect to fall back ever. If the generals would let them, the men would run to Paris instead of walking there." So spoke one of the leaders of that huge invading host, the main part of which was now heading straight for the British line. A second part, unseen and unsuspected, were working round by Tournai to the west, hurrying hard to strike in upon the British flank and rear. The German is a great marcher as well as a great fighter, and the average rate of progress was little less than thirty miles a day.

It was after ten o'clock when scouting cavalry were observed falling back. Then the distant sound of a gun was heard, and a few seconds later a shell burst some hundreds of yards behind the British lines. The British guns one by one roared into action. A cloud of smoke rose along the line of the woods in front from the bursting shrapnel, but nothing could be seen of the German gunners. The defending guns were also well concealed. Here and there, from observation points upon buildings and slag-heaps, the controllers of the batteries were able to indicate targets and register hits unseen by the gunners themselves. The fire grew warmer and warmer as fresh batteries dashed up and unlimbered on either side. The noise was horrible, but no enemy had been seen by the infantry, and little damage done.

But now an ill-omened bird flew over the British lines. Far aloft across the deep blue sky skimmed the dark Taube, curved, turned, and sailed northwards again. It had marked the shells bursting beyond the trenches. In an instant, by some devilish cantrip of signal or wireless, it had set the range right. A rain of shells roared and crashed along the lines of the shallow trenches. The injuries were not yet numerous, but they were inexpressibly ghastly. Men who had hardly seen worse than a cut finger in their lives gazed with horror at the gross mutilations around them. " One dared not look sideways," said one of them. Stretcher-bearers bent and heaved while wet, limp forms were hoisted upwards by their comrades. Officers gave short, sharp words of encouragement or advice. The minutes seemed very long, and still the shells came raining down. The men shoved the five-fold clips down into their magazines and waited with weary patience. A senior officer peering over the end of a trench leaned tensely forward and rested his glasses upon the grassy edge. " They're coming ! " he whispered to his neighbour. It ran from lip to lip along the line of crouching men. Heads were poked up here and there above the line of broken earth. Soon, in spite of the crashing shells overhead, there was a fringe of peering faces. And there at last in front of them was the German enemy. After all the centuries, Briton and Teuton faced each other at last for the test of battle.

A stylist among letter-writers has described that oncoming swarm as grey clouds drifting over green fields. They had deployed under cover whilst the batteries were preparing their path, and now over an extended front to the north-west of Mons they

F

were breaking out from the woods and coming rapidly onwards. The men fidgeted with their triggers, but no order came to fire. The officers were gazing with professional interest and surprise at the German formations. Were these the tactics of the army which had claimed to be the most scientific in Europe ? British observers had seen it in peace-time and had conjectured that it was a screen for some elaborate tactics held up for the day of battle. Yet here they were, advancing in what in old Soudan days used to be described as the twenty-acre formation, against the best riflemen in Europe. It was not even a shoulder to shoulder column, but a mere crowd, shredding out in the front and dense to the rear. There was nothing of the swiftly weaving lines, the rushes of alternate companies, the twinkle and flicker of a modern attack. It was mediaeval, and yet it was impressive also in its immediate display of numbers and the ponderous insistence of its onward flow. It was not many weeks before the stern lesson of war taught very different formations to those of the grand Kaiser manœuvres.

The men, still fingering their triggers, gazed expectantly at their officers, who measured intently the distance of the approaching swarms. The Germans had already begun to fire in a desultory fashion. Shrapnel was bursting thickly along the head of their columns but they were coming steadily onwards. Suddenly a rolling wave of independent firing broke out from the British position. At some portions of the line the enemy were at eight hundred, at others at one thousand yards. The men, happy in having something definite to do, snuggled down earnestly to their work and fired swiftly but deliberately into the approaching mass. Rifles, machine-guns, and field-pieces were all roaring together, while the incessant crash of the shells overhead added to the infernal uproar. Men lost all sense of time as they thrust clip after clip into their rifles. The German swarms staggered on bravely under that leaden sleet. Then they halted, vacillated, and finally thinned, shredded out, and drifted backwards like a grey fog torn by a gale. The woods absorbed them once again, whilst the rain of shells upon the British trenches became thicker and more deadly.

There was a lull in the infantry attack, and the British, peering from their shelters, surveyed with a grim satisfaction the patches and smudges of grey which showed the effect of their fire. But the rest was not a long one. With fine courage the German battalions re-formed under the shelter of the trees, while fresh troops from the rear pushed forward to stiffen the shaken lines. "Hold your fire!" was the order that ran down the ranks. With the confidence bred of experience, the men waited and still waited, till the very features of the Germans could be distinguished. Then once more the deadly fire rippled down the line, the masses shredded and dissolved, and the fugitives hurried to the woods. Then came the pause under shell fire, and then once again the emergence of the infantry, the attack, the check, and the recoil. Such were the general characteristics of the action at Mons over a large portion of the British line—that portion which extended along the actual course of the canal.

It is not to be supposed, however, that there was a monotony of attack and defence over the whole of the British position. A large part of the force, including the whole of the First Army Corps, was threatened rather than seriously engaged, while the opposite end of the line was also out of the main track of the storm. It beat most dangerously, as had been foreseen, upon the troops to the immediate west and north of Mons, and especially upon those which defended the impossible peninsula formed by the loop of the canal.

There is a road which runs from Mons due north through the village of Nimy to Jurbise. The defences to the west of this road were in the hands of the 9th Brigade. The 4th Royal Fusiliers, with the Scots Fusiliers, were the particular battalions which held the trenches skirting this part of the peninsula, while half the Northumberland Fusiliers were on the straight canal to the westward. To the east of Nimy are three road bridges—those of Nimy itself, Lock No. 5, and Aubourg Station. All these three bridges were defended by the 4th Middlesex, who had made shallow trenches which commanded them. The Gordons were on their immediate right. The field of fire was much interfered with by the mines and buildings which faced them, so that at this point the Germans could get up unobserved to the very front. It has also been already explained that the German artillery could enfilade the peninsula from each side, making the defence most difficult. A rush of German troops came between eleven and twelve o'clock across the Aubourg Station Bridge. It was so screened up to the moment of the advance that neither the rifles nor the machine-guns of the Middlesex could stop it. It is an undoubted fact that this rush was preceded by a great crowd of women and children, through which the leading files of the

Germans could hardly be seen. At the same time, or very shortly afterwards, the other two bridges were forced in a similar manner, but the Germans in all three cases as they reached the farther side were unable to make any rapid headway against the British fire, though they made the position untenable for the troops in trenches between the bridges. The whole of the 8th Brigade, supported by the 2nd Irish Rifles from McCracken's 7th Brigade, which had been held in reserve at Ciply, were now fully engaged, covering the retirement of the Middlesex and Gordons. At some points the firing between the two lines of infantry was across the breadth of a road. Two batteries of the 40th Artillery Brigade, which were facing the German attack at this point, were badly mauled, one of them, the 23rd R.F.A., losing its gun teams. Major Ingham succeeded in reconstituting his equipment and getting his guns away.

It is well to accentuate the fact that though this was the point of the most severe pressure there was never any disorderly retirement, and strong reserves were available had they been needed. The 8th Brigade, at the time of the general strategical withdrawal of the Army, made its arrangements in a methodical fashion, and General Doran kept his hold until after nightfall upon Bois la Haut, which was an elevation to the east of Mons from which the German artillery might have harassed the British retreat, since it commanded all the country to the south. The losses of the brigade had, however, been considerable, amounting to not less than three hundred and fifty in the case of the 4th Middlesex, many being killed or wounded in the defence, and some cut off in the trenches between the various bridge-heads. Majors

Davey and Abell of the Middlesex were respectively wounded and killed, with thirteen other officers.

It has already been said that the line of the 4th Royal Fusiliers extended along the western perimeter up to Nimy Road Bridge, where Colonel MacMahon's section ended and that of Colonel Hull, of the Middlesex Regiment, began. To the west of this point was the Nimy Railway Bridge, defended also by Captain Ashburner's company of the 4th Royal Fusiliers. This was assaulted early, and was held for nearly five hours against an attack of several German battalions. The British artillery was unable to help much in the defence, as the town of Mons behind offered no positions for guns, but the 107th Battery in the immediate rear did good work. The defence was continued until the Germans who had already crossed to the east were advancing on the flank. Lieutenant Maurice Dease, five times wounded before he was killed, worked his machine-gun to the end, and every man of his detachment was hit. Lieutenant Dease and Private Godley both received the Victoria Cross. The occupants of one trench, including Lieutenant Smith, who was wounded, were cut off by the rush. Captain Carey commanded the covering company and the retirement was conducted in good order, though Captain Bowden Smith, Lieutenant Mead, and a number of men fell in the movement. Altogether, the Royal Fusiliers lost five officers and about two hundred men in the defence of the bridge, Lieutenant Tower having seven survivors in his platoon of sixty. Captain Byng's company at the Glin Bridge farther east had severe losses and was driven in in the same way. As the infantry retired a small party of engineers under Captain Theodore

THE BATTLE OF MONS

Wright endeavoured to destroy this and other bridges. Lieutenant Day was twice wounded in his attempt upon the main Nimy Bridge. Corporal Jarvis received the V.C. for his exertions in preparing the Jemappes bridge for destruction to the west of Nimy. Captain Wright, with Sergeant Smith, made an heroic endeavour under terrific fire to detonate the charge, but was wounded and fell into the canal. Lieutenant Holt, a brave young officer of reserve engineers, also lost his life in these operations.

Having held on as long as was possible, the front line of the 9th Brigade fell back upon the prepared position on high ground between Mons and Frameries, where the 107th R.F.A. was entrenched. The 4th Royal Fusiliers passed through Mons and reached the new line in good order and without further loss. The 1st Royal Scots Fusiliers, however, falling back to the same point on a different route through Flenu, came under heavy machine-gun fire from a high soil heap, losing Captain Rose and a hundred men.

The falling back of the 8th and 9th Brigades from the Nimy Peninsula had an immediate effect upon Cuthbert's 13th Brigade, which was on their left holding the line up to the railway bridge just east of St. Ghislain. Of this brigade two battalions, the 1st West Kent on the right and the 2nd Scottish Borderers on the left, were in the trenches while the 2nd West Riding and the 2nd Yorkshire Light Infantry were in support, having their centre at Boussu. The day began by some losses to the West Kent Regiment, who were probably, apart from cavalry patrols, the first troops to suffer in the great war. A company of the regiment under Captain Lister was sent across the canal early as a support to some advancing

CHAPTER III.

The Battle of Mons.

cavalry, and was driven in about eleven o'clock with a loss of two officers and about a hundred men. From this time onwards the German attacks were easily held, though the German guns were within twelve hundred yards. The situation was changed when it was learned later in the day that the Germans were across to the right and had got as far as Flenu on the flank of the brigade. In view of this advance, General Smith-Dorrien, having no immediate supports, dashed off on a motor to Sir Douglas Haig's headquarters some four miles distant, and got his permission to use Haking's 5th Brigade, which pushed up in time to re-establish the line.

It has been shown that the order of the regiments closely engaged in the front line was, counting from the east, the 1st Gordons, the 4th Middlesex, the 4th Royal Fusiliers, the 1st Scots Fusiliers, half the 1st Northumberland Fusiliers, the 1st West Kents, and the 2nd Scottish Borderers, the other regiments of these brigades being in reserve. The last-named battalion, being opposite a bridge, was heavily engaged all day, losing many men, but holding its position intact against repeated advances. On the left hand or western side of the Scottish Borderers, continuing the line along the canal, one would come upon the front of the 14th Brigade (Rolt's), which was formed by the 1st Surrey on the right and the 1st Duke of Cornwall's on the left. The German attack upon this portion of the line began about 1 P.M., and by 3 P.M. had become so warm that the reserve companies were drawn into the firing line. Thanks to their good work, both with rifles and with machine-guns, the regiments held their own until about six o'clock in the evening, when the retirement of the troops on

THE BATTLE OF MONS

their right enabled the Germans to enfilade the right section of the East Surreys at close range. They were ordered to retire, but lost touch with the left section, which remained to the north of the canal where their trench was situated. Captain Benson of this section had been killed and Captain Campbell severely wounded, but the party of one hundred and ten men under Lieutenant Morritt held on most gallantly and made a very fine defence. Being finally surrounded, they endeavoured to cut their way out with cold steel, Lieutenant Ward being killed and Morritt four times wounded in the attempt. Many of the men were killed and wounded, and the survivors were taken. Altogether the loss of the regiment was five officers and one hundred and thirty-four men.

On the left of the East Surreys, as already stated, lay the 1st Duke of Cornwall's of the same brigade. About four o'clock in the afternoon the presence of the German outflanking corps first made itself felt. At that hour the Cornwalls were aware of an advance upon their left as well as their front. The Cornwalls drew in across the canal in consequence, and the Germans did not follow them over that evening.

The chief point defended by the 14th Brigade upon this day had been the bridge and main road which crosses the canal between Pommeroeul and Thulin, some eight or nine miles west of Mons. In the evening, when the final order for retreat was given, this bridge was blown up, and the brigade fell back after nightfall as far as Dour, where it slept.

By the late afternoon the general position was grave, but not critical. The enemy had lost very heavily, while the men in the trenches were, in comparison, unscathed. Here and there, as we have seen, the Germans had obtained a lodgment in the British position, especially at the salient which had always appeared to be impossible to hold, but, on the other hand, the greater part of the Army, including the whole First Corps, had not yet been seriously engaged, and there were reserve troops in the immediate rear of the fighting line who could be trusted to make good any gap in the ranks before them. The German artillery fire was heavy and well-directed, but the British batteries had held their own. Such was the position when, about 5 P.M., a telegram from General Joffre was put into Sir John French's hand, which must have brought a pang to his heart. From it he learned that all his work had been in vain, and that far from contending for victory, he would be fortunate if he saved himself from utter defeat.

There were two pieces of information in this fatal message, and each was disastrous. The first announced that instead of the two German corps whom he had reason to think were in front of him, there were four—the Third, Fourth, Seventh, and Fourth Reserve Corps—forming, with the second and fourth cavalry divisions, a force of nearly 200,000 men, while the Second Corps were bringing another 40,000 round his left flank from the direction of Tournai. The second item was even more serious. Instead of being buttressed up with French troops on either side of him, he learned that the Germans had burst the line of the Sambre, and that the French armies on his right were already in full retreat, while nothing substantial lay upon his left. It was a most perilous position. The British force lay exposed and unsupported amid converging foes who far outnumbered it in men and guns. What was the profit of one day of successful defence if the morrow would dawn upon a British Sedan? There was only one course of action, and Sir John decided upon it in the instant, bitter as the decision must have been. The Army must be extricated from the battle and fall back until it resumed touch with its Allies.

But it is no easy matter to disengage so large an army which is actually in action and hard-pressed by a numerous and enterprising enemy. The front was extensive and the lines of retreat were limited. That the operation was carried out in an orderly fashion is a testimony to the skill of the General, the talents of the commanders, and the discipline of the units. If it had been done at once and simultaneously it would certainly have been the signal for a vigorous German advance and a possible disaster. The positions were therefore held, though no efforts were made to retake those points where the enemy had effected a lodgment. There was no possible use in wasting troops in regaining positions which would in no case be held. As dusk fell, a dusk which was lightened by the glare of burning villages, some of the regiments began slowly to draw off to the rear. In the early morning of the 24th the definite order to retire was conveyed to the corps commanders, whilst immediate measures were taken to withdraw the impedimenta and to clear the roads.

Such, in its bare outlines, was the action of Mons upon August 23, interesting for its own sake, but more so as being the first clash between the British and German armies. One or two questions call for discussion before the narrative passes on. The most obvious of these is the question of the bridges. Why were they not blown up in the dangerous peninsula?

CHAPTER III.

The Battle of Mons.

Without having any special information upon the point, one might put forward the speculation that the reason why they were not at once blown up was that the whole of Joffre's advance was an aggressive movement for the relief of Namur, and that the bridges were not destroyed because they would be used in a subsequent advance. It will always be a subject for speculation as to what would have occurred had the battle been fought to a finish. Considering the comparative merits of British and German infantry as shown in many a subsequent encounter, and allowing for the advantage that the defence has over the attack, it is probable that the odds might not have been too great and that Sir John French might have remained master of the field. That, however, is a matter of opinion. What is not a matter of opinion is that the other German armies to the east would have advanced on the heels of the retiring French, that they would have cut the British off from their Allies, and that they would have been hard put to it to reach the coast. Therefore, win or lose, the Army had no possible course open but to retire. The actual losses of the British were not more than three or four thousand, the greater part from the 8th, 9th, and 13th Brigades. There are no means as yet by which the German losses can be taken out from the general returns, but when one considers the repeated advances over the open and the constant breaking of the dense attacking formations, it is impossible that they should have been fewer than from seven to ten thousand men. Each army had for the first time an opportunity of forming a critical estimate of the other. German officers have admitted with soldierly frankness that the efficiency of the British came to them as a revelation, which is

THE BATTLE OF MONS

not surprising after the assurances that had been made to them. On the other hand, the British bore away a very clear conviction of the excellence of the German artillery and of the plodding bravery of the German infantry, together with a great reassurance as to their own capacity to hold their own at any reasonable odds.

After a night of flames and of uproar the day dawned, a day of great anxiety to the British commanders and of considerable pressure upon a portion of the troops. Sir John French had given instructions that the First Corps, which had been only slightly engaged the day before, should pretend to assume the offensive upon the extreme right wing in the direction of Binche, whilst the Second Corps began its retirement. The enemy was following up rapidly, however, along the whole length of the British line, both flanks of which were exposed. Shortly after dawn the evacuated positions had been occupied, and Mons itself was in the hands of the advancing Germans. The Second Corps began its retreat, helped by the feint which was carried out by General Haig upon the right, and by the bulk of the batteries of both corps, but the pursuit was vigorous and the shell-fire incessant. A shell from the rear is more intimidating than twenty in the front. Hamilton's Third Division, including the 8th and 9th Brigades, who had done such hard work the day before, sustained the most severe losses, especially at Frameries, four miles south of Mons. The 2nd Royal Scots of the 8th Brigade about midnight had been attacked by a heavy German column which got so near that the swish of their feet through the long grass put the regiment on the alert. The attack was

CHAPTER III.

The Battle of Mons.

The rearguard actions of Frameries, Wasmes, and Dour.

78   THE BRITISH CAMPAIGN, 1914

Chapter III.

The Battle of Mons.

blown back by a volley at close quarters. The 9th Brigade (Shaw's), which covered the retreat, was closely pressed from dawn by the pursuing Germans, and was subjected to a very heavy shell-fire. A barricade, erected in the village and manned by Captain Sandilands, of the Northumberlands, with his company, held up the German advance, and they were never permitted to reach the line nor to hustle the retirement. Butler's 23rd Artillery Brigade helped with its fire. The chief losses in this skilful covering action fell upon the 1st Lincolns and upon the 1st Northumberland Fusiliers, each of which lost about 150 men, including Captain Rose, Lieutenants Bulbe, Welchman, and others. There was a stational ambulance in the village of Frameries, and a foreign nurse in its employ has left a vivid picture of the wounded British rushing in grimy and breathless to have their slighter wounds dressed and then running out, rifle in hand, to find their place in the firing line.

The remaining brigade of the Third Division, McCracken's 7th Brigade, had detached one regiment, the 2nd Irish Rifles, upon the day before to reinforce the 8th Brigade, and this regiment had, as already mentioned, some severe fighting, holding back the German advance after the retirement from the Nimy Peninsula of the Middlesex and the Gordons. It did not find its way back to its brigade until the evening of the 24th. The brigade itself, during the first day of the retreat, held a position near Ciply, to the south of Mons, where it was heavily attacked in the early morning, and in some danger as its flank was exposed. At ten o'clock it was ordered to retire *via* Genly towards Bavai, and it carried out this difficult movement in the face of a pushful enemy in

THE BATTLE OF MONS

perfect order, covered by the divisional artillery. The principal losses fell upon the 2nd South Lancashire Regiment, which came under heavy fire from German machine-guns posted upon slag-heaps. This regiment was very hard hit, losing several hundred men. The brigade faced round near Bavai and held off the pursuit.

Cuthbert's 13th Brigade, keeping in line with their comrades on the right, halted at Wasmes, some four miles from the canal, where they prepared some hasty entrenchments. Here, at the dawn of day, they were furiously attacked by the German vanguard at the same time that the 9th Brigade was hustled in Frameries, but for two hours the assailants were beaten back with heavy losses. The brunt of the fighting fell upon the 2nd West Riding Regiment, who lost heavily, were at one time nearly surrounded, and finally, with dour Yorkshire pertinacity, shook themselves clear. Their losses included their commander, Colonel Gibbs, their adjutant, 300 men, and all their officers save five. The 1st West Kents also lost about 100 men and several officers, including Major Pack-Beresford. For the remainder of the day and for the whole of the 25th the brigade, with the rest of the Fifth Division, fell back with little fighting *via* Bavai to the Le Cateau line.

On the evening of the 23rd the 14th Brigade, still farther to the west, had fallen back to Dour, blowing up the bridge and road over the canal. After dark the Germans followed them, and Gleichen's 15th Brigade, which had not yet been engaged, found itself in the position of rearguard and immediately exposed to the pressure of the German flanking movement. This was now threatening to envelop the

80   THE BRITISH CAMPAIGN, 1914

CHAPTER III.
The Battle of Mons.

whole of Ferguson's Fifth Division. The situation was particularly difficult, since this General had to make a flank movement in the face of the enemy in order to close up with his comrades of the Third Division. He was soon compelled to call for assistance, and Allenby, with his cavalry division, was advanced to help him. It was evidently the intention of the enemy to strike in upon the western side of the division and pin it to its ground until it could be surrounded.

The charge of the Lancers.

The first menacing advance in the morning of the 24th was directed against the flank of the British infantry who were streaming down the Elouges-Dour high road. The situation was critical, and a portion of De Lisle's 2nd Cavalry Brigade was ordered to charge near Andregnies, the hostile infantry being at that time about a thousand yards distant, with several batteries in support. The attack of the cavalry was vigorously supported by L Battery of Horse Artillery. The charge was carried out by three squadrons of the 9th Lancers, Colonel Campbell at their head. The 4th Dragoon Guards under Colonel Mullens was in support. The cavalry rode forward amidst a heavy but not particularly deadly fire until they were within a few hundred yards of the enemy, when, being faced by a wire fence, they swung to the right and rallied under the cover of some slag-heaps and of a railway embankment. Their menace and rifle fire, or the fine work of Major Sclater-Booth's battery, had the effect of holding up the German advance for some time, and though the cavalry were much scattered and disorganised they were able to reunite without any excessive loss, the total casualties being a little over two hundred. Some

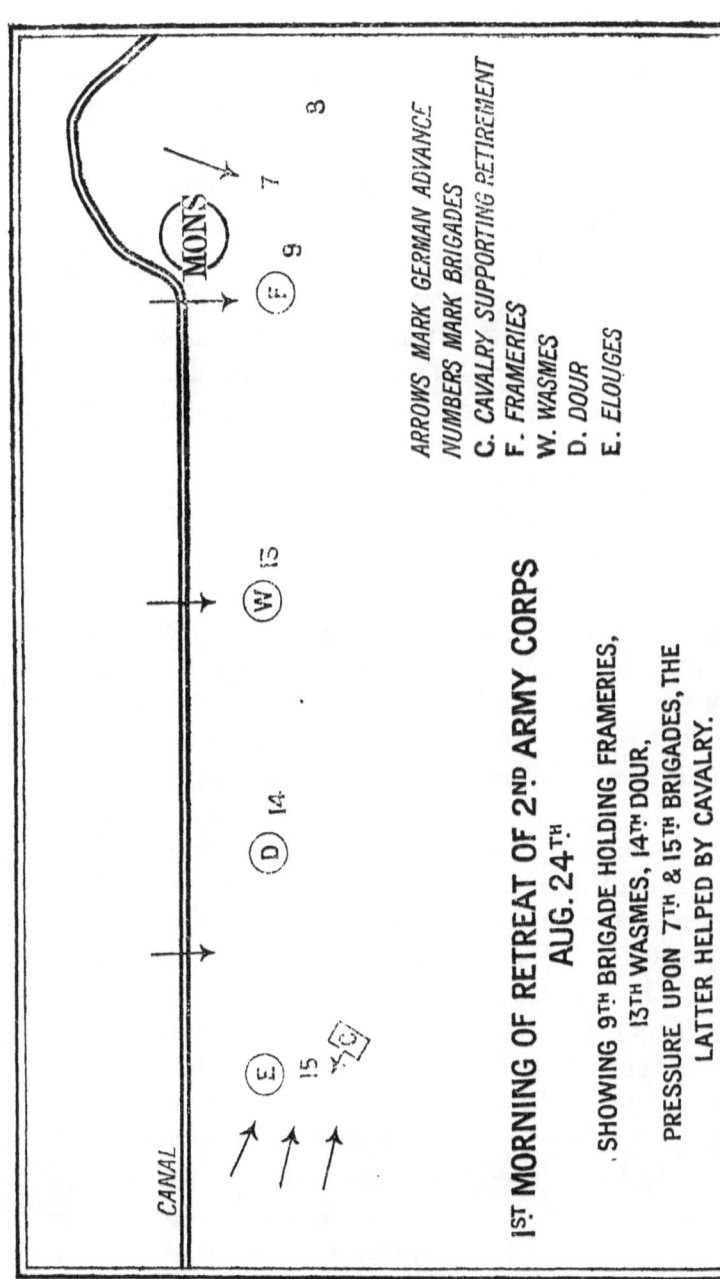

82   THE BRITISH CAMPAIGN, 1914

CHAPTER III.
The Battle of Mons.

hours later the enemy's pressure again became heavy upon Ferguson's flank, and the 1st Cheshires and 1st Norfolks, of Gleichen's 15th Brigade, which formed the infantry flank-guard, incurred heavy losses. It was in this defensive action that the 119th R.F.A., under Major Alexander, fought itself to a standstill with only three unwounded gunners by the guns. The battery had silenced one German unit and was engaged with three others. Only Major Alexander and Lieutenant Pollard with a few men were left. As the horses had been destroyed the pieces had to be man-handled out of action. Captain the Hon. F. Grenfell, of the 9th Lancers, bleeding from two wounds, with several officers, Sergeants Davids and Turner, and some fifty men of the regiment, saved these guns under a terrible fire, the German infantry being within close range. During the whole long, weary day the batteries and horsemen were working hard to cover the retreat, while the surgeons exposed themselves with great fearlessness, lingering behind the retiring lines in order to give first aid to the men who had been hit by the incessant shell-fire. It was in this noble task—the noblest surely within the whole range of warfare—that Captain Malcolm Leckie, and other brave medical officers, met with a glorious end, upholding to the full the traditions of their famous corps.

The fate of the Cheshires.

It has been stated that the 1st Cheshires, in endeavouring to screen the west flank of the Second Corps from the German pursuit, were very badly punished. This regiment, together with the Norfolks, occupied a low ridge to the north-east side of the village of Elouges, which they endeavoured to hold against the onflowing tide of Germans. About three in the afternoon it was seen

THE BATTLE OF MONS 83

that there was danger of this small flank-guard being entirely cut off. As a matter of fact an order had actually been sent for a retreat, but had not reached them. Colonel Boger of the Cheshires sent several messengers, representing the growing danger, but no answer came back. Finally, in desperation, Colonel Boger went himself and found that the enemy held the position previously occupied by the rest of Gleichen's Brigade, which had retired. The Cheshires had by this time endured dreadful losses, and were practically surrounded. A bayonet charge eased the pressure for a short time, but the enemy again closed in and the bulk of the survivors, isolated amidst a hostile army corps, were compelled to surrender. Some escaped in small groups and made their way through to their retreating comrades. When roll was next called, there remained 5 officers and 193 men out of 27 officers and 1007 of all ranks who had gone into action. It speaks volumes for the discipline of the regiment that this remnant, under Captain Shore, continued to act as a useful unit. These various episodes, including the severe losses of Gleichen's 15th Brigade, the attack of the 2nd Cavalry Brigade, and the artillery action in which the 119th Battery was so severely handled, group themselves into a separate little action occurring the day after Mons and associated either with the villages of Elouges or of Dour. The Second German Corps continued to act upon the western side of the Second British Corps, whilst the rest of General von Kluck's army followed it behind. With three corps close behind him, and one snapping at his flank, General Smith-Dorrien made his way southwards, his gunners and cavalry labouring hard to relieve the ever-increasing

84   THE BRITISH CAMPAIGN, 1914

CHAPTER III.

The Battle of Mons.

pressure, while his rear brigades were continually sprayed by the German shrapnel.

It is to be noted that Sir John French includes the Ninth German Corps in Von Kluck's army in his first dispatch, and puts it in Von Bulow's second army in his second dispatch. The French authorities are of opinion that Von Kluck's army consisted of the Second, Third, Fourth, Seventh, and Fourth Reserve Corps, with two divisions of cavalry. If this be correct, then part of Von Bulow's army was pursuing Haig, while the *whole* of Von Kluck's was concentrated upon Smith-Dorrien. This would make the British performance even more remarkable than it has hitherto appeared, since it would mean that during the pursuit, and at the subsequent battle, ten German divisions were pressing upon three British ones.

It is not to be supposed that so huge a force was all moving abreast, or available simultaneously at any one point. None the less a General can use his advance corps very much more freely when he knows that every gap can be speedily filled.

A tiny reinforcement had joined the Army on the morning after the battle of Mons. This was the 19th Brigade under General Drummond, which consisted of the 1st Middlesex, 1st Scots Rifles, 2nd Welsh Fusiliers, and 2nd Argyll and Sutherland Highlanders. This detached brigade acted, and continued to act during a large part of the war, as an independent unit. It detrained at Valenciennes on August 23, and two regiments, the Middlesex and the Cameronians, may be said to have taken part in the battle of Mons, since they formed up at the east of Condé, on the extreme left of the British position, and received, together with the Queen's Bays, who were scouting in front of them, the first impact of the German flanking corps. They fell back with the Army upon the 24th and 25th, keeping the line Jenlain—Solesmes, finally reaching Le Cateau, where they eventually took up their position on the right rear of the British Army.

As the Army fell back, the border fortress of Maubeuge with its heavy guns offered a tempting haven of rest for the weary and overmatched troops, but not in vain had France lost her army in Metz. Sir John French would have no such protection, however violently the Germans might push him towards it. "The British Army invested in Maubeuge" was not destined to furnish the head-line of a Berlin special edition. The fortress was left to the eastward, and the tired troops snatched a few hours of rest near Bavai, still pursued by the guns and the searchlights of their persistent foemen. At an early hour of the 25th the columns were again on the march for the south, and for safety.

It may be remarked that in all this movement what made the operation most difficult and complicated was, that in the retirement the Army was not moving direct to the rear, but diagonally away to the west, thus making the west flank more difficult to cover as well as complicating the movements of transport. It was this oblique movement which caused the Third Division to change places with the Fifth, so that from now onwards it was to the west of the Army.

The greater part of the Fourth Division of the Third Army Corps, coming up from the lines of communication, brought upon this day a welcome reinforcement to the Army and did yeoman work in covering the retirement. The total composition of this division was as follows :—

THIRD ARMY CORPS

GENERAL PULTENEY.

DIVISION IV.—General SNOW.

10*th Infantry Brigade—General Haldane.*
1st Warwicks.
2nd Seaforths.
1st Irish Fusiliers.
2nd Dublin Fusiliers.

11*th Infantry Brigade—General Hunter-Weston.*
1st Somerset L. Infantry.
1st East Lancashires.
1st Hants.
1st Rifle Brigade.

12*th Infantry Brigade—General Wilson.*
1st Royal Lancaster Regiment.
2nd Lancs. Fusiliers.
2nd Innis. Fusiliers.
2nd Essex.

Artillery—General Milne.
XIV. Brig. R.F.A. 39, 68, 88.
XXIX.   ,,   ,   125, 126, 127.
XXXII. ,,   ,,   27, 134, 135.
XXXVII. ,, (How.) 31, 35, 55.
Heavy R.G.A. 31 Battery.
R.E. 7, 9 Field Cos.

These troops, which had been quartered in the Ligny and Montigny area, received urgent orders at one in the morning of the 25th that they should advance northwards. They marched that night to Briastre, where they covered the retreat of the Army, the Third Division passing through their lines. The Fourth Division then retired south again, having great difficulty in getting along, as the roads were choked with transport and artillery, and fringed with exhausted men. The 12th Brigade (Wilson's) was acting as rearguard, and began to experience pressure from the pursuers, the Essex men being shelled out of the village of Bethencourt, which they held until it was nearly surrounded by the German cavalry. The line followed by the division was Briastre—Viesly—Bethencourt—Caudry—Ligny and Haucourt, the latter village marking the general position which they were to take up on the left of the Army at the line of Le Cateau. Such reinforcements were mere handfuls when compared with the pursuing hosts, but their advent heartened up the British troops and relieved them of some of the pressure. It has been remarked by officers of the Fourth Division that they and their men were considerably taken aback by the worn appearance of the weary regiments from Mons which passed through their ranks. Their confidence was revived, however, by the undisturbed demeanour of the General Headquarters Staff, who came through them in the late afternoon of the 25th. "General French himself struck me as being extremely composed, and the staff officers looked very cheerful." These are the imponderabilia which count for much in a campaign.

Tuesday, August 25, was a day of scattered rearguard actions. The weary Army had rested upon the evening of the 24th upon the general line Maubeuge—Bavai—Wargnies. Orders were issued for the retirement to continue next day to a position already partly prepared, in front of the centre of which stood the town of Le Cateau. All rearguards were to be clear of the above-mentioned line by 5.30 A.M. The general conception was that the inner flanks of the two corps should be directed upon Le Cateau.

The intention of the Commander-in-Chief was that the Army should fight in that position next day,

88   THE BRITISH CAMPAIGN, 1914

CHAPTER III.
The Battle of Mons.

the First Corps occupying the right and the Second Corps the left of the position. The night of the 25th found the Second Corps in the position named, whilst their comrades were still at Landrecies, eight miles to the north-east, with a cavalry brigade endeavouring to bridge the gap between. It is very certain, in the case of so ardent a leader as Haig, that it was no fault upon his part which kept him from Smith-Dorrien's side upon the day of battle. It can only be said that the inevitable delays upon the road experienced by the First Corps, including the rearguard actions which it fought, prevented the ensuing battle from being one in which the British Army as a whole might have stemmed the rush of Von Kluck's invading host.

The 7th Brigade at Solesmes.

Whilst the whole Army had been falling back upon the position which had been selected for a stand, it was hoped that substantial French reinforcements were coming up from the south. The roads were much blocked during the 25th, for two divisions of French territorials were retiring along them, as well as the British Army. As a consequence progress was slow, and the German pressure from the rear became ever more severe. Allenby's cavalry and horse-guns covered the retreat, continually turning round and holding off the pursuers. Finally, near Solesmes, on the evening of the 25th, the cavalry were at last driven in, and the Germans came up against McCracken's 7th Brigade, who held them most skilfully until nightfall with the assistance of the 42nd Brigade R.F.A. and the 30th Howitzer Brigade. Most of the fighting fell upon the 1st Wiltshires and 2nd South Lancashires, both of which had substantial losses. The Germans could make no further progress,

THE BATTLE OF MONS 89

and time was given for the roads to clear and for the artillery to get away. The 7th Brigade then followed, marching, so far as possible, across country and taking up its position, which it did not reach until after midnight, in the village of Caudry, on the line of the Le Cateau—Courtrai road. As it faced north once more it found Snow's Fourth Division upon its left, while on its immediate right were the 8th and the 9th Brigades, with the Fifth Division on the farther side of them. One unit of the 7th Brigade, the 2nd Irish Rifles, together with the 41st R.F.A., swerved off in the darkness and confusion and went away with the cavalry. The rest were in the battle line. Here we may leave them in position while we return to trace the fortunes of the First Army Corps.

Sir Douglas Haig's corps, after the feint of August 24, in which the Second Division appeared to be attacking with the First in support, was cleverly disengaged from the enemy and fell back by alternate divisions. It was not an easy operation, and it was conducted under a very heavy shell-fire, which fell especially upon the covering guns of Colonel Sandilands' 34th Artillery Brigade. These guns were exposed to a concentration of fire from the enemy, which was so intense that a thick haze of smoke and dust blotted out the view for long periods at a time. It was only with difficulty and great gallantry that they were got away. An officer of the 6th Brigade, immediately behind them, writes: "Both going in and coming back the limbers passed my trench at a tearing gallop, the drivers lying low on the horses' necks and screaming at them to go faster, while on the return the guns bounded about on the stubble

CHAPTER III.

The Battle of Mons.

field like so many tin cans behind a runaway dog." The guns having been drawn in, the corps retired by roads parallel to the Second Corps, and were able to reach the line Bavai—Maubeuge by about 7 P.M. upon that evening, being on the immediate eastern flank of Smith-Dorrien's men. It is a striking example of the historical continuity of the British Army that as they marched that day many of the regiments, such as the Guards and the 1st King's Liverpool, passed over the graves of their predecessors who had died under the same colours at Malplaquet in 1709, two hundred and six years before.

On August 25 General Haig continued his retreat. During the day he fell back to the west of Maubeuge by Feignies to Vavesnes and Landrecies. The considerable forest of Mormal intervened between the two sections of the British Army. On the forenoon of this day the vanguard of the German infantry, using motor transport, overtook Davies' 6th Brigade, which was acting as rearguard to the corps. They pushed in to within five hundred yards, but were driven back by rifle-fire. Other German forces were coming rapidly up and enveloping the wings of the British rearguard, but the brigade, through swift and skilful handling, disengaged itself from what was rapidly becoming a dangerous situation. The weather was exceedingly hot during the day, and with their heavy packs the men were much exhausted, many of them being barely able to stagger. In the evening, footsore and weary, they reached the line of Landrecies, Maroilles, and Pont-sur-Sambre. The 4th Brigade of Guards, consisting of Grenadiers, Coldstream, and Irish, under General Scott-Kerr, occupied the town of Landrecies. During the day they had seen little of the enemy, and they had no reason to believe that the forest, which extended up to the outskirts of the town, was full of German infantry pressing eagerly to cut them off. The possession of vast numbers of motor lorries for infantry transport introduces a new element into strategy, especially the strategy of a pursuit, which was one of those disagreeable first experiences of up-to-date warfare which the British Army had to undergo. It ensures that the weary retreating rearguard shall ever have a perfectly fresh pursuing vanguard at its heels.

The Guards at Landrecies were put into the empty cavalry barracks for a much-needed rest, but they had hardly settled down before there was an alarm that the Germans were coming into the town. It was just after dusk that a column of infantry debouched from the shadow of the trees and advanced briskly towards the town. A company of the 3rd Coldstream under Captain Monck gave the alarm, and the whole regiment stood to arms, while the rest of the brigade, who could not operate in so confined a space, defended the other entrances of the town. The van of the approaching Germans shouted out that they were French, and seemed to have actually got near enough to attack the officer of the picket and seize a machine-gun before the Guardsmen began to fire. There is a single approach to the village, and no means of turning it, so that the attack was forced to come directly down the road.

Possibly the Germans had the impression that they were dealing with demoralised fugitives, but if so they got a rude awakening. The advance party, who were endeavouring to drag away the machine-gun, were all shot down, and their comrades who stormed up to the houses were met with a steady and murderous fire which drove them back into the shadows of the wood. A gun was brought up by them, and fired at a range of five hundred yards with shrapnel, but the Coldstream, reinforced by a second company, lay low or flattened themselves into the doorways for protection, while the 9th British Battery replied from a position behind the town. Presently, believing that the way had been cleared for them, there was a fresh surge of dark masses out of the wood, and they poured into the throat of the street. The Guards had brought out two machine-guns, and their fire, together with a succession of volleys from the rifles, decimated the stormers. Some of them got near enough to throw hand bombs among the British, but none effected a lodgment among the buildings.

From time to time there were fresh advances during the night, designed apparently rather to tire out the troops than to gain the village. Once fire was set to the house at the end of the street, but the flames were extinguished by a party led by Corporal Wyatt, of the 3rd Coldstream. The Irish Guards after midnight relieved the Coldstream of their vigil, and in the early morning the tired but victorious brigade went forward unmolested upon their way. They had lost 170 of their number, nearly all from the two Coldstream companies. Lord Hawarden and the Hon. Windsor Clive of the Coldstream and Lieut. Vereker of the Grenadiers were killed, four other officers were wounded. The Germans in their close attacking formation had suffered very much more heavily. Their enterprise was a daring one, for they had pushed far forward to get command of the Landrecies Bridge, but their audacity became foolhardy when faced by steady, unshaken infantry. History has shown many times before that a retreating British Army still retains a sting in its tail.

At the same time as the Guards' Brigade was attacked at Landrecies there was an advance from the forest against Maroilles, which is four miles to the eastward. A troop of the 15th Hussars guarding a bridge over the Sambre near that point was driven in by the enemy, and two attempts on the part of the 1st Berkshires, of Davies' 6th Brigade, to retake it were repulsed, owing to the fact that the only approach was by a narrow causeway with marshland on either side, where it was not possible for infantry to deploy. The 1st Rifles were ordered to support the Berkshires, but darkness had fallen and nothing could be done. The casualties in this skirmish amounted to 124 killed, wounded, or missing. The Landrecies and Maroilles wounded were left behind with some of the medical staff. At this period of the war the British had not yet understood the qualities of the enemy, and several times made the mistake of trusting surgeons and orderlies to their mercy, with the result that they were inhumanly treated, both by the authorities at the front and by the populace in Germany, whither they were conveyed as starving prisoners of war. Five of them, Captains Edmunds and Hamilton, Lieut. Danks (all of the Army Medical Corps), with Dr. Austin and Dr. Elliott, who were exchanged in January 1915, deposed that they were left absolutely without food for long periods. It is only fair to state that at a later date, with a few scandalous exceptions, such as that of Wittenberg, the German treatment of prisoners, though often harsh, was no longer barbarous. For the first six months, however, it was brutal in the extreme, and frequently accompanied by torture as well as neglect. A Spanish prisoner, incarcerated by mistake, has given very clear neutral evidence of the abominable punishments of the prison camps. His account reads more like the doings of Iroquois than of a Christian nation.

A small mishap—small on the scale of such a war, though serious enough in itself—befell a unit of the First Army Corps on the morning after the Landrecies engagement. The portion of the German army who pursued General Haig had up to now been able to effect little, and that little at considerable cost to themselves. Early on August 26, however, a brisk action was fought near Pont-sur-Sambre, in which the 2nd Connaughts, of Haking's Fifth Brigade, lost six officers, including Colonel Abercrombie, who was taken prisoner, and 280 men. The regiment was cut off by a rapidly advancing enemy in a country which was so thickly enclosed that there was great difficulty in keeping touch between the various companies or in conveying their danger to the rest of the brigade. By steadiness and judgment the battalion was extricated from a most difficult position, but it was at the heavy cost already quoted. In this case again the use by the enemy of great numbers of motor lorries in their pursuit accounts for the suddenness and severity of the attacks which now and afterwards fell upon the British rearguards.

Dawn broke upon August 26, a day upon which the exhausted troops were destined to be tried to the limit of human endurance. It was the date of Von Kluck's exultant telegram in which he declared that he held them surrounded, a telegram which set Berlin fluttering with flags. On this day the First Army Corps was unmolested in its march, reaching the Venerolles line that night. There was woody country upon the west of it, and from beyond this curtain of trees they heard the distant roar of a terrific cannonade, and knew that a great battle was in progress to the westward. It was on Smith-Dorrien's Second Corps and upon the single division of the Third Corps that the full storm of the German attack had broken. In a word, a corps and a half of British troops, with 225 guns, were assailed by certainly four and probably five German corps, with 600 guns. It is no wonder that the premature tidings of a great German triumph were forwarded that morning to make one more item in that flood of good news which from August 21 to the end of the month was pouring in upon the German people. A glittering mirage lay before them. The French lines had been hurled back from the frontier, the British were in full retreat, and now were faced with absolute disaster. Behind these breaking lines lay the precious capital, the brain and heart of France. But God is not always with the big battalions, and the end was not yet.

CHAPTER IV

THE BATTLE OF LE CATEAU

The order of battle at Le Cateau—The stand of the 2nd Suffolks—Major Yate's V.C.—The fight for the quarries—The splendid work of the British guns—Difficult retirement of the Fourth Division—The fate of the 1st Gordons—Results of the battle—Exhaustion of the Army—The destruction of the 2nd Munsters—A cavalry fight—The news in Great Britain—The views of General Joffre—Battery L—The action of Villars-Cotteret—Reunion of the Army.

CHAPTER IV.

The Battle of Le Cateau.

REFERENCE has already been made to the retirement of Smith-Dorrien's Second Corps, covered by Allenby's cavalry, throughout the 25th. The heads of the columns arrived at the Le Cateau position at about 3 P.M., but the rearguards were fighting into the night, and came in eventually in an exhausted condition. The Fourth Division, which was still quite fresh, did good and indeed vital service by allowing the tired units to pass through its ranks and acting as a pivot upon which the cavalry could fall back.

Sir John French had reconsidered the idea of making a stand at Le Cateau, feeling, no doubt, that if his whole Army could not be consolidated there the affair would be too desperate. He had moved with his staff during the evening of the 25th to St. Quentin, leaving word that the retirement should be continued early next morning. Smith-Dorrien spent the afternoon and evening going round the position, but it was

THE BATTLE OF LE CATEAU 97

not until 2 A.M. upon the morning of the 26th that he was able to ascertain the whereabouts of all his scattered and weary units. About that time General Allenby reported that his cavalry had been widely separated, two and a half brigades being at Chatillon, six miles east of Le Cateau, the other one and a half brigades being near Ligny, four miles west of the same town. General Smith-Dorrien was in the position that his troops were scattered, weary, and in danger of losing their *morale* through continued retreat in the presence of an ever-pressing enemy. Even with the best soldiers such an experience too long continued may turn an army into a rabble. He therefore made urgent representations by telephone to the Commander-in-Chief, pointing out that the only hope of checking the dangerous German pursuit was to stagger them by a severe counter. "The only thing for the men to do when they can't stand is to lie down and fight," said he. Sir John assented to the view, with the proviso that the retirement should be continued as soon as possible. Smith-Dorrien, taking under his orders the cavalry, the Fourth Division, and the 19th Brigade, as well as his own corps, issued instructions for the battle which he knew must begin within a few hours.

Owing to the gap of eight miles between the nearest points of the two corps, both flanks of the position were in the air. Smith-Dorrien therefore requested the cavalry brigades from Chatillon to move in and guard the east flank, while the rest of the cavalry watched the west. He was less anxious about the latter, as he knew that Sordet's French cavalry was in that direction.

The exhausted infantry, who had now been march-

H

ing for about a week, and fighting for three days and the greater part of three nights, flung themselves down where best they could, some to the north-east of Le Cateau, some in the town, and some along the line of very inadequate trenches hastily prepared by civilian labour. In the early dawn they took up their position, the Fifth Division being to the right near the town. Of this division, the 14th Brigade (Rolt's) was on the extreme right, the 13th (Cuthbert's) to the left of it, and the 15th (Gleichen's) to the left again. To the west of the Fifth Division lay the Third, their trenches covering the villages of Troisville (9th Brigade), Audencourt (8th Brigade), and Caudry (7th Brigade). Behind Caudry one and a half brigades of cavalry were in reserve to strengthen the left wing. From Caudry the line was thrown back to meet a flanking movement and extended to Haucourt. This portion was held by Snow's Fourth Division. Sordet's cavalry had passed across the rear of the British position the day before, and lay now to the left flank and rear of the Army. There were rumours of approaching French forces from the south, which put heart into the weary men, but, as a matter of fact, they had only their own brave spirits upon which to depend. Their numbers, putting every unit at its full complement, were about 70,000 men. Their opponents were four army corps at the least, with two divisions of cavalry—say, 170,000 men with an overpowering artillery. Subsequent reports showed that the guns of all five army corps had been concentrated for the battle.

It has been said that Rolt's 14th Brigade was at the extreme right of the line. This statement needs some expansion. The 14th Brigade consisted of the

THE BATTLE OF LE CATEAU

1st East Surrey, 2nd Suffolk, 2nd Manchester, and 1st Cornwalls. Of these four regiments, half of the East Surrey had been detached on escort duty and the other half, under Colonel Longley, with the whole of the Cornwalls, bivouacked in the northern suburbs of Le Cateau on the night of the 25th. In the early morning of the 26th the enemy's advanced guard got into the town, and this detachment of British troops were cut off from their comrades and fired upon as they assembled in the streets of the town. They made their way out, however, in orderly fashion and took up a position to the south-east of the town, where they fought an action on their own account for some hours, quite apart from the rest of the Army, which they could hear but not see. Eventually the division of cavalry fell back from Chatillon to join the Army and picked up these troops *en route*, so that the united body was able to make its way safely back to their comrades. These troops were out of the main battle, but did good work in covering the retreat. The whole signal section of the 14th Brigade was with them, which greatly hampered the brigade during the battle. Two companies of the 1st East Surreys under Major Tew had become separated from their comrades after Mons, but they rejoined the British line at Troisville, and on the morning of August 26 were able to fall in on the rear of the 14th Brigade, where, as will be seen later, they did good service.

The 19th Brigade had also bivouacked in Le Cateau and was nearly cut off, as the two regiments of the 14th Brigade had been, by the sudden intrusion of the enemy. It had been able to make its way out of the town, however, without being separated from the rest of the Army, and it took up its position on

CHAPTER IV.

The Battle of Le Cateau.

the right rear of the infantry line, whence it sent help where needed and played the part of a reserve until towards the close of the action its presence became very vital to the Fifth Division. At the outset the 2nd Argyll and Sutherlands were in the front line of this brigade and the 1st Middlesex supporting them, while the other two battalions, the 2nd Welsh Fusiliers and 1st Scots Rifles, with a battery of artillery had been taken as a reserve by the force commander. No trenches had been prepared at this point, and the losses of the two front battalions from shell-fire were, from the beginning, very heavy. The other two battalions spent a day of marching rather than fighting, being sent right across to reinforce the Fourth Division and then being brought back to the right flank once more.

The stand of the 2nd Suffolks.

It was the Fifth Division, on the right of the line, who first experienced the full effect of the heavy shelling which about seven o'clock became general along the whole position, but was always most severe upon the right. There was a dangerous salient in the trenches at the cross-roads one mile west of Le Cateau which was a source of very great weakness. Every effort was made to strengthen the trenches, the 15th Brigade and 59th Company R.E. working especially hard in the Troisville section. The Germans were moving round upon this right wing, and the murderous hail of missiles came from the flank as well as from the front, being supplemented by rifle and machine-gun fire. The 2nd Suffolks and 2nd Manchesters, the remaining half of Rolt's 14th Brigade, being on the extreme right of the line, suffered the most. The guns immediately supporting them, of the 28th Artillery Brigade, were quite overmatched and were

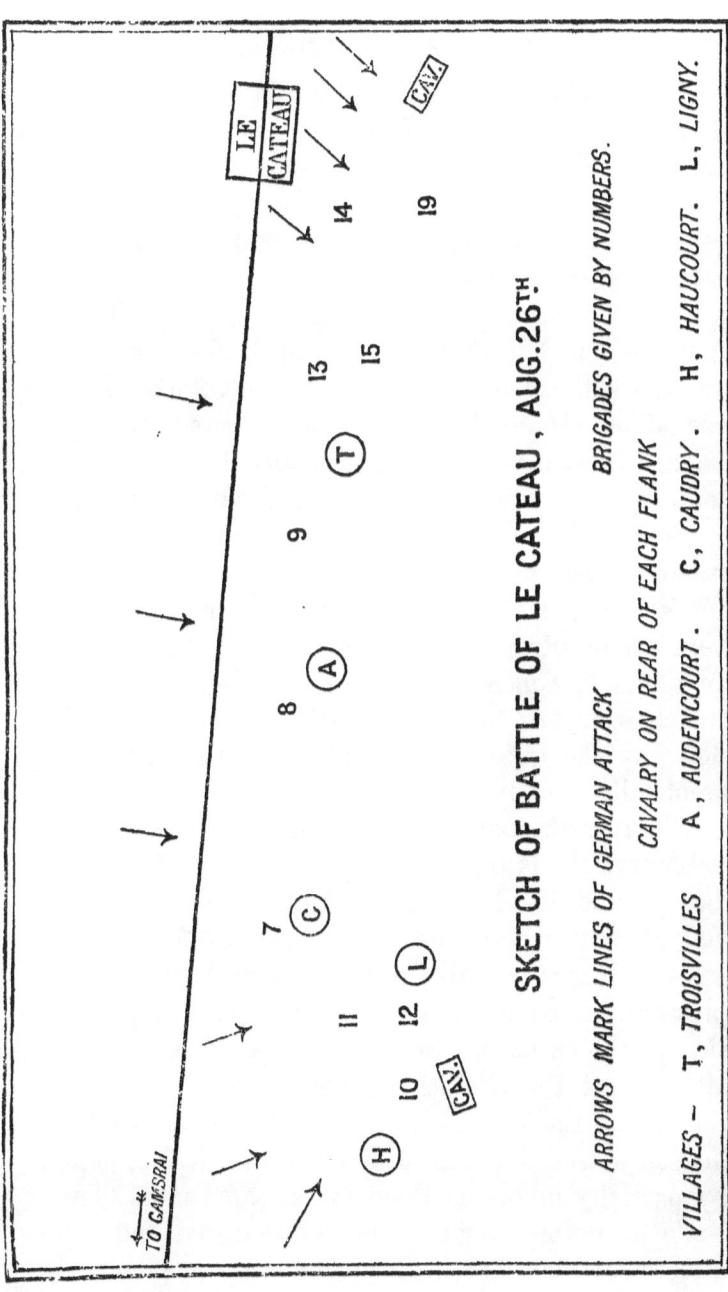

CHAPTER IV.

The Battle of Le Cateau.

overwhelmed by the devastating rain of shells, many of them being put out of action. A heavy battery, the 108th, some little distance behind the line, kept up a steady and effective fire which long held back the German advance. The pressure, however, was extreme, and growing steadily from hour to hour until it became well-nigh intolerable. Especially it fell upon the 2nd Suffolks, who held their shallow trenches with splendid tenacity. Their colonel, Brett, was killed, Major Doughty was wounded in three places, Captains Orford and Cutbill, with eight lieutenants, were on the ground. Finally, when the position of the brigade became untenable and it was ordered to retreat, the gallant Suffolks held on to their line with the desire of saving the disabled guns, and were eventually all killed, wounded, or taken, save for about 250 men, while their neighbours, the 2nd Manchesters, lost 14 officers and 350 of their men. In this way the extreme right of the British line was practically destroyed.

The 19th Brigade, in the rear of the 14th, were able to observe the fate of their comrades, and about midday the 2nd Argyll and Sutherland Highlanders, who had already lost a good many men from shell-fire, advanced in the chivalrous hope of relieving the pressure. The battalion went forward as if on parade, though the casualties were numerous. They eventually gained the shelter of some trenches near the remains of the 14th Brigade, but their gallant effort, instead of averting the threatened destruction, ended by partially involving them in the same fate. They could do nothing against the concentrated and well-directed artillery fire of the enemy. When eventually they fell back, part of two companies were cut off in their trench and taken. The rest of the regiment, together with the 1st Middlesex and two companies of the Royal Scots Fusiliers from the 9th Brigade, formed a covering line on a ridge in the rear and held back the German advance for a long time. This line did not retire until 5 P.M., when it was nearly enveloped. General Drummond, commanding the 19th Brigade, had met with an injury in the course of the action, and it was commanded during the latter part by Colonel Ward, of the Middlesex.

The retirement or destruction of the 14th Brigade exposed the flank of the 13th (Cuthbert's) to a murderous enfilade fire, which fell chiefly upon the 2nd Yorkshire Light Infantry. This brigade had defended itself successfully for six hours against various frontal attacks, but now the flank-fire raked it from end to end and practically destroyed the Yorkshiremen, who were the most exposed to it. On them and on the 2nd Scottish Borderers fell the great bulk of the losses, for the West Kents and the survivors of the West Ridings were in reserve. Of the two companies of the Yorkshire Light Infantry who held the foremost trenches, that on the right had only fifteen men left, with whom Major Yate attempted a final charge, finding his Victoria Cross in the effort, while the next company, under Major Trevor, had only forty-one survivors, the whole losses of the battalion being 600 men, with 20 officers. Both the Yorkshire and the Scottish Border battalions lost their colonels in the action. Their losses were shared by the two companies of the 1st East Surreys under Major Tew, who had been placed between the 14th and 13th Brigades, and

104   THE BRITISH CAMPAIGN, 1914

CHAPTER IV.

The Battle of Le Cateau.

who fought very steadily in shallow trenches, holding on to the last possible moment.

Whilst the battle was going badly on the right, the Third Division in the centre and the Fourth Division on the left had held their own against a succession of attacks. The 8th and 9th Brigades drove off the German infantry with their crushing rifle-fire, and endured as best they might the shelling, which was formidable and yet very much less severe than that to which the Fifth Division had been exposed. In the case of the 7th Brigade (McCracken's) the village of Caudry, which it defended, formed a salient, since the Fourth Division on the left was thrown back. The attack upon this brigade from daylight onwards was very severe, but the assailants could neither drive in the line nor capture the village of Caudry. They attacked on both flanks at short rifle range, inflicting and also enduring heavy losses. In this part of the field the British guns held their own easily against the German, the proportion of numbers being more equal than on the right of the line.

Whilst the right flank was crumbling before the terrific concentration of German guns, and while the centre was stoutly holding its own, farther to the west, in the Haucourt—Ligny direction, the Second German Army Corps was beating hard against Snow's Fourth Division, which was thrown back to protect the left flank of the Army, and to cover the Cambrai—Esnes road. Hunter-Weston's 11th Brigade was on the right, south of Fontaine, with Wilson's 12th upon its left, and Haldane's 10th in reserve at Haucourt. As the German attack came from the left, or western flank, the 12th Brigade received the

THE BATTLE OF LE CATEAU

first impact. The artillery of the division had not yet come up, and the 1st Royal Lancasters, stretched in a turnip patch, endured for some time a severe fire which cost them many casualties, including their Colonel Dykes, and to which little reply could be made. There were no cavalry scouts in front of the infantry, so that working parties and advanced posts were cut up by sudden machine-gun fire. Some of the covering parties both of the Lancasters and of the 2nd Lancashire Fusiliers were never seen again. At about seven the British guns came up, the 14th Brigade R.F.A. on the left, the 29th in the centre, and the 32nd on the right, with the howitzers of the 37th behind the right centre on the high ground near Selvigny. From this time onward they supported the infantry in the most self-sacrificing way. The German infantry advance began shortly afterwards, and was carried out by wave after wave of men. A company of the 2nd Essex Regiment, under Captain Vandeleur, upon the British left, having good cover and a clear field of fire, inflicted very heavy losses on the Germans, though they were finally overwhelmed, their leader having been killed. The 2nd Lancashire Fusiliers in the front line were also heavily attacked, and held their own for several hours. About ten o'clock the pressure was so great that the defence was driven in, and two battalions lost their machine-guns, but a new line was formed in the Haucourt—Esnes road, the retirement being skilfully covered by Colonel Anley, of the Essex, and Colonel Griffin, of the Lancashire Fusiliers. There the 2nd Inniskilling Fusiliers, the 1st Royal Lancasters, the 2nd Lancashire Fusiliers, and the 2nd Essex held firmly on until the afternoon under very heavy and

106   THE BRITISH CAMPAIGN, 1914

CHAPTER IV.

The Battle of Le Cateau.

incessant fire, while the 11th Brigade upon their right were equally involved in the fight. Two battalions of the 10th Brigade (Haldane's), the 1st Irish Fusiliers and 2nd Seaforths, had dug themselves in on the high ground just north of Selvigny and repulsed every attack, but two others, the 2nd Dublins and 1st Warwicks, had got involved with the 12th Brigade and could not be retrieved. The Signal Corps had not yet arrived, and the result was that General Snow had the greatest difficulty in ensuring his connections with his brigadiers, the orders being carried by his staff officers. At two o'clock, as there was a lull in the German advance, Wilson of the 12th Brigade made a spirited counter-attack, recovering many of the wounded, but being finally driven back to the old position by intense artillery and machine-gun fire.

It is worth recording that during this advance the Essex men found among the German dead many Jaeger with the same Gibraltar badge upon their caps which they bore themselves. It was a Hanoverian battalion who had been comrades with the old 56th in the defence of the fortress one hundred and fifty years before.

The fight for the quarries.

The 11th Brigade (Hunter-Weston), on the right of the 12th, had meanwhile played a very vital part in the fight. This brigade was defending a position called Les Carrières, or the quarry pits, which was east of Fontaine and to the north of the village of Ligny. It was a desperate business, for the British were four times driven out of it and four times came back to their bitter work amid a sleet of shells and bullets. Parties of the 1st Somersets and of the 1st East Lancashires held the quarries with the 1st

Hants and 1st Rifle Brigade in immediate support, all being eventually drawn into the fight. Major Rickman, of the latter regiment, distinguished himself greatly in the defence, but was seriously wounded and left behind in the final retirement. Besides incessant gun-fire, the defenders were under infantry fire of a very murderous description from both flanks. In spite of this, the place was held for six hours until the retirement of the line in the afternoon caused it to be untenable, as the enemy was able to get behind it. The brigade then fell back upon Ligny under heavy shrapnel-fire, moving steadily and in good order. The Germans at once attacked the village from the east and north-east. Could they have taken it, they would have been upon the flank of the British line of retirement. They were twice driven back, however, by the fire of the infantry, losing very heavily upon both occasions. About four o'clock, the Army being in full retreat, the brigade received orders to abandon Ligny and march upon Malincourt. The effect of a heavy shrapnel-fire was minimised by this movement being carried out in small columns of fours. A loss of 30 officers and 1115 men in a single day's fighting showed how severe had been the work of Hunter-Weston's brigade. The 12th Brigade had also lost about a thousand men. Many of the guns had run short of shells. A spectator has described how he saw the British gunners under a heavy fire, sitting in gloomy groups round the guns which they had neither the shells to work, nor the heart to abandon.

Such was the general fortune of the British left. At the extreme edge of it, in the gap between the left of the Fourth Division and the town of Cambrai,

108   THE BRITISH CAMPAIGN, 1914

CHAPTER IV.

The Battle of Le Cateau.

Sordet's French cavalry had been fighting to prevent the British wing from being turned. There was some misconception upon this point at the time, but in justice to our Ally it should be known that General Smith-Dorrien himself galloped to this flank in the course of the afternoon and was a witness of the efforts of the French troopers, who had actually marched 40 miles in order to be present at the battle.

The narrative has now taken the movements of the left wing up to the point of its retirement, in order to preserve the continuity of events in that portion of the field, but the actual abandonment of their position by Snow's Fourth Division was due to circumstances over which they had no control, and which had occurred at a considerable distance. Both the centre and the left of the Army could have held its own, though it must be admitted that the attack to which they were exposed was a very violent one gallantly pushed home.

All might have gone well had the Germans not been able to mass such an overpowering artillery attack upon the right of the line. It was shortly after mid-day that this part of the position began to weaken, and observers from the centre saw stragglers retiring over the low hill in the Le Cateau direction. At that hour the artillery upon the right of the British line was mostly silenced, and large masses of the German infantry were observed moving round the right flank. The salient of the Suffolks was in the possession of the enemy, and from it they could enfilade the line. It was no longer possible to bring up ammunition or horses to the few remaining guns. The greater part of the troops held on none the less most doggedly to their positions. A steady downpour

THE BATTLE OF LE CATEAU 109

of rain was a help rather than a discomfort, as it enabled the men to moisten their parched lips. But the situation of the Fifth Division was growing desperate. It was plain that to remain where they were could only mean destruction. And yet to ask the exhausted men to retire under such a rain of shells would be a dangerous operation. Even the best troops may reach their snapping point. Most of them had by the afternoon been under constant shrapnel-fire for eight hours on end. Some were visibly weakening. Anxious officers looked eagerly over their shoulders for any sign of reinforcement, but an impassable gap separated them from their comrades of the First Army Corps, who were listening with sinking hearts to the rumble of the distant cannonade. There was nothing for it but to chance the retirement. About three o'clock commanders called to officers and officers to men for a last great effort. It was the moment when a leader reaps in war the love and confidence which he has sown in peace. Smith-Dorrien had sent his meagre reserve, which consisted of one battery and two battalions, to take up a rearguard position astride the Le Cateau—St. Quentin road. Every available detail, that could pull a trigger, down to Hildebrand's signallers of the Headquarters Staff, who had already done wonderful work in their own particular line, were thrust into the covering line. One by one the dishevelled brigades were drawn off towards the south. One section of the heavy guns of the 108th Heavy Battery was ordered back to act with two battalions of the 19th Brigade in covering the Reumont—Maritz road, while the 1st Norfolks were put in echelon behind the right flank for the same purpose.

110   THE BRITISH CAMPAIGN, 1914

CHAPTER IV.

The Battle of Le Cateau.

The splendid work of the British guns.

The Fifth Division, with the 15th Brigade as rearguard, considerably disorganised by its long hammering, retreated along the straight Roman road via Maritz and Estrees. The Third Division fell back through Berthy and Clary to Beaurevoir, the 9th Brigade forming a rearguard. The cavalry, greatly helped by Sordet's French cavalry upon the west, flung itself in front of the pursuit, while the guns sacrificed themselves to save the retiring infantry. Every British battery was an inferno of bursting shells, and yet every one fought on while breech-block would shut or gunner could stand. Many batteries were in the state of the 61st R.F.A., which fired away all its own shells and then borrowed from the limbers of other neighbouring batteries, the guns of which had been put out of action. Had the artillery gone the Army would have gone. Had the Army gone the Germans had a clear run into Paris. It has been said that on the covering batteries of Wing, Milne, and Headlam may, on that wet August afternoon, have hung the future history of Europe.

Wing's command included the 23rd, 30th, 40th, and 42nd Brigades, with the 48th Heavy Battery; Headlam's were the 15th, 27th, 28th, and 8th, with the 108th Heavy; Milne's, the 14th, 29th, 32nd, and 37th, with the 31st Heavy. These numbers deserve to be recorded, for every gun of them did great service, though many were left in ruins on the field. Some, like those of the 37th R.F.A., were plucked from under the very noses of the Germans, who were within a hundred yards of them when they were withdrawn, a deed of valour for which Captain Reynolds of that battery received the Cross. One by one those batteries which could move were drawn off, the cavalry cover-

THE BATTLE OF LE CATEAU   111

ing the manœuvre by their rifle-fire, and sometimes man-handling the gun from the field. Serving one day as charging cavaliers, another as mounted infantry in covering a retreat, again as sappers in making or holding a trench, or when occasion called for it as gun-teams to pull on the trace of a derelict gun, the cavalry have been the general utility men of the Army. The days of pure cavalry may have passed, but there will never be a time when a brave and handy fighting man who is mobile will not be invaluable to his comrades.

It was about four o'clock that the Fourth Division, on the left flank, who had been maintaining the successful defensive already described, were ordered to begin their retirement. The 12th Brigade was able to withdraw with no great difficulty along the line Walincourt—Villiers—Vendhuile, reaching the latter village about nine-thirty. The doings of the 11th Brigade have been already described. There was considerable disintegration but no loss of spirit. One of the regiments of the 12th, the 2nd Royal Lancasters, together with about three hundred Warwicks, from the 10th Brigade, and some detachments of other regiments, were by some mischance, isolated in the village of Haucourt with no definite orders, and held on until ten o'clock at night, when the place was nearly surrounded. They fought their way out, however, in a most surprising fashion, and eventually made good their retreat. One party, under Major Poole of the Warwicks, rejoined the Army next day. Captain Clutterbuck, with a small party of Royal Lancasters, wandered into Haumont after it was occupied by the Germans. Summoned to surrender the gallant officer refused, and was shot

CHAPTER IV.

The Battle of Le Cateau.

Difficult retirement of the Fourth Division.

dead, but his men charged with the bayonet and fought their way clear to a post which was held by Major Parker of the same regiment, to the immediate south of the village. This officer, finding that he was the last rearguard, withdrew in the face of heavy German forces. Being joined by Major Christie of the Warwicks with 200 men, they followed the Army, and, finally, by a mixture of good luck and good leadership, picked their way through the German advance guards, and on the third day rejoined the colours at Noyon.

Haldane's 10th Brigade had got split up during the confused fighting of the day, half of it, the 1st Warwicks and 2nd Dublins, getting involved with the 12th Brigade in the fighting on the Haucourt Ridge. The other two battalions, the 2nd Seaforths and 1st Royal Irish Fusiliers, kept guard as a reserve over the left flank of the division. Towards evening General Haldane, finding it hopeless to recover control of his lost regiments, collected the rest of his brigade, and endeavoured to follow the general line of retreat. He lost touch with the remainder of the Army, and might well have been cut off, but after a most exhausting experience he succeeded in safely rejoining the division at Roisel upon the 27th. It may be said generally that the reassembling of the Fourth Division after the disintegration they had experienced was a remarkable example of individualism and determination.

It is impossible to doubt that the Germans, in spite of their preponderating numbers, were staggered by the resistance which they had encountered. In no other way can one explain the fact that their pursuit, which for three days had been incessant, should now, at the most critical instant, have eased off. The cavalry and guns staved off the final blow, and the stricken infantry staggered from the field. The strain upon the infantry of the Fifth Division may be gathered from the fact that up to this point they had lost, roughly, 143 officers, while the Third Division had lost 92 and the Fourth 70. For the time they were disorganised as bodies, even while they preserved their *moral* as individuals.

CHAPTER IV.

The Battle of Le Cateau.

When extended formations are drawn rapidly in under the conditions of a heavy action, it is often impossible to convey the orders to men in outlying positions. Staying in their trenches and unconscious of the departure of their comrades, they are sometimes gathered up by the advancing enemy, but more frequently fall into the ranks of some other corps, and remain for days or weeks away from their own battalion, turning up long after they have helped to swell some list of casualties. Regiments get intermingled and pour along the roads in a confusion which might suggest a rout, whilst each single soldier is actually doing his best to recover his corps. It is disorganisation—but not demoralisation.

It has been remarked above that in the widespread formations of modern battles it is difficult to be sure of the transmission of orders. An illustration of such a danger occurred upon this occasion, which gave rise to an aftermath of battle nearly as disastrous as the battle itself. This was the episode which culminated in the loss of a body of troops, including a large portion of the 1st Gordon Highlanders. This distinguished corps had been engaged with the rest of Beauchamp Doran's 8th Brigade at Mons and again upon the following day, after which they

The fate of the 1st Gordons.

CHAPTER IV.

The Battle of Le Cateau.

retreated with the rest of their division. On the evening of the 25th they bivouacked in the village of Audencourt, just south of the Cambrai—Le Cateau highway, and on the morning of the 26th they found themselves defending a line of trenches in front of this village. From nine o'clock the Gordons held their ground against a persistent German attack. About 3.30 an order was given for the battalion to retire. This message only reached one company, which acted upon it, but the messenger was wounded *en route*, and failed to reach battalion headquarters. Consequently the remainder of the battalion did not retire with the Army, but continued to hold its trenches, greatly helped by the flank (D) Company of Royal Scots, until long after nightfall, when the enemy in great force had worked round both of its flanks. It should be understood that the withdrawal of the Royal Scots was under direct order emanating from brigade headquarters, but an officer of the Gordons, not knowing that such an order had been issued, and perceiving that their flank would be exposed if D Company left their trench, said a few words to them which had such an effect upon their fiery souls that they rushed back to stand by the Highlanders, their Captain being shot dead as he waved his men back into their trench. From that time onwards this company of Royal Scots, finely led by two young lieutenants, Graves and Graham Watson, shared all the dangers and the ultimate fate of the Gordons, as did a handful of Royal Irish upon the other flank. When it was dusk it became clear to Colonel Gordon, who was now in command of the mixed detachment, that he and his men were separated from the Army and surrounded

THE BATTLE OF LE CATEAU 115

on every side by the advancing Germans. At that time the men, after supreme exertion for several days, had been in action for twelve hours on end. He therefore decided, as against annihilation in the morning, that retreat was the only course open. The wounded were left in the trenches. The transport, machine-guns, and horses had already been destroyed by the incessant shelling. The detachment made a move towards the south, the operation being a most difficult one in pitch darkness with the enemy within a few hundred yards. The success attained in this initial stage was largely due to the way in which the Master of Saltoun conveyed the orders which drew in the flanks to the centre. Having made good the Audencourt—Caudry road at 1 A.M. on August 27, the troops managed to traverse some miles of road, with blazing villages all about them, and had a fair chance of reaching safety when unfortunately at Montigny they took a wrong turn, which brought them into Bertry which was held by the Germans. Some confusion was caused by the latter challenging in French. A confused fight followed in the darkness, in the course of which many individual acts of great bravery and devotion were performed. The enemy were now all round the Highlanders, and though the struggle continued for fifty minutes, and there was no official surrender, the little body of men was embedded in Von Kluck's army, and no escape could be found. The utmost discipline and gallantry were shown by all ranks. It must be some consolation to the survivors to know that it is freely admitted that their resistance in the trenches for so long a period undoubtedly facilitated the safe withdrawal of the Third, and to some extent of the Fourth Divisions.

CHAPTER IV.

The Battle of Le Cateau.

Major Leslie Butler, Brigade-Major of the 8th Brigade, who had made a gallant effort to ride to the Gordons and warn them of their danger, was entangled among the Germans, and only succeeded six days later in regaining the British lines.

Results of the battle.

So ended the perilous, costly, and almost disastrous action of Le Cateau. The loss to the British Army, so far as it can be extracted from complex figures and separated from the other losses of the retreat, amounted to between seven and eight thousand killed, wounded, and missing, while at the time of the action, or in the immediate retreat, a considerable quantity of transport and thirty-six field-pieces, mostly in splinters, were abandoned to the enemy. It was an action which could hardly have been avoided, and from which the troops were extricated on better terms than might have been expected. It will always remain an interesting academic question what would have occurred had it been possible for the First Corps to line up with the rest of the Army. The enemy's preponderance of artillery would probably have prevented a British victory, and the strategic position would in any case have made it a barren one, but at least the Germans would have been hard hit and the subsequent retreat more leisurely. As it stood, it was an engagement upon which the weaker side can look back without shame or dishonour. One result of it was to give both the Army and the country increased confidence in themselves and their leaders. Sir John French has testified to the splendid qualities shown by the troops, while his whole-hearted tribute to Smith-Dorrien, in which he said, "The saving of the left wing of the Army could never have been accomplished unless a commander of rare and unusual

THE BATTLE OF LE CATEAU 117

coolness, intrepidity, and determination had been present to personally conduct the operation," will surely be endorsed by history.

It is difficult to exaggerate the strain which had been thrown upon this commander. On him had fallen the immediate direction of the action at Mons; on him also had been the incessant responsibility of the retreat. He had, as has been shown in the narrative, been hard at work all night upon the eve of the battle; he superintended that trying engagement, he extricated his forces, and finally motored to St. Quentin in the evening, went on to Noyon, reached it after midnight, and was back with his Army in the morning, encouraging every one by the magnetism of his presence. It was a very remarkable feat of endurance.

Exhausted as the troops were, there could be no halt or rest until they had extricated themselves from the immediate danger. At the last point of human endurance they still staggered on through the evening and the night time, amid roaring thunder and flashing lightning, down the St. Quentin road. Many fell from fatigue, and having fallen, continued to sleep in ditches by the roadside, oblivious of the racket around them. A number never woke until they found themselves in the hands of the Uhlan patrols. Others slumbered until their corps had disappeared, and then, regaining their senses, joined with other straggling units so as to form bands, which wandered over the country, and eventually reached the railway line about Amiens with wondrous Bill Adams tales of personal adventures which in time reached England, and gave the impression of complete disaster. But the main body were, as a matter of fact, holding well

Chapter IV.
The Battle of Le Cateau.

Exhaustion of the Army.

together, though the units of infantry had become considerably mixed and so reduced that at least four brigades, after less than a week of war, had lost 50 per cent of their *personnel*. Many of the men threw away the heavier contents of their packs, and others abandoned the packs themselves, so that the pursuing Germans had every evidence of a rout before their eyes. It was deplorable that equipment should be discarded, but often it was the only possible thing to do, for either the man had to be sacrificed or the pack. Advantage was taken of a forked road to station an officer there who called out, " Third Division right, Fifth Division left," which greatly helped the reorganisation. The troops snatched a few hours of rest at St. Quentin, and then in the breaking dawn pushed upon their weary road once more, country carts being in many cases commandeered to carry the lame and often bootless infantry. The paved *chaussées*, with their uneven stones, knocked the feet to pieces, and caused much distress to the tired men, which was increased by the extreme heat of the weather.

In the case of some of the men the collapse was so complete that it was almost impossible to get them on. Major Tom Bridges, of the 4th Royal Irish Dragoons, being sent to round up and hurry forward 250 stragglers at St. Quentin, found them nearly comatose with fatigue. With quick wit he bought a toy drum, and, accompanied by a man with a penny whistle, he fell them in and marched them, laughing in all their misery, down the high road towards Ham. When he stopped he found that his strange following stopped also, so he was compelled to march and play the whole way to Roupy. Thus by one man's com-

THE BATTLE OF LE CATEAU   119

pelling personality 250 men were saved for the Army. But such complete collapse was rare. The men kept their *moral*. "Beneath the dirt and grime and weariness I saw clear eyes and grim jaws even when the men could hardly walk." So spoke Coleman, the gallant American volunteer.

Up to now nothing had been seen of the French infantry, and the exposed British force had been hustled and harried by Von Kluck's great army without receiving any substantial support. This was through no want of loyalty, but our gallant Allies were themselves hard pressed. Sir John French had sent urgent representations, especially to General Sordet, the leader of the cavalry operating upon the western side, and he had, as already shown, done what he could to screen Smith-Dorrien's flank. Now at last the retiring Army was coming in touch with those supports which were so badly needed. But before they were reached, on the morning of the 27th, the Germans had again driven in the rearguard of the First Corps.

Some delay in starting had been caused that morning by the fact that only one road was available for the whole of the transport, which had to be sent on in advance. Hence the rearguard was exposed to increased pressure. This rearguard consisted of the 1st Brigade. The 2nd Munsters were the right battalion. Then came the 1st Coldstream, the 1st Scots Guards, and the 1st Black Watch in reserve. The front of the Munsters, as it faced round to hold back the too pushful Germans, was from the north of Fesmy to Chapeau Rouge, but Major Charrier, who was in command, finding no French at Bergues, as he had been led to expect, sent B and D

CHAPTER IV.

The Battle of Le Cateau.

The destruction of the 2nd Munsters.

Companies of Munsters with one troop of the 15th Hussars to hold the cross-roads near that place.

At about 12.30 a message reached Major Charrier to the effect that when ordered to retire he should fall back on a certain line and act as flank-guard to the brigade. He was not to withdraw his two companies from Chapeau Rouge until ordered. The Germans were already in force right on the top of the Irishmen, the country being a broken one with high hedges which restricted the field of fire. A section of guns of the 118th R.F.A. were served from the road about fifty yards behind the line of the infantry. A desperate struggle ensued, in the course of which the Munsters, suffering heavily, overlapped on each flank, and utterly outnumbered, held on bravely in the hope of help from the rest of the brigade. They did not know that a message had already been dispatched to them to the effect that they should come on, and that the other regiments had already done so. Still waiting for the orders which never came, they fell back slowly through Fesmy before the attack, until held up at a small village called Etreux, where the Germans cut off their retreat. Meanwhile the Brigadier, hearing that the Munsters were in trouble, gave orders that the Coldstream should reinforce them. It was too late, however. At Oisy Bridge the Guards picked up sixty men, survivors of C Company. It was here at Oisy Bridge that the missing order was delivered at 3 P.M., the cycle orderly having been held up on his way. As there was no longer any sound of firing, the Coldstream and remnant of Munsters retired, being joined some miles back by an officer and some seventy men. Together with the transport guard this brought the

THE BATTLE OF LE CATEAU

total survivors of that fine regiment to 5 officers and 206 men. All the rest had fought to the end and were killed, wounded, or captured, after a most desperate resistance, in which they were shot down at close quarters, making repeated efforts to pierce the strong German force at Etreux. To their fine work and that of the two lost guns and of a party of the 15th Hussars, under Lieutenant Nicholson, who covered the retreat it may have been due that the pursuit of the First Corps by the Germans from this moment sensibly relaxed. Nine gallant Irish officers were buried that night in a common grave. Major Charrier was twice wounded, but continued to lead his men until a third bullet struck him dead, and deprived the Army of a soldier whose career promised to be a brilliant one. Among others who fell was Lieutenant Chute, whose masterly handling of a machine-gun stemmed again and again the tide of the German attack. One of the most vivid recollections of the survivors was of this officer lying on his face in six inches of water—for the action was partly fought in tropical rain—and declaring that he was having "the time of his life." The moral both of this disaster and that of the Gordons must be the importance of sending a message in duplicate, or even in triplicate, where the withdrawal of a regiment is concerned. This, no doubt, is a counsel of perfection under practical conditions, but the ideal still remains.

During the retreat of the First Corps its rear and right flank had been covered by the 5th Cavalry Brigade (Chetwode). On August 28 the corps was continuing its march towards La Fère and the cavalry found itself near Cerizy. At this point the pursuing German horsemen came into touch with it. At about

CHAPTER IV.

The Battle of Le Cateau.

five in the afternoon three squadrons of the enemy advanced upon one squadron of the Scots Greys, which had the support of J Battery. Being fired at, the Germans dismounted and attempted to advance upon foot, but the fire was so heavy that they could make no progress and their led horses stampeded. They retired, still on foot, followed up by a squadron of the 12th Lancers on their flank. The remainder of the 12th Lancers, supported by the Greys, rode into the dismounted dragoons with sword and lance, killing or wounding nearly all of them. A section of guns had fired over the heads of the British cavalry during the advance into a supporting body of German cavalry, who retired, leaving many dead behind them. The whole hostile force retreated northwards, while the British cavalry continued to conform to the movements of the First Corps. In this spirited little action the German regiment engaged was, by the irony of fate, the 1st Guard Dragoons, Queen Victoria's Own. The British lost 43 killed and wounded. Among the dead were Major Swetenham and Captain Michell of the 12th Lancers. Colonel Wormald of the same regiment was wounded. The excited troopers rode back triumphantly between the guns of J Battery, the cavalrymen exchanging cheers with the horse-gunners as they passed, and brandishing their blood-stained weapons.

On the evening before this brisk skirmish, the flank-guards of the British saw a considerable body of troops in dark clothing upon their left, and shortly afterwards perceived the shell-bursts of a rapid and effective fire over the pursuing German batteries. It was the first contact with the advancing French. These men consisted of the Sixty-first and Sixty-

THE BATTLE OF LE CATEAU 123

second French Reserve Divisions, and were the van of a considerable army under General D'Amade. From that moment the British forces were at last enabled, after a week of constant marching, covering sometimes a good thirty miles a day, and four days of continual fighting against extreme odds, to feel that they had reached a zone of comparative quiet.

The German cavalry still followed the Army upon its southerly march, but there was no longer any fear of a disaster, for the main body of the Army was unbroken, and the soldiers were rather exasperated than depressed by their experience. On the Friday and Saturday, however, August 28 and 29, considerable crowds of stragglers and fugitives, weary and often weaponless, appeared upon the lines of communication, causing the utmost consternation by their stories and their appearance. Few who endured the mental anxiety caused in Great Britain by the messages of Sunday, August 30, are likely to forget it. The reports gave an enormous stimulus to recruiting, and it is worthy of record and remembrance that, in the dark week which followed before the true situation was clearly discerned, every successive day brought as many recruits to the standards as are usually gained in a year. Such was the rush of men that the authorities, with their many preoccupations, found it very difficult to deal with them. A considerable amount of hardship and discomfort was the result, which was endured with good humour until it could be remedied. It is to be noted in this connection that it was want of arms which held back the new armies. He who compares the empty arsenals of Britain with the huge extensions of Krupp's, undertaken during the years before the war, will find the final proof as to which Power deliberately planned it.

The Battle of Le Cateau. To return to the fortunes of the men retreating from Le Cateau, the colonels and brigadiers had managed to make order out of what was approaching to chaos on the day that the troops left St. Quentin. The feet of many were so cut and bleeding that they could no longer limp along, so some were packed into a few trains available and others were hoisted on to limbers, guns, wagons, or anything with wheels, some carts being lightened of ammunition or stores to make room for helpless men. In many cases the whole kits of the officers were deliberately sacrificed. Many men were delirious from exhaustion and incapable of understanding an order. By the evening of the 27th the main body of the troops were already fifteen miles south of the Somme river and canal, on the line Nesle—Ham—Flavy. All day there was distant shelling from the pursuers, who sent their artillery freely forward with their cavalry.

On the 28th the Army continued its retreat to the line of the Oise near Noyon. Already the troops were re-forming, and had largely recovered their spirits, being much reassured by the declarations of the officers that the retreat was strategic to get them in line with the French, and that they would soon turn their faces northwards once more. As an instance of reorganisation it was observed that the survivors of a brigade of artillery which had left its horses and guns at Le Cateau still marched together as a single disciplined unit among the infantry. All day the enemy's horse artillery, cavalry, and motor-infantry hung on the skirts of the British, but were unable to make much impression. The work of the Staff was excellent, for

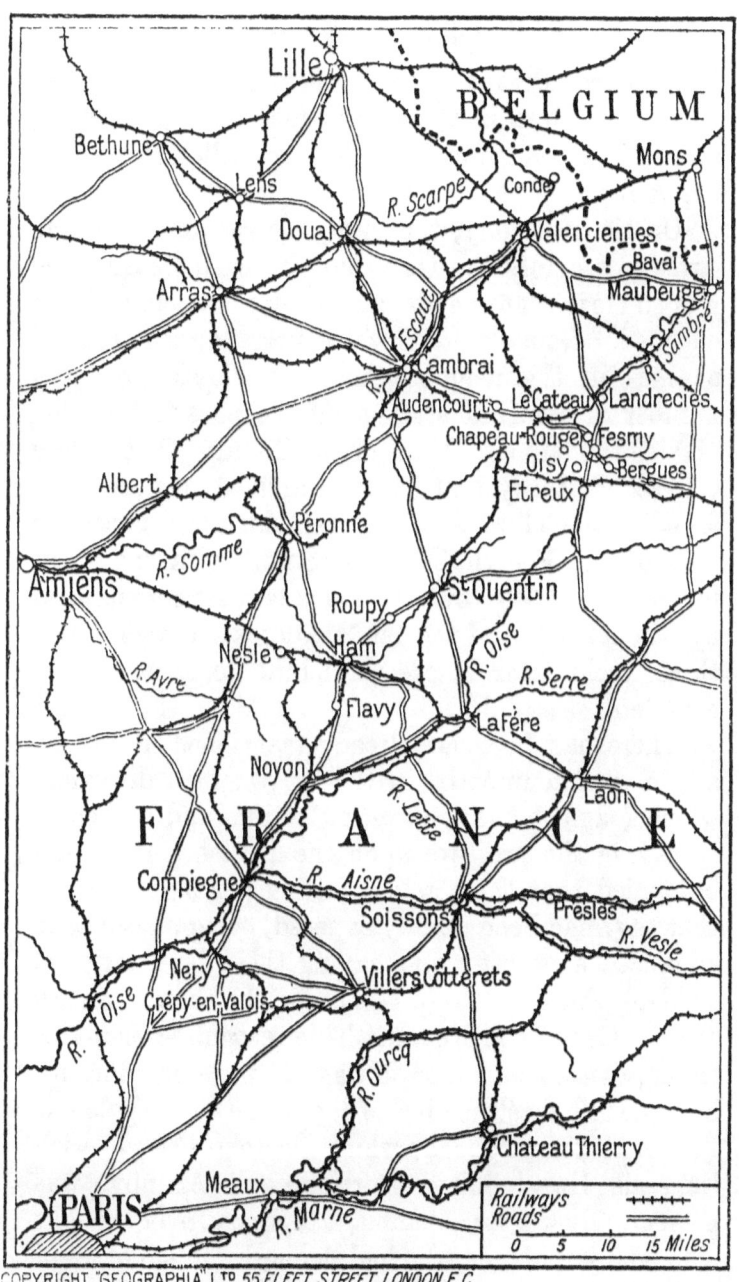

LINE OF RETREAT FROM MONS

126   THE BRITISH CAMPAIGN, 1914

CHAPTER IV.
The Battle of Le Cateau.

it is on record that many of them had not averaged two hours' sleep in the twenty-four for over a week, and still they remained the clear and efficient brain of the Army.

On the next day, the 29th, the remainder of the Army got across the Oise, but the enemy's advance was so close that the British cavalry was continually engaged. Gough's 3rd Cavalry Brigade made several charges in the neighbourhood of Plessis, losing a number of men but stalling off the pursuit and dispersing the famous Uhlans of the Guard. On this day General Pulteney and his staff arrived to take command of the Third Army Corps, which still consisted only of the Fourth Division (Snow) with the semi-independent 19th Infantry Brigade, now commanded by Colonel Ward, of the 1st Middlesex. It was nearly three weeks later before the Third Corps was made complete.

The views of General Joffre.

There had been, as already mentioned, a French advance of four corps in the St. Quentin direction, which fought a brave covering action, and so helped to relieve the pressure upon the British. It cannot be denied that there was a feeling among the latter that they had been unduly exposed, being placed in so advanced a position and having their flank stripped suddenly bare in the presence of the main German army. General Joffre must have recognised that this feeling existed and that it was not unreasonable, for he came to a meeting on this day at the old Napoleonic Palace at Compiègne, at which Sir John French, with Generals Haig, Smith-Dorrien, and Allenby, was present. It was an assemblage of weary, overwrought men, and yet of men who had strength enough of mind and sufficient sense of justice to realise that whatever weight had been thrown upon them, there was even more upon the great French engineer whose spirit hovered over the whole line from Verdun to Amiens. Each man left the room more confident of the immediate future. Shortly afterwards Joffre issued his kindly recognition of the work done by his Allies, admitting in the most handsome fashion that the flank of the long French line of armies had been saved by the hard fighting and self-sacrifice of the British Army.

On August 30, the whole Army having crossed the Oise, the bridges over that river were destroyed, an operation which was performed under a heavy shell-fire, and cost the lives of several sapper officers and men. No words can exaggerate what the Army owed to Wilson's sappers of the 56th and 57th Field Companies and 3rd Signal Company, as also to Tulloch's, of the 17th and 59th Companies and 5th Signal Company, whose work was incessant, fearless, and splendid.

The Army continued to fall back on the line of the Aisne, the general direction being almost east and west through Crépy-en-Valois. The aeroplanes, which had conducted a fine service during the whole of the operations, reported that the enemy was still coming rapidly on, and streaming southwards in the Compiègne direction. That they were in touch was shown in dramatic fashion upon the early morning of September 1. The epic in question deserves to be told somewhat fully, as being one of those incidents which are mere details in the history of a campaign, and yet may live as permanent inspirations in the life of an army.

The 1st Cavalry Brigade, greatly exhausted after screening the retreat so long, was encamped near Nery,

CHAPTER IV.

The Battle of Le Cateau.

to the south of Compiègne, the bivouac being a somewhat extended one. Two units were close to each other and to the brigade headquarters of General Briggs. These were the hard-worked 2nd Dragoon Guards (the Bays) and L Battery of Horse Artillery. *Réveillé* was at four o'clock, and shortly after that hour both troopers and gunners were busy in leading their horses to water. It was a misty morning, and, peering through the haze, an officer perceived that from the top of a low hill about seven hundred yards away three mounted men were looking down upon them. They were the observation officers of three four-gun German batteries. Before the British could realise the situation the guns dashed up and came into action with shrapnel at point-blank range. The whole twelve poured their fire into the disordered bivouac before them. The slaughter and confusion were horrible. Numbers of the horses and men were killed or wounded, and three of the guns were dismounted. It was a most complete surprise, and promised to be an absolute disaster. A body of German cavalry had escorted the guns, and their rifles added to the volume of fire.

It is at such moments that the grand power of disciplined valour comes to bring order out of chaos. Everything combined to make defence difficult—the chilling hour of the morning, the suddenness of the attack, its appalling severity, and the immediate loss of guns and men. A sunken road ran behind the British position, and from the edge of this the dismounted cavalrymen brought their rifles and their machine-gun into action. They suffered heavily from the pelting gusts of shrapnel. Young Captain de Crespigny, the gallant cadet of a gallant family,

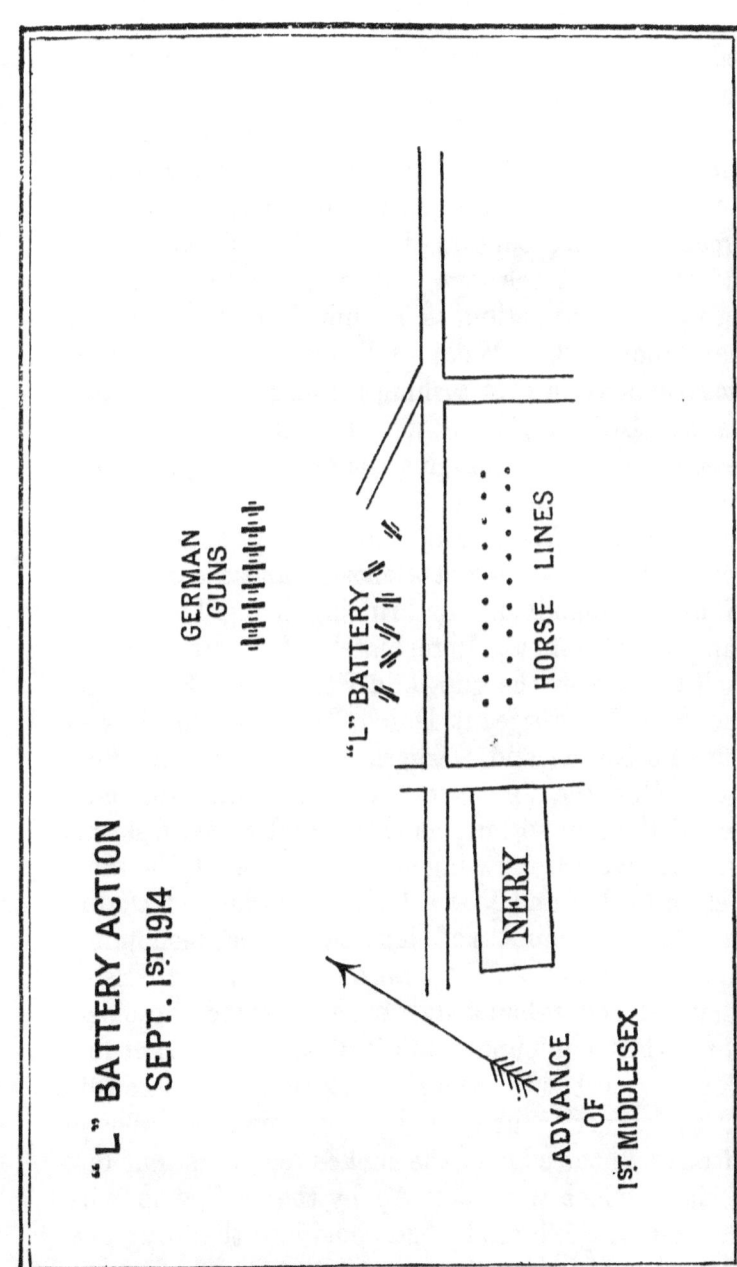

and many other good men were beaten down by it. The sole hope lay in the guns. Three were utterly disabled. There was a rush of officers and men to bring the other three into action. Sclater-Booth, the major of the battery, and one lieutenant were already down. Captain Bradbury took command and cheered on the men. Two of the guns were at once put out of action, so all united to work the one that remained. What followed was Homeric. Lieutenant Giffard in rushing forward was hit in four places. Bradbury's leg was shattered, but he lay beside the trail encouraging the others and giving his directions. Lieutenant Mundy, standing wide as observation officer, was mortally wounded. The limber could not be got alongside and the shell had to be man-handled. In bringing it up Lieutenant Campbell was shot. Immediately afterwards another shell burst over the gun, killed the heroic Bradbury, and wounded Sergeant Dorell, Driver Osborne, and Gunners Nelson and Derbyshire, the only remaining men. But the fight went on. The bleeding men served the gun so long as they could move, Osborne and Derbyshire crawling over with the shells while Nelson loaded and Dorell laid. Osborne and Derbyshire fainted from loss of blood and lay between limber and gun. But the fight went on. Dorell and Nelson, wounded and exhausted, crouched behind the shield of the thirteen-pounder and kept up an incessant fire. Now it was that the amazing fact became visible that all this devotion had not been in vain. The cluster of Bays on the edge of the sunken road burst out into a cheer, which was taken up by the staff, who, with General Briggs himself, had come into the firing-line. Several of the German pieces had gone out of action.

THE BATTLE OF LE CATEAU 131

The dying gun had wrought good work, as had the Maxim of the Bays in the hands of Lieutenant Lamb. Some at least of its opponents had been silenced before the two brave gunners could do no more, for their strength had gone with their blood. Not only had the situation been saved, but victory had been assured.

About eight in the morning news of the perilous situation had reached the 19th Brigade. The 1st Middlesex, under Colonel Rowley, was hurried forward, followed by the 1st Scottish Rifles. Marching rapidly upon the firing, after the good old maxim, the Middlesex found themselves in a position to command the German batteries. After two minutes of rapid fire it was seen that the enemy had left their guns. Eight guns were captured, two of them still loaded. About a dozen German gunners lay dead or wounded round them. Twenty-five of the escort were captured, as was an ambulance with some further prisoners a mile in the rear. The cavalry, notably the 11th Hussars, endeavoured to follow up the success, but soon found themselves in the presence of superior forces. New wheels and new wheelers were found for the injured guns, and Battery L came intact out of action—intact save for the brave acolytes who should serve her no more. Bradbury, Nelson, and Dorell had the Victoria Cross, and never was it better earned. The battery itself was recalled to England to refit and the guns were changed for new ones. It is safe to say that for many a long year these shrapnel-dinted thirteen-pounders will serve as a monument of one of those deeds which, by their self-sacrifice and nobility, do something to mitigate the squalors and horrors of war.

The success was gained at the cost of many valuable

lives. Not only had the *personnel* of the battery been destroyed, but the Bays lost heavily, and there were some casualties among the rest of the brigade who had come up in support. The 5th Dragoon Guards had 50 or 60 casualties, and lost its admirable commander, Colonel Ansell, who was shot down in a flanking movement which he had initiated. Major Cawley, of the staff, also fell. The total British loss was not far short of 500 killed and wounded, but the Germans lost heavily also, and were compelled to abandon their guns.[1]

The German advance guards were particularly active upon this day, September 1, the anniversary of Sedan. Although the Soissons Bridge had been destroyed they had possession of another at Vic, and over this they poured in pursuit of the First Corps, overtaking about 8 A.M. near Villars-Cotteret the rearguard, consisting of the Irish Guards and the 2nd Coldstream. The whole of the 4th Guards Brigade was drawn into the fight, which resolved itself into a huge rifle duel amid thick woods, Scott-Kerr, their Brigadier, riding up and down the firing line. The Guards retired slowly upon the 6th Infantry Brigade (Davies), which was aided by Lushington's 41st Brigade of Artillery, just south of Pisseleux. The Germans had brought up many guns, but could make no further progress, and the British position was held until 6 P.M., when the rearguard closed up with the rest of the Army. Lushington's guns had fought with no infantry in front of them, and it was a matter of great difficulty in the end to get them off, but it was

[1] The German cavalry were the Fourth Cavalry Division, including the 2nd Cuirassiers, 9th Uhlans, 17th and 18th Dragoons. They published in their losses for the "Combat of Néry" 643 casualties. This is not the complete loss, as the artillery does not seem to have been included.

accomplished by some very brilliant work under an infernal fire. After this sharp action, in which Colonel Morris of the Irish Guards lost his life, the retreat of the First Army Corps was not seriously interfered with. The losses at that date in this corps amounted to 81 officers and 2180 of all ranks.

So much attention is naturally drawn to the Second Army Corps, which both at Mons and at Le Cateau had endured most of the actual fighting, that there is some danger of the remarkable retreat effected by the First Corps having less than its fair share of appreciation. The actual fighting was the least of the difficulties. The danger of one or both flanks being exposed, the great mobility of the enemy, the indifferent and limited roads, the want of rest, the difficulty of getting food cooked, the consequent absolute exhaustion of the men, and the mental depression combined to make it an operation of a most trying character, throwing an enormous strain upon the judgment and energy of General Haig, who so successfully brought his men intact and fit for service into a zone of safety.

On the night of September 1, the First and Second Army Corps were in touch once more at Betz, and were on the move again by 2 A.M. upon the 2nd. On this morning the German advance was curiously interlocked with the British rear, and four German guns were picked up by the cavalry near Ermenonville. They are supposed to have been the remaining guns of the force which attacked Battery L at Nery. The movements of the troops during the day were much impeded by the French refugees, who thronged every road in their flight before the German terror. In spite of these obstructions, the rearward services

CHAPTER IV.

The Battle of Le Cateau.

of the Army—supply columns, ammunition columns, and medical transport—were well conducted, and the admiration of all independent observers. The work of all these departments had been greatly complicated by the fact that, as the Channel ports were now practically undefended and German troops, making towards the coast, had cut the main Calais-Boulogne line at Amiens, the base had been moved farther south from Havre to St. Nazaire, which meant shifting seventy thousand tons of stores and changing all arrangements. In spite of this the supplies were admirable. It may safely be said that if there is one officer more than another for whom the whole British Army felt a glow of gratitude, it was for Sir William Robertson, the Chief of the Commissariat, who saw that the fighting man was never without his rations. Greatly also did they appreciate the work of his subordinates, who, wet or fine, through rainfall or shell-fall, passed the food forward to the weary men at the front.

A difficult movement lay in front of the Army which had to cross the Marne, involving a flank march in the face of the enemy. A retirement was still part of the general French scheme of defence, and the British Army had to conform to it, though it was exultantly whispered from officer to sergeant and from sergeant to private that the turn of the tide was nearly due. On this day it was first observed that the Germans, instead of pushing forward, were swinging across to the east in the direction of Chateau-Thierry. This made the task of the British a more easy one, and before evening they were south of the Marne and had blown up the bridges. The movement of the Germans brought them down to the river, but at a point some ten miles east of the British position. They were reported to be crossing the river at La Ferté, and Sir John French continued to fall back towards the Seine, moving after sundown, as the heat had been for some days very exhausting. The troops halted in the neighbourhood of Presles, and were cheered by the arrival of some small drafts, numbering about 2000, a first instalment towards refilling the great gaps in the ranks, which at this date could not have been less than from 12,000 to 15,000 officers and men. Here for a moment this narrative may be broken, since it has taken the Army to the farthest point of its retreat and reached that moment of advance for which every officer and man, from Sir John French to the drummer-boys, was eagerly waiting. With their left flank resting upon the extreme outer forts of Paris, the British troops had finally ended a retreat which will surely live in military history as a remarkable example of an army retaining its cohesion and courage in the presence of an overpowering adversary, who could never either cut them off or break in their rearguard. The British Army was a small force when compared with the giants of the Continent, but when tried by this supreme test it is not mere national complacency for us to claim that it lived up to its own highest traditions. "It was not to forts of steel and concrete that the Allies owed their strength," said a German historian, writing of this phase of the war, "but to the magnificent qualities of the British Army." We desire no compliments at the expense of our brothers-in-arms, nor would they be just, but at least so generous a sentence as this may be taken as an advance from that contemptuous view of the British Army with which the campaign had begun.

136 THE BRITISH CAMPAIGN, 1914

CHAPTER IV.

The Battle of Le Cateau.

Before finally leaving the consideration of this historical retreat, where a small army successfully shook itself clear from the long and close pursuit of a remarkably gallant, mobile, and numerous enemy, it may be helpful to give a chronology of the events, that the reader may see their relation to each other.

HAIG'S FIRST CORPS.	SMITH-DORRIEN'S SECOND CORPS.
August 22.	
Get into position to the east of Mons, covering the line Mons—Bray.	Get into position to the west of Mons, covering the line Mons—Condé.
August 23.	
Artillery engagement, but no severe attack. Ordered to retreat in conformity with Second Corps.	Strongly attacked by Von Kluck's army. Ordered to abandon position and fall back.
August 24.	
Retreat with no serious molestation upon Bavai. Here the two Corps diverged and did not meet again till they reached Betz upon September 1.	Retreat followed up by the Germans. Severe rearguard actions at Dour, Wasmes, Frameries. Corps shook itself clear and fell back on Bavai.
August 25.	
Marching all day. Overtaken in evening at Landrecies and Maroilles by the German pursuit. Sharp fighting.	Marching all day. Reinforced by Fourth Division. Continual rearguard action becoming more serious towards evening, when Cambrai—Le Cateau line was reached.
August 26.	
Rearguard actions in morning. Marching south all day, halting at the Venerolles line.	Battle of Le Cateau. German pursuit stalled off at heavy cost of men and guns. Retreat on St. Quentin.

THE BATTLE OF LE CATEAU 137

August 27.

Rearguard action in which Munsters lost heavily. Marching south all day.	Marching south. Reach the line Nesle—Ham—Flavy.

August 28.

Cavalry actions to stop German pursuit. Marching south on La Fere.	Marching south, making for the line of the Oise near Noyon. Light rearguard skirmishes.

August 29, 30, and 31.

Marching on the line of the Aisne, almost east and west.	Crossed Oise. Cavalry continually engaged. General direction through Crépy-en-Valois.

September 1.

Sharp action at Nery with German vanguard. Later in the day considerable infantry action at Villars—Cotteret. Unite at Betz.	Retreat upon Paris continued. Late this night the two Corps unite once more at Betz.

September 2.

Crossed the Marne and began to fall back on the Seine. Halted near Presles.	Crossed the Marne and began to fall back on the Seine.

CHAPTER IV.
The Battle of Le Cateau.

CHAPTER V

THE BATTLE OF THE MARNE

The general situation—" Die grosse Zeit "—The turn of the tide—The Battle of the Ourcq—The British advance—Cavalry fighting—The 1st Lincolns and the guns—6th Brigade's action at Hautvesnes — 9th Brigade's capture of Germans at Vinly—The problem of the Aisne—Why the Marne is one of the great battles of all time.

<small>Chapter V.</small>
<small>The Battle of the Marne.</small>
<small>The general situation.</small>

There are several problems connected with the strategical opening of the great war which will furnish food for debate among military critics for many years to come. One of these, already alluded to, is the French offensive taken in Alsace and Lorraine. It ended in check in both cases, and yet its ultimate effects in confusing the German plans and deflecting German armies which might have been better used elsewhere may be held to justify the French in their strategy.

Another remarkable and questionable move now obtrudes itself, this time upon the part of the Germans. Very shortly after the outbreak of war, the Russians had pushed their covering armies over the frontier of East Prussia, and had defeated a German force at Gumbinnen, with a loss of prisoners and guns. A few days later the left wing of the widespread, and as yet only partially mobilised, Russian army struck

THE BATTLE OF THE MARNE 139

heavily at the Austrians in the south near Lemberg, where after a week of fighting they gained a great victory, with prisoners, which amounted to over 70,000 men and a large booty of guns and supplies. Before this blow had befallen their cause, and influenced only by the fact that the Russian right wing was encroaching upon the sacred soil of the Fatherland, a considerable force was detached from the invading armies in France and dispatched to the Eastern front. These men were largely drawn from the Third (Saxon) Army of Von Haussen. Such a withdrawal at such a time could only mean that the German general staff considered that the situation in France was assured, and that they had still sufficient means to carry on a victorious invasion. Events were to show that they were utterly mistaken in their calculation. It is true that, aided by these reinforcements, Von Hindenburg succeeded on August 31 in inflicting a severe defeat upon the Russians at the battle of Tannenberg, but subsequent events proved that such a victory could have no decisive result, while the weakening of the armies in France may have had a permanent effect upon the whole course of the war. At the very moment that the Germans were withdrawing troops from their Western front the British and French were doing all they could to thicken their own line of resistance, especially by the transference of armies from Alsace and the south. Thus the net result was that, whereas the Germans had up to August 25 a very marked superiority in numbers, by the beginning of September the forces were more equal. From that moment the chance of their taking Paris became steadily more and more remote.

The first month of the war represented a very

remarkable military achievement upon the part of Germany. In her high state of preparation as compared with the Allies, it was to be expected that the beginning of hostilities would be all in her favour, but the reality exceeded what could have been foreseen. Her great armies were ready to the last button. Up to the eve of war the soldiers did not themselves know what their field uniform was like. At the last moment two millions of men filed into the depots and emerged in half an hour clad in grey, with new boots, equipment, and every possible need for the campaign. On her artillery surprises she set special store, and they were upon a vast scale. The machine-gun had been developed to an extent unknown by other armies, and of these deadly little weapons it is certain that very many thousands were available. From the tiny quick-firer, carried easily by two men upon a stretcher, to the vast cannon with a diameter of sixteen and a half inches at the mouth, taking three railway trucks for its majestic portage, every possible variety of man-killing engine was ready in vast profusion. So, too, was the flying service, from the little Taube to the huge six-hundred-foot Zeppelin. From these latter devices great results were expected which were not destined to materialise, for, apart from reconnaissances, they proved themselves to be machines rather for the murder of non-combatants than for honest warfare.

Making every allowance for the huge advantage which the nation that *knows* war is coming must always enjoy over those which merely fear that it may come, it would be foolish to deny the vast military achievement of Germany in the month of August. It reflects great credit upon the bravery

THE BATTLE OF THE MARNE 141

and energy of her troops, as well as upon the foresight of her organisers and the capacity of her leaders. Though we are her enemies, our admiration would have been whole-hearted were it not for the brutalities which marked her advance both in Poland, in Belgium, and in France. Consider that wonderful panorama of victory which was known all over the Fatherland as "*Die grosse Zeit*." On August 10 fell the great fortress of Liége, on the 22nd the great fortress of Namur, early in September that of Maubeuge, while the smaller strongholds went down as if they were open cities. On August 10 was a considerable victory at Mülhausen, on the 20th the Belgians were defeated at Tirlemont, on the same day Brussels was occupied. On the 22nd the French central army of ten corps was defeated in a great battle near Charleroi, losing, according to the Germans, some 20,000 prisoners and 200 guns. On the left flank the Crown Prince's army won the battle of Longwy, taking 10,000 prisoners and many more guns. On August 23 the Duke of Würtemberg won a battle in the Ardennes. Upon the same date the British were driven from their position at Mons. Upon the 26th they were defeated at Le Cateau. Most of Belgium and the North of France were overrun. Scattered parties of Uhlans made their way to the shores of the Atlantic spreading terror along the Channel coast. The British bases were in such danger that they had to be moved.

Finally, upon the last day of the month, a great battle took place at Tannenberg in East Prussia, in which the Russian invading army was almost completely destroyed. I do not know where in history such a succession of victories is to be found, and our

CHAPTER V.

The Battle of the Marne.

142 THE BRITISH CAMPAIGN, 1914

CHAPTER V.

The Battle of the Marne.

horror of the atrocities of Louvain, Aerschot, Dinard, and so many other places must not blind us to the superb military achievement.

It was not, it is true, an unbroken series of successes even in the West. The French in the early days won a victory at Dornach in Alsace, and another smaller one at Dinant in the Ardennes. They held the enemy in the neighbourhood of Nancy, fought a fairly equal battle at St. Quentin in taking the pressure off the British at the end of August, and had a success at Guise. These, however, were small matters as compared with the sweeping tide of German victory. But gradually the impetus of the rush was being stayed. Neither the French nor the British lines were broken. They grew stronger from compression, whilst the invaders grew weaker from diffusion. Even as they hoped to reach the climax of their success, and the huge winning-post of the Eiffel Tower loomed up before their racing armies, the dramatic moment arrived, and the dauntless, high-hearted Allies had the reward of their constant, much-enduring valour.

The turn of the tide.

September 6 was a day of great elation in the armies of the Allies, for it marked the end of the retreat and the beginning of their victorious return. It is clear that they could in no case have gone farther south without exposing Paris to the danger of an attack. The French Government had already been transferred to Bordeaux and the city put into a state which promised a long and stubborn defence, but after the surprising rapidity of the capture of Namur there was a general distrust of fortresses, and it was evident that if only one or two of the outer ring of forts should be overwhelmed by the German fire, the enemy would be in a position to do terrible damage to the city, even if they failed to occupy it. The constant dropping of bombs from German aeroplanes, one of which had already injured the Cathedral of Notre Dame, gave a sinister forecast of the respect which the enemy was likely to show to the monuments of antiquity.

Fortunately, the problem of investing Paris while the main French armies remained unbeaten in the field proved to be an insuperable one. The first German task, in accordance with the prophet Clausewitz, was to break the French resistance. Everything would follow after that, and nothing could precede it. Von Kluck, with his army, comprising originally something over 200,000 men, had lost considerably in their conflicts with the British, and were much exhausted by rapid marching, but they were still in good heart, as the roads over which they passed seemed to offer ample evidence that their enemy was in full flight before them. Knowing that they had hit the British hard, they hoped that, for a time at least, they might disregard them, and, accordingly, they ventured to close in, by a flank march, on to the other German armies to the east of them, in order to combine against the main line of French resistance and to make up the gaps of those corps which had been ordered to East Prussia. But the bulldog, though weary and somewhat wounded, was still watching with bloodshot eyes. He now sprang suddenly upon the exposed flank of his enemy and got a grip which held firm for many a day to come.

Without going into complicated details of French strategy, which would be outside the scope of this work, it may be generally stated that the whole

CHAPTER V.

The Battle of the Marne.

CHAPTER V.

The Battle of the Marne.

French line, which had stretched on August 22 from Namur along the line of the Sambre to Charleroi and had retired with considerable loss before the German advance, was now extended in seven separate armies from Verdun to the west of Paris.

General Joffre had assembled Maunoury's Sixth Army, which consisted of the Seventh Regular Corps, one reserve corps, and three territorial divisions, with Sordet's cavalry, in the neighbourhood of Amiens, and at the end of the month they lay with their right upon Roye. Thus, when Von Kluck swerved to his left, this army was on the flank of the whole great German line which extended to Verdun. Next to this Sixth Army and more to the south-east were the British, now no longer unsupported, but with solid French comrades upon either side of them. Next to the British, counting from the left or westward end of the defensive line, was the Fifth French Army under General d'Esperey, of four corps, with Conneau's cavalry forming the link between. These three great bodies, the French Sixth, the British, and the French Fifth, were in touch during the subsequent operations, and moved forward in close co-operation upon September 6. Their operations were directed against the First (Von Kluck's) and Second (Von Bülow's) Armies. On the right of the Fifth French Army came another extra, produced suddenly by the prolific Joffre and thrust into the centre of the line. This was General Foch's Seventh, three corps strong, which joined to the eastward General Langlé de Cary's Fourth Army. Opposed to them were the remains of Von Haussen's Third Saxon Army and the Prince of Würtemberg's Fourth Army. Eastward of this, on the farther side of the great plain of

THE BATTLE OF THE MARNE

Chalons, a place of evil omen for the Huns, were the Third (Sarrail), Second (Castelnau), and First (Dubail) French Armies, which faced the Fifth, Sixth, and Seventh German, commanded respectively by the Crown Prince of Prussia, the Crown Prince of Bavaria, and General von Heeringen. Such were the mighty lines which were destined to swing and sway for an eventful week in the strain of a close-locked fight.

Chapter V.

The Battle of the Marne.

The eastern portion of this great battle is outside the scope of this account, but it may briefly be stated that after murderous fighting neither the French nor the German lines made any marked advance in the extreme east, but that the Crown Prince's army was driven back by Dubail, Sarrail, and Castelnau from all its advanced positions, and held off from Nancy and Verdun, which were his objectives. It was at the western end of the Allied line that the strategical position was most advantageous and the result most marked. In all other parts of that huge line the parallel battle prevailed. Only in the west were the Germans outflanked, and the shock of the impact of the Sixth French Army passed down from Meaux to Verdun as the blow of the engine's buffer sends the successive crashes along a line of trucks. This French army was, as already stated, upon the extreme outside right of Von Kluck's army, divided from it only by the River Ourcq. This was the deciding factor in the subsequent operations.

The Battle of the Ourcq.

By mid-day upon September 6, according to the dispatch of Sir John French, the Germans had realised their dangerous position. The British Army, consisting of five divisions and five cavalry brigades, with its depleted ranks filled up with reinforcements and some of its lost guns replaced, was advancing

L

CHAPTER V.

The Battle of the Marne.

from the south through the forest of Crécy, men who had limped south with bleeding feet at two miles an hour changing their gait to three or four now that they were bound northward. The general movement of the Army cannot, however, be said to have been rapid. Von Kluck had placed nothing more substantial than a cavalry screen of two divisions in front of them, while he had detached a strong force of infantry and artillery to fight a rearguard action against the Sixth French Army and prevent it from crossing the Ourcq.

The desperate struggle of September 6, 7, 8, and 9 between Von Kluck and Maunoury may be looked upon as the first turning-point of the war. Von Kluck had originally faced Maunoury with his Fourth Reserve Corps on the defensive. Recognising how critical it was that Maunoury should be crushed, he passed back two more army corps—the Seventh and Second—across the Ourcq, and fell upon the French with such violence that for two days it was impossible to say which side would win. Maunoury and his men fought magnificently, and the Germans showed equal valour. At one time the situation seemed desperate, but 20,000 men, odds and ends of every kind—Republican Guards, gendarmes, and others—were rushed out from Paris in a five-mile line of automobiles, and the action was restored. Only on the morning of the 10th did the Germans withdraw in despair, held in their front by the brave Maunoury, and in danger of being cut off by the British to the east of them.

The British advance.

The advance of the British upon September 6 was made in unison with that of the Fifth French Army (D'Esperey's) upon the right, and was much facilitated

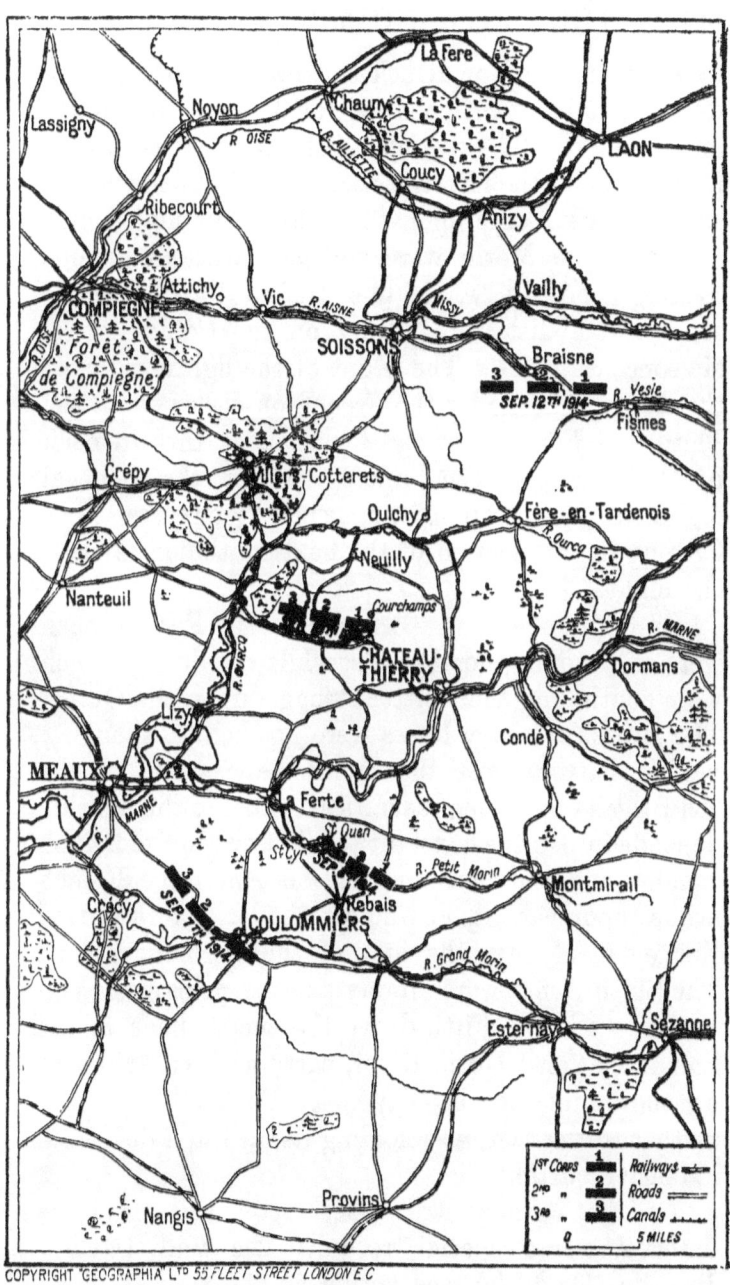

BRITISH ADVANCE DURING THE BATTLE OF THE MARNE

148   THE BRITISH CAMPAIGN, 1914

CHAPTER V.

The Battle of the Marne.

by the fact that Von Kluck had to detach the strong force already mentioned to deal with Maunoury upon the left. The British advanced with the Fourth Division upon the left, the Second Corps in the centre and the First Corps upon the right. The high banks of the Grand Morin were occupied without serious fighting, and the whole line pushed forward for a considerable distance, halting on the Coulommiers-Maisoncelles front. The brunt of the fighting during the day was borne by the French on either wing, the Third and Fourth German Corps being thrown back by D'Esperey's men, among whom the Senegal regiments particularly distinguished themselves. The fighting in this section of the field continued far into the night.

On September 7 the British and the Fifth French were still moving northwards, while the Sixth French were continuing their bitter struggle upon the Ourcq. The British infantry losses were not heavy, though a hidden battery cost the South Lancashires of the 7th Brigade forty-one casualties. Most of the fighting depended upon the constant touch between the British cavalry and the German. It was again the French armies upon each flank who did the hard work during this eventful day, the first of the German retreat. The Sixth Army were all day at close grips with Von Kluck, while the Fifth drove the enemy back to the line of the Petit Morin River, carrying Vieux-Maisons at the point of the bayonet. Foch's army, still farther to the east, was holding its own in a desperate defensive battle.

Cavalry fighting.

Of the cavalry skirmishes upon this day one deserves some special record. The 2nd Cavalry Brigade (De Lisle) was acting at the time as flank

THE BATTLE OF THE MARNE 149

guard with the 9th Lancers in front. Coming into contact with some German dragoons near the village of Moncel, there followed a face-to-face charge between two squadrons, each riding through the other. The American, Coleman, who saw the encounter, reckons the odds in numbers to have been two to one against the Lancers. The British Colonel Campbell was wounded, and the adjutant, Captain Reynolds, transfixed through the shoulder by a lance. While drawing the weapon out Captain Allfrey was killed. The other casualties were slight, and those of the German dragoons were considerably greater. This example of shock tactics was almost instantly followed by an exhibition of those mounted rifleman tactics which have been cultivated of late years. A squadron of the 18th Hussars, having dismounted, was immediately charged by a German squadron in close order. About 70 Germans charged, and 32 were picked up in front of the dismounted Hussars, while the few who passed through the firing line were destroyed by the horse-holders. It may fairly be argued that had the two squadrons met with shock tactics, no such crushing effect could possibly have been attained. It is interesting that in one morning two incidents should have occurred which bore so directly upon the perennial dispute between the partisans of the *arme blanche* and those of the rifle.

On the 8th the orders were to advance towards Château-Thierry and to endeavour to reach the Marne. The Germans were retreating fast, but rather on account of their generally faulty strategical position than from tactical compulsion, and they covered themselves with continual rearguard actions, especially along the line of the Petit Morin. It is one of

CHAPTER V.

The Battle of the Marne.

the noticeable results, however, of the use of aircraft that the bluff of a rearguard has disappeared and that it is no longer possible to make such a retreat as Masséna from Torres Vedras, where the pursuer never knew if he were striking at a substance or a shadow. Gough's Second Cavalry Division, which consisted of the 3rd and 5th Brigades, swept along, and the infantry followed hard at the heels of the horses, Doran's 8th Brigade suffering the loss of about 100 men when held up at the crossing of the Petit Morin River near Orly, which they traversed eventually under an effective covering fire from J Battery, R.H.A.

The First Army Corps upon this day forced the Petit Morin at two places, both near La Trétoire, north of Rebaix. The First Division secured the passage at Sablonnières, where the Black Watch seized the heights, causing the German rearguard some losses and taking 60 prisoners. The Second Division met with considerable resistance, but the 2nd Worcesters got over at Le Gravier and the 2nd Grenadier Guards at La Forge. The enemy was then driven from the river bank into the woods, where they were practically surrounded and had eventually to surrender. Eight machine-guns and 350 prisoners, many of them from the Guards' Jaeger Battalion, were captured. Six of these machine-guns fell to the Irish Guards.

The Second Army Corps passed the Petit Morin near St. Cyr and St. Ouen, the 13th Brigade attacking the former and the 14th the latter, both being villages on the farther side of the river. Such fighting as there was in this quarter came largely to the 1st East Surrey and 1st Cornwalls, of the 14th Brigade,

THE BATTLE OF THE MARNE 151

but the resistance was not great, and was broken by the artillery fire. To the soldiers engaged the whole action was more like a route march with occasional deployments than a battle.

Chapter V.

The Battle of the Marne.

On the 9th the Army was up to the Marne and was faced with the problem of crossing it. The operations extending over many miles were unimportant in detail, though of some consequence in the mass. The real hard fighting was falling upon the Sixth French Army north of Ligny, which was still in desperate conflict with the German right, and upon Foch's army, which was fighting magnificently at Fère-Champenoise. The advance of the British, and their own exertions, caused the Germans to retire and cleared the passage over the Ourcq for our Allies. The chief losses during the day upon the British side fell upon the Guards' Brigade, the 1st Lincolns, and the 1st Cornwalls, most of which were inflicted by invisible quick-firing batteries shrouded by the woods which flank the river. The latter regiment lost Colonel Turner, Major Cornish-Bowden, and a number of other killed or wounded in a brilliant piece of woodland fighting, where they drove in a strong German rearguard. The 1st East Surrey, who were very forward in the movement, were also hard hit, having 6 officers and about 120 men out of action.

The British infantry was able on this day to show that woods may serve for other purposes besides hiding batteries. The 1st Lincolns, being held up by a rapid and accurate fire from invisible guns, dispatched two companies, C and D, to make in single file a *détour* under the shelter of the trees. Coming behind the battery, which appears to have had no immediate support, they poured in a rapid fire at

The 1st Lincolns and the guns.

CHAPTER V.

The Battle of the Marne.

two hundred and fifty yards, which laid every man of the German gunners upon the ground. The whole battery was captured. The casualties of the Lincolns in this dashing exploit, which included Captains Hoskyns and Ellison, with Lieutenant Thruston, were unavoidably caused by British shrapnel, our gunners knowing nothing of the movement.

On this date (September 9) both the First and the Second Army Corps were across the Marne, and advanced some miles to the north of it, killing, wounding, or capturing many hundreds of the enemy. The Sixth French Army was, as stated, fighting hard upon the Ourcq, but the Fifth had won a brilliant success near Montmirail and driven the enemy completely over the river.

Pulteney's Third Corps, still a division short, had been held up by the destruction of the bridges at La Ferté, but on September 10 they were across and the whole Army sweeping northwards. The cavalry overrode all resistance and rounded up a number of prisoners, over 2000 in all. It was a strange reversal of fortune, for here within a fortnight were the same two armies playing the converse parts, the British eagerly pushing on with a flushed consciousness of victory, while the Germans, tired and dispirited, scattered in groups among the woods or were gathered up from the roadsides. It was a day of mist and rain, with muddy, sodden roads, but all weather is fine weather to the army that is gaining ground. An impression of complete German demoralisation became more widespread as transport, shells, and even guns were found littering the high-roads, and yet there was really even less cause for it than when the same delusion was held by the Germans. The

THE BATTLE OF THE MARNE 153

enemy were actually making a hurried but orderly retreat, and these signs of disaster were only the evidence of a broken rearguard resistance. German armies do not readily dissolve. There is no more cohesive force in the world. But they were undoubtedly hard pressed.

Chapter V.
The Battle of the Marne.

About eight o'clock upon the morning of the 10th the 6th Brigade (Davies') observed a column of the enemy's infantry on a parallel road near the village of Hautvesnes. Artillery fire was at once opened upon them, and a vigorous infantry attack, the 1st Rifles advancing direct with the 1st Berkshires on their right, whilst the 1st King's Liverpool worked round each flank in Boer fashion. The 2nd Staffords were in support. The Germans had taken refuge in a sunken road, but they were mercilessly lashed by shrapnel, and 400 of them ran forward with their hands up. The sunken road was filled with their dead and wounded. Some hundreds streamed away across country, but these were mostly gathered up by the Third Division on the left.

6th Brigade's action at Hautvesnes.

In this brisk little action the 50th R.F.A., and later the whole of the 34th Brigade R.F.A., put in some fine work, the shrapnel-fire being most deadly and accurate. The British had pushed their guns freely forward with their cavalry and did much execution with them, though they had the misfortune on this same date, the 10th, to lose, by the answering shell-fire of the enemy, General Findlay, artillery commander of the First Division. In this second action, in which the German rearguard, infantry as well as artillery, was engaged, the 2nd Sussex Regiment, which was leading the First Division, sustained considerable losses near Courchamps or

154   THE BRITISH CAMPAIGN, 1914

CHAPTER V.

The Battle of the Marne.

Priez, as did the 1st Northamptons and the 1st North Lancashires. Some 300 of Bulfin's 2nd Brigade were hit altogether, among whom was Colonel Knight, of the North Lancashires. The enemy came under heavy fire, both from the infantry and from the guns, so that their losses were considerable, and several hundred of them were captured. The country was very hilly, and the roads so bad that in the exhausted state of men and horses the pursuit could not be sufficiently pressed. Thirty large motor cars were seen at Priez in front of the 2nd Brigade, carrying the enemy's rearguard.

9th Brigade's capture of Germans at Vinly.

On this same date the 9th Brigade captured 600 German infantry, the survivors of a battalion, at the village of Vinly. This seems to have been an incident of the same character as the loss of the Cheshires or of the Munsters in the British retreat, where a body of troops fighting a covering action was left too long, or failed to receive the orders for its withdrawal. The defence was by no means a desperate one, and few of the attacking infantry were killed or wounded. On this date the Fifth and Sixth French Armies were hardly engaged at all, and the whole Allied Force, including General Foch's Seventh French Army on the right of the Fifth, were all sweeping along together in a single rolling steel-crested wave, composed of at least twelve army corps, whilst nine German corps (five of Von Kluck and four of Bülow) retired swiftly before them, hurrying towards the chance of re-forming and refitting which the Aisne position would afford them.

On September 11 the British were still advancing upon a somewhat narrowed front. There was no opposition and again the day bore a considerable

THE BATTLE OF THE MARNE

crop of prisoners and other trophies. The weather had become so foggy that the aircraft were useless, and it is only when these wonderful scouters are precluded from rising that a general realises how indispensable they have become to him. As a wit expressed it, they have turned war from a game of cards into a game of chess. It was still very wet, and the Army was exposed to considerable privation, most of the officers and men having neither change of clothing, overcoats, nor waterproof sheets, while the blowing up of bridges on the lines of communication had made it impossible to supply the wants. The undefeatable commissariat, however, was still working well, which means that the Army was doing the same. On the 12th the pursuit was continued as far as the River Aisne. Allenby's cavalry occupied Braine in the early morning, the Queen's Bays being particularly active, but there was so much resistance that the Third Division was needed to make the ground good. Gough's Cavalry Division also ran into the enemy near Chassemy, killing or capturing several hundred of the German infantry. In these operations Captain Stewart, whose experience as an alleged spy has been mentioned, met with a soldier's death. On this day the Sixth French Army was fighting a considerable action upon the British left in the vicinity of Soissons, the Germans making a stand in order to give time for their impedimenta to get over the river. In this they succeeded, so that when the Allied Forces reached the Aisne, which is an unfordable stream some sixty yards from bank to bank, the retiring army had got across it, had destroyed most of the bridges, and showed every sign of being prepared to dispute the crossing.

Missy Bridge, facing the Fifth Division, appeared at first to be intact, but a daring reconnaissance by Lieutenant Pennecuick, of the Engineers, showed that it was really badly damaged. Condé Bridge was intact, but was so covered by a high horse-shoe formation of hills upon the farther side that it could not be used, and remained throughout under control of the enemy. Bourg Bridge, however, in front of the First Army Corps, had for some unexplained reason been left undamaged, and this was seized in the early morning of September 13 by De Lisle's cavalry, followed rapidly by Bulfin's 2nd Brigade. It was on the face of it a somewhat desperate enterprise which lay immediately in front of the British general. If the enemy were still retreating he could not afford to slacken his pursuit, while, on the other hand, if the enemy were merely making a feint of resistance, then, at all hazards, the stream must be forced and the rearguard driven in. The German infantry could be seen streaming up the roads on the farther bank of the river, but there were no signs of what their next disposition might be. Air reconnaissance was still precluded, and it was impossible to say for certain which alternative might prove to be correct, but Sir John French's cavalry training must incline him always to the braver course. The officer who rode through the Boers to Kimberley and threw himself with his weary men across the path of the formidable Kronje was not likely to stand hesitating upon the banks of the Aisne. His personal opinion was that the enemy meant to stand and fight, but none the less the order was given to cross.

September 13 was spent in arranging this dashing

THE BATTLE OF THE MARNE 157

and dangerous movement. The British got across eventually in several places and by various devices. Bulfin's men, followed by the rest of the First Division of Haig's Army Corps, passed the canal bridge of Bourg with no loss or difficulty. The 11th Brigade of Pulteney's Third Corps got across by a partially demolished bridge and ferry at Venizel. They were followed by the 12th Brigade, who established themselves near Bucy. The 13th Brigade was held up at Missy, but the 14th got across and lined up with the men of the Third Corps in the neighbourhood of Ste. Marguerite, meeting with a considerable resistance from the Germans. Later, Count Gleichen's 15th Brigade also got across. On the right Hamilton got over with two brigades of the Third Division, the 8th Brigade crossing on a single plank at Vailly and the 9th using the railway bridge, while the whole of Haig's First Corps had before evening got a footing upon the farther bank. So eager was the advance and so inadequate the means that Haking's 5th Brigade, led by the Connaught Rangers, was obliged to get over the broad and dangerous river, walking in single file along the sloping girder of a ruined bridge, under a heavy, though distant, shell-fire. The night of September 13 saw the main body of the Army across the river, already conscious of a strong rear-guard action, but not yet aware that the whole German Army had halted and was turning at bay. On the right De Lisle's cavalrymen had pushed up the slope from Bourg Bridge and reached as far as Vendresse, where they were pulled up by the German lines.

It has been mentioned above that the 11th and 12th Brigades of the Fourth Division had passed the

CHAPTER V.

The Battle of the Marne.

river at Venizel. These troops were across in the early afternoon, and they at once advanced, and proved that in that portion of the field the enemy were undoubtedly standing fast. The 11th Brigade, which was more to the north, had only a constant shell-fall to endure, but the 12th, pushing forward through Bucy-le-long, found itself in front of a line of woods from which there swept a heavy machine-gun- and rifle-fire. The advance was headed by the 2nd Lancashire Fusiliers, supported by the 2nd Inniskilling Fusiliers. It was across open ground and under heavy fire, but it was admirably carried out. In places where the machine-guns had got the exact range the stricken Fusiliers lay dead or wounded with accurate intervals, like a firing-line on a field-day. The losses were heavy, especially in the Lancashire Fusiliers. Colonel Griffin was wounded, and 5 of his officers with 250 men were among the casualties. It should be recorded that fresh supplies of ammunition were brought up at personal risk by Colonel Seely, late Minister of War, in his motor-car. The contest continued until dusk, when the troops waited for the battle of next day under such cover as they could find.

The crossing of the stream may be said, upon the one side, to mark the end of the battle and pursuit of the Marne, while, on the other, it commenced that interminable Battle of the Aisne which was destined to fulfil Bloch's prophecies and to set the type of all great modern engagements. The prolonged struggles of the Manchurian War had prepared men's minds for such a development, but only here did it first assume its full proportions and warn us that the battle of the future was to be the siege of the past.

THE BATTLE OF THE MARNE

Men remembered with a smile Bernhardi's confident assertion that a German battle would be decided in one day, and that his countrymen would never be constrained to fight in defensive trenches.

The moral effect of the Battle of the Marne was greater than its material gains. The latter, so far as the British were concerned, did not exceed 5000 prisoners, 20 guns, and a quantity of transport. The total losses, however, were very heavy. The Germans had perfected a method of burning their dead with the aid of petrol. These numerous holocausts over the country-side were found afterwards by the peasants to have left mounds of charred animal matter which were scattered by their industrious hands on the fields which they might help to fertilise. The heat of cremation had dissolved the bones, but the teeth in most cases remained intact, so that over an area of France it was no uncommon thing to see them gleaming in the clods on either side of the new-cut furrow. Had the ring of high-born German criminals who planned the war seen in some apocalyptic vision the detailed results of their own villainy, it is hard to doubt that even their hearts and consciences would have shrunk from the deed.

Apart from the losses, the mere fact that a great German army had been hustled across thirty miles of country, had been driven from river to river, and had finally to take refuge in trenches in order to hold their ground, was a great encouragement to the Allies. From that time they felt assured that with anything like equal numbers they had an ascendancy over their opponents. Save in the matter of heavy guns and machine-guns, there was not a single arm

THE BATTLE OF THE MARNE.

CHAPTER V.

in which they did not feel that they were the equals or the superiors. Nor could they forget that this foe, whom they were driving in the open and holding in the trenches, was one who had rushed into the war with men and material all carefully prepared for this day of battle, while their own strength lay in the future. If the present was bright, it would surely be incomparably brighter when the reserves of France and the vast resources of the British Empire were finally brought into line. There had never from the beginning been a doubt of final victory, but from this time on it became less an opinion and more a demonstrable and mathematical certainty.

Why the Marne is one of the great battles of all time.

The battle must also be regarded as a fixed point in military history, since it was the first time since the days of the great Napoleon that a Prussian army had been turned and driven. In three successive wars—against the Danes, the Austrians, and the French—they had lived always in the warm sunshine of success. Now, at last, came the first chill of disaster. Partly from their excellent military qualities, but even more on account of their elaborate and methodical preparations, joined with a want of scruple which allowed them to force a war at the moment when they could take their adversary at a disadvantage, they had established a legend of invincibility. This they left behind them with their cannon and their prisoners between the Marne and the Aisne. It had been feared that free men, trained in liberal and humane methods, could never equal in military efficiency those who had passed through the savage discipline which is the heritage of the methods that first made Prussia great at the expense of her neighbours. This shadow was henceforth for ever lifted from men's minds, and it was shown that the kindly comradeship which exists in the Western armies between officers and men was not incompatible with the finest fighting qualities of which any soldiers are capable.

Chapter V.

The Battle of the Marne.

CHAPTER VI

THE BATTLE OF THE AISNE

The hazardous crossing of the Aisne—Wonderful work of the sappers—The fight for the sugar factory—General advance of the Army—The 4th (Guards) Brigade's difficult task—Cavalry as a mobile reserve—The Sixth Division—Hardships of the Army—German breach of faith—*Tâtez toujours*—The general position—Attack upon the West Yorks—Counter-attack by Congreve's 18th Brigade—Rheims Cathedral—Spies—The siege and fall of Antwerp.

<small>CHAPTER VI.
The Battle of the Aisne.
The hazardous crossing of the Aisne.</small>

THE stretch of river which confronted the British Army when they set about the hazardous crossing of the Aisne was about fifteen miles in length. It lay as nearly as possible east and west, so that the advance was from south to north. As the British faced the river the First Army Corps was on the right of their line, together with half the cavalry. In the centre was the Second Corps, on the left the Third Corps, which was still without one of its divisions (the Sixth), but retained, on the other hand, the 19th Brigade, which did not belong to it. Each of these British corps covered a front of, roughly, five miles. Across the broad and swift river a considerable German army with a powerful artillery was waiting to dispute the passage. On the right of the British were the French Fifth and Seventh Armies, and on their left, forming the extremity of the Allied line, was the French Sixth Army, acting in such close co-operation

THE BATTLE OF THE AISNE 163

with the British Third Corps in the Soissons region that their guns were often turned upon the same point. This Sixth French Army, with the British Army, may be looked upon as the left wing of the huge Allied line which stretched away with many a curve and bend to the Swiss frontier. During all this hurried retreat from the Marne, it is to be remembered that the Eastern German armies had hardly moved at all. It was their four armies of the right which had swung back like a closing door, the Crown Prince's Fifth Army being the hinge upon which it turned. Now the door had ceased to swing, and one solid barrier presented itself to the Allies. It is probable that the German preponderance of numbers was, for the moment, much lessened or even had ceased to exist, for the losses in battle, the detachments for Russia, and the operations in Belgium had all combined to deplete the German ranks.

The Belgian Army had retired into Antwerp before the fall of Brussels, but they were by no means a force to be disregarded, being fired by that sense of intolerable wrong which is the most formidable stimulant to a virile nation. From the shelter of the Antwerp entrenchments they continually buzzed out against the German lines of communication, and although they were usually beaten back, and were finally pent in, they still added to the great debt of gratitude which the Allies already owed them by holding up a considerable body, two army corps at least, of good troops. On the other hand, the fortress of Maubeuge, on the northern French frontier, which had been invested within a few days of the battle of Mons, had now fallen before the heavy German guns, with the result that at least a corps of troops under

CHAPTER VI.

The Battle of the Aisne.

Wonderful work of the sappers.

Von Zwehl and these same masterful guns were now released for service on the Aisne.

The more one considers the operation of the crossing of the Aisne with the battle which followed it, the more one is impressed by the extraordinary difficulty of the task, the swift debonair way in which it was tackled, and the pushful audacity of the various commanders in gaining a foothold upon the farther side. Consider that upon the 12th the Army was faced by a deep, broad, unfordable river with only one practicable bridge in the fifteen miles opposite them. They had a formidable enemy armed with powerful artillery standing on the defensive upon a line of uplands commanding every crossing and approach, whilst the valley was so broad that ordinary guns upon the corresponding uplands could have no effect, and good positions lower down were hard to find. There was the problem. And yet upon the 14th the bulk of the Army was across and had established itself in positions from which it could never afterwards be driven. All arms must have worked well to bring about such a result, but what can be said of the Royal Engineers, who built under heavy fire in that brief space nine bridges, some of them capable of taking heavy traffic, while they restored five of the bridges which the enemy had destroyed! September 13, 1914, should be recorded in their annals as a marvellous example of personal self-sacrifice and technical proficiency.

Sir John French, acting with great swiftness and decision, did not lose an hour after he had established himself in force upon the northern bank of the river in pushing his men ahead and finding out what was in front of him. The weather was still very wet,

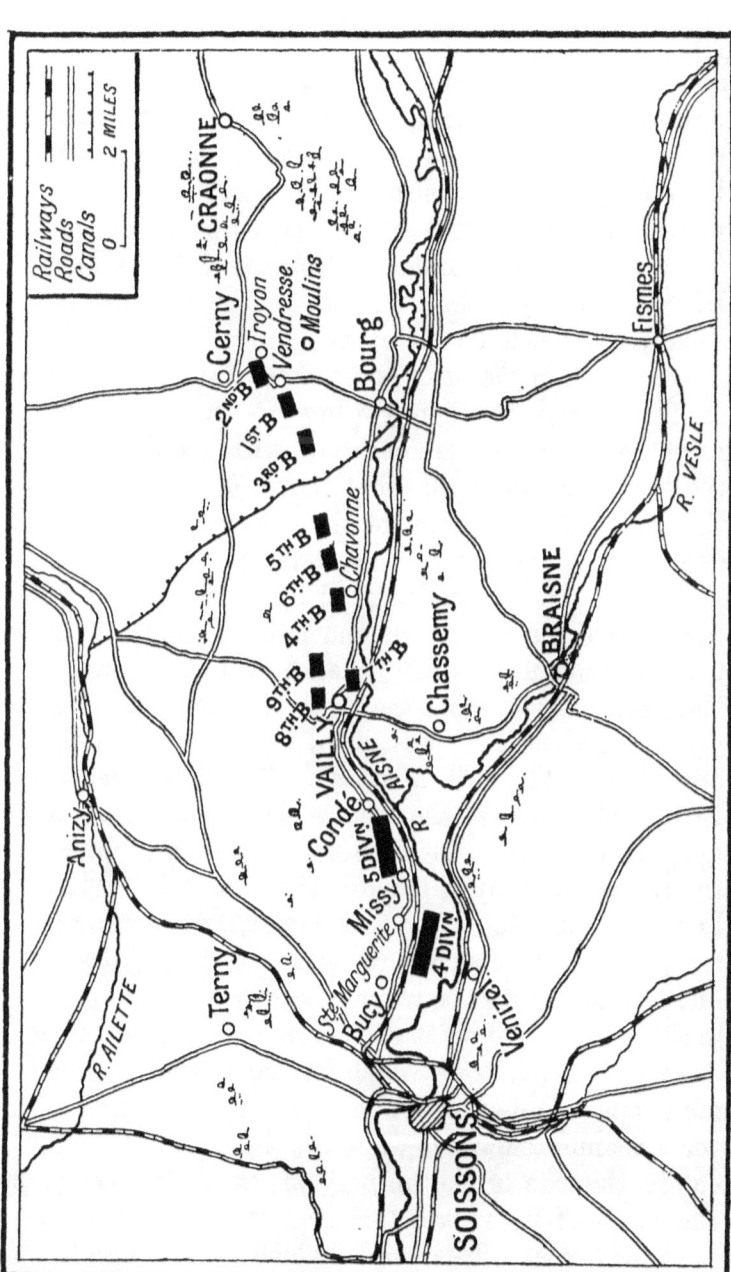

British Advance at the Aisne

CHAPTER VI.
The Battle of the Aisne.

and heavy mists drew a veil over the German dispositions, but the advance went forward. The British right wing, consisting of the First Division of the First Corps, had established itself most securely, as was natural, since it was the one corps which had found an unbroken bridge in front of it. The First Division had pushed forward as far as Moulins and Vendresse, which lie about two miles north of the river. Now, in the early hours of the 14th, the whole of the Second Division got over. The immediate narrative, therefore, is concerned with the doings of the two divisions of the First Corps, upon which fell the first and chief strain of the very important and dangerous advance upon that date.

On the top of the line of chalk hills which faced the British was an ancient and famous highway, the Chemin-des-dames, which, like all ancient highways, had been carried along the crest of the ridge. This was in the German possession, and it became the objective of the British attack. The 2nd Infantry Brigade (Bulfin's) led the way, working upwards in the early morning from Moulins and Vendresse through the hamlet of Troyon towards the great road. This brigade, consisting of the 2nd Sussex, 1st Northamptons, 1st North Lancashire, and 2nd Rifles, drawn mostly from solid shire regiments, was second to none in the Army. Just north of Troyon was a considerable deserted sugar factory, which formed a feature in the landscape. It lay within a few hundred yards of the Chemin-des-dames, while another winding road, cut in the side of the hill, lay an equal distance to the south of it, and was crossed by the British in their advance. This road, which was somewhat sunken in the chalk, and thus offered some cover

THE BATTLE OF THE AISNE

to a crouching man, played an important part in the operations.

Lieutenant Balfour and a picket of the 2nd Rifles, having crept up and reconnoitred the factory, returned with the information that it was held by the Germans, and that twelve guns were in position three hundred yards to the east of it. General Bulfin then—it was about 3.30 in the morning of a wet, misty day—sent the 2nd Rifles, the 2nd Sussex Regiment, and the 1st Northamptons forward, with the factory and an adjoining whitewashed farmhouse as their objective. The 1st North Lancashires remained in reserve at Vendresse. The attacking force was under the immediate command of Colonel Serocold of the Rifles. The three advanced regiments drove in the pickets of the Germans, and after a severe fight turned the enemy out of his front trench, A Company of the Sussex capturing several hundred prisoners. A number of men, however, including Colonel Montresor and Major Cookson, were shot while rounding up these Germans and sending them to the rear. The advanced line had suffered severely, so the North Lancashires were called up and launched at the sugar factory, which they carried with a magnificent bayonet attack in spite of a fierce German resistance. Their losses were very heavy, including Major Lloyd, their commander, but their victory was a glorious one. The two batteries of the enemy were now commanded by machine-guns, brought up to the factory by Lieutenant Dashwood of the Sussex. The enemy made a brave attempt to get these guns away, but the teams and men were shot down, and it was a German Colenso. The British, however, unlike the Boers, were unable to get away the prizes of their victory. The factory

CHAPTER VI.

The Battle of the Aisne.

The fight for the sugar factory.

CHAPTER VI.

The Battle of the Aisne.

was abandoned as it was exposed to heavy fire, and the four regiments formed a firing-line, taking such cover as they could find, but a German shell fire developed which was so deadly that they were unable to get forward.

A small party of Rifles, under Cathcart and Foljambe, clung hard to the captured guns, sending repeated messages: "For God's sake bring horses and fetch away these pieces!" No horses were, however, available, and eventually both the guns and the buildings were regained by the Germans, the former being disabled before they were abandoned by their captors, and the factory being smashed by the shells. Major Green and a company of the Sussex, with some of the Coldstream under Major Grant, had got as far forward as the Chemin-des-dames, but fell back steadily when their flank was finally exposed. Two companies of the 1st Coldstream, under Colonel Ponsonby, had also pushed on to the road, and now came back. Nothing could exceed the desperate gallantry of officers and men. Major Jelf, severely wounded, cheered on his riflemen until evening. Major Warre of the same regiment and Major Phillips rallied the hard-pressed line again and again. Lieutenant Spread, of the Lancashires, worked his machine-gun until it was smashed, and then, wounded as he was, brought up a second gun and continued the fight. Major Burrows rallied the Lancashires when their leader, Major Lloyd, was hit. Brigade-Major Watson, of the Queen's, was everywhere in the thick of the firing. No men could have been better led, nor could any leaders have better men. A large number of wounded, both British and Germans, lay under the

THE BATTLE OF THE AISNE 169

shelter of some haystacks between the lines, and crawled slowly round them for shelter, as the fire came from one side or the other—a fitting subject surely for a Verestschagin!

Meanwhile, it is necessary to follow what had been going on at the immediate left of Bulfin's Brigade. Maxse's 1st Brigade had moved up in the face of a considerable fire until it came to be nearly as far north as the factory, but to the west of it. The 1st Coldstream had been sent across to help the dismounted cavalry to cover Bulfin's right, since the main German strength seemed to be in that quarter. The 1st Scots Guards was held in reserve, but the other regiments of the 1st Brigade, the 1st Black Watch and the 1st Camerons, a battalion which had taken the place of the brave but unfortunate Munsters, lined up on the left of the factory and found themselves swept by the same devastating fire which had checked the advance. This fire came from the fringe of the woods and from a line of trenches lying north-east of the factory on the edge of the Chemin-des-dames. Up to this time the British had no artillery support on account of the mist, but now Geddes' 25th Brigade R.F.A., comprising the 113th, 114th, and 115th Batteries, was brought to its assistance. It could do little good in such a dim light, and one battery, the 115th, under Major Johnstone, which pushed up within eight hundred yards of the enemy's position, was itself nearly destroyed. The 116th R.F.A., under Captain Oliver, also did great work, working its way up till it was almost in the infantry line, and at one time in advance of it. The whole infantry line, including a mixture of units, men of the Rifles, Sussex, and

CHAPTER
VI.

The Battle of the Aisne.

General advance of the Army.

CHAPTER VI.
The Battle of the Aisne.

North Lancashires, with a sprinkling of Guardsmen and Black Watch from the 1st Brigade, came slowly down the hill—"sweating blood to hold their own," as one of them described it—until they reached the sunken road which has been already mentioned. There General Bulfin had stationed himself with the reserve, and the line steadied itself, re-formed, and, with the support of the guns, made head once more against the advancing Germans, who were unable to make any progress against the fire which was poured into them. With such spades and picks as could be got, a line of shallow trenches was thrown up, and these were held against all attacks for the rest of the day.[1] It was the haphazard line of these hurriedly dug shelters which determined the position retained in the weeks to come. As this was the apex of the British advance and all the corps upon the left were in turn brought to a standstill and driven to make trenches, the whole line of the First Corps formed a long diagonal slash across the hillside, with its right close to the Chemin-des-dames and its left upon the river in the neighbourhood of Chavonne. The result was that now and always the trenches of the 2nd Brigade were in an extremely exposed position, for they were open not only to the direct fire of the Germans, which was not very severe, but to an enfilading fire from more distant guns upon each flank. Their immediate neighbours upon the right were the 1st Queen's Surrey, acting as flank-

[1] Until an accurate German military history of the war shall appear, it is difficult to compute the exact rival forces in any engagement, but in this attack of the 2nd Brigade, where six British regiments may be said to have been involved, there are some data. A German officer, describing the same engagement, says that, apart from the original German force, the reinforcements amounted to fourteen battalions, from the Guards' Jaeger, the 4th Jaeger Battalion, 65th, 13th Reserve, and 13th and 16th Landwehr Regiments.

THE BATTLE OF THE AISNE 171

guard, and a Moroccan corps from the Fifth French Army, which had not reached so advanced a position, but was in echelon upon their right rear.

It has already been shown how the 1st Brigade was divided up, the 1st Coldstream being on the right of the 2nd Brigade. The rest of the 1st Brigade had carried out an advance parallel to that described, and many of the Black Watch, who were the right-hand regiment, got mixed with Bulfin's men when they were driven back to what proved to be the permanent British line. This advance of the 1st Brigade intercepted a strong force of the enemy which was creeping round the left flank of the 2nd Brigade. The counter-stroke brought the flank attack to a standstill. The leading regiments of the 1st Brigade suffered very severely, however, especially the Cameron Highlanders, whose gallantry carried them far to the front. This regiment lost Lieutenant-Colonel MacLachlan, 2 majors, Maitland and Nicholson, 3 captains, 11 lieutenants, and about 300 rank and file in the action. Some of these fell into the hands of the enemy, but the great majority were killed or wounded. The 1st Scots Guards upon the left of the brigade had also heavy casualties, while the Black Watch lost their Colonel, Grant Duff, their Adjutant, Rowan Hamilton, and many men. When the line on their right fell back, they conformed to the movement until they received support from two companies of the 1st Gloucesters from the 3rd Brigade upon their left rear.

The 4th (Guards) Brigade, forming the left of the Second Division, was across the river in battle array by ten o'clock in the morning and moving northwards towards the village of Ostel.

Chapter VI.

The Battle of the Aisne.

The 4th (Guards) Brigade's difficult task.

Its task was a supremely difficult one. Dense woods faced it, fringed with the hostile riflemen, while a heavy shell-fire tore through the extended ranks. It is safe to say that such an advance could not have been carried out in the heavy-handed German fashion without annihilating losses. As it was, the casualties were heavy, but not sufficient to prevent a continuance of the attack, which at one o'clock carried the farm and trenches which were its objective. The steep slopes and the thick woods made artillery support impossible, though one section of a battery did contrive to keep up with the infantry. The 3rd Coldstream being held up in their advance on the Soupir front, the 1st Irish were moved up on their right flank, but the line could do little more than hold its own. Captain Berners, Lord Guernsey, Lord Arthur Hay, and others were killed at this point. The German infantry advanced several times to counter-attack, but were swept back by the fire of the Guards.

At one period it was found that the general German advance, which had followed the holding of the British attack, was threatening to flow in between the two divisions of the First Army Corps. The 3rd Brigade (Landon's) was therefore deployed rapidly from the point about a mile south of Vernesse where it had been stationed. Two regiments of the brigade, the 2nd Welsh and the 1st South Wales Borderers, were flung against the heavy German column advancing down the Beaulne ridge and threatening to cut Haig's corps in two. The Welshmen, worthy successors of their ancestors who left such a name on the battlefields of France, succeeded in heading it off and driving it back so that they were

THE BATTLE OF THE AISNE 173

able to extend and get in touch with the right of the Second Division. This consisted of the 5th Brigade (Haking's) with the 6th (Davies') upon its left. Both of these brigades had to bear the brunt of continual German counter-attacks, involving considerable losses, both from shell and rifle fire. In spite of this they won their way for a mile or more up the slopes, where they were brought to a standstill and dug themselves into temporary shelter, continuing the irregular diagonal line of trenches which had been started by the brigades upon the right.

It is impossible not to admire the way in which the German general in command observed and attempted to profit by any gap in the British line. It has already been shown how he tried to push his column between the two divisions of the First Corps and was only stopped by the deployment of the 3rd Brigade. Later, an even fairer chance presented itself, and he was quick to take advantage of it. The advance of the Guards Brigade to the Ostel ridge had caused a considerable gap between them and the nearest unit of the Second Corps, and also between the First Corps and the river. A German attack came swarming down upon the weak spot. From Troyon to Ostel, over five miles of ground, Haig's corps was engaged to the last man and pinned down in their positions. It was not possible to fill the gap. Not to fill it might have meant disaster—disaster under heavy shell-fire with an unfordable river in the rear. Here was a supreme example of the grand work that was done when our cavalry were made efficient as dismounted riflemen. Their mobility brought them quickly to the danger spot. Their training turned them in an instant from horse-

CHAPTER VI.

The Battle of the Aisne.

men to infantry. The 15th Hussars, the Irish Horse, the whole of Briggs' 1st Cavalry Brigade, and finally the whole of De Lisle's 2nd Cavalry Brigade, were thrown into the gap. The German advance was stayed and the danger passed. From now onwards the echelon formed by the units of the First Corps ended with these cavalry brigades near Chavonne to the immediate north of the river.

The Third Division of the Second Corps, being on the immediate left of the operations which have been already described, moved forward upon Aizy, which is on about the same level as Ostel, the objective of the Guards. The 8th (Doran's) Brigade moved north by a tributary stream which runs down to the Aisne, while the 9th (Shaw's) tried to advance in line with it on the plateau to the right. Both brigades found it impossible to get any farther, and established themselves in entrenchments about a mile north of Vailly, so as to cover the important bridge at that place, where the 7th Brigade was in reserve. The three Fusilier regiments of the 9th Brigade all lost heavily, and the Lincolns had at one time to recross the river, but recovered their position.

The attack made by the Fifth Division near Missy was held up by a very strong German position among the woods on the Chivres heights which was fronted by wire entanglements. The regiments chiefly engaged were the Norfolks and Bedfords of the 15th Brigade, with the Cornwalls and East Surreys of the 14th Brigade, the remains of the Cheshires being in close support. They crossed the wire and made good progress at first, but were eventually brought to a stand by heavy fire at close range from a trench upon their right front. It was already dusk, so the

THE BATTLE OF THE AISNE 175

troops ended by maintaining the position at Missy and Ste. Marguerite, where there were bridges to be guarded.

The Fourth Division of Pulteney's Third Corps had no better success, and was only able to maintain its ground. It may be remarked, as an example of valiant individual effort, that this division was largely indebted for its ammunition supply to the efforts of Captain Johnston of the Sappers, who, upon a crazy raft of his own construction, aided by Lieutenant Flint, spent twelve hours under fire ferrying over the precious boxes. The familiar tale of stalemate was to be told of the Sixth French Army in the Soissons section of the river. Along the whole Allied line the position was the same, the greatest success and probably the hardest fighting having fallen to the lot of the Eighteenth French Corps, which had taken, lost, and finally retaken Craonne, thus establishing itself upon the lip of that formidable plateau which had been the objective of all the attacks.

In the Vailly region the 5th Cavalry Brigade found itself in a difficult position, for it had crossed the stream as a mounted unit in expectation of a pursuit, and now found itself under heavy fire in the village of Vailly with no possibility of getting forward. The only alternative was to recross the river by the single narrow bridge, which was done at a later date under very heavy fire, the troopers leading their horses over in single file. This difficult operation was superintended by Captain Wright of the Engineers, the same brave officer who had endeavoured to blow up the bridge at Mons. Unhappily, he was mortally wounded on this occasion. On the afternoon of the 14th—it being found that the British artillery was

176   THE BRITISH CAMPAIGN, 1914

Chapter VI.
The Battle of the Aisne.

shelling our own advanced trenches—Staff-Captain Harter of the 9th Brigade galloped across the bridge and informed the gunners as to the true position.

Towards evening, in spite of the fact that there were no reserves and that all the troops had endured heavy losses and great fatigue, a general advance was ordered in the hope of gaining the high ground of the Chemin-des-dames before night. It was nearly sunset when the orders were given, and the troops responded gallantly to the call, though many of them had been in action since daybreak. The fire, however, was very heavy, and no great progress could be made. The First Division gained some ground, but was brought to a standstill. The only brigade which made good headway was Haking's 5th, which reached the crest of the hill in the neighbourhood of Tilleul-de-Courtecon. General Haking sent out scouts, and finding German outposts upon both his flanks, he withdrew under cover of darkness.

Thus ended the sharp and indecisive action of September 14, the Germans holding their ground, but being in turn unable to drive back the Allies, who maintained their position and opposed an impassable obstacle to the renewed advance upon Paris. The battle was marked by the common features of advance, arrest, and entrenchment, which occurred not only in the British front, but in that of the French armies upon either flank. When the action ceased, the 1st Northamptons and the 1st Queen's, sent to guard the pressure point at the extreme right of the line, had actually reached the Chemin-des-dames, the British objective, and had dug themselves in upon the edge of it. From this very advanced spot the British line extended diagonally across the hillside for many miles until it reached the river. Several hundred prisoners and some guns were taken in the course of the fighting. When one considers the predominant position of the Germans, and that their artillery was able to give them constant assistance, whereas that of the British and French was only brought up with the utmost difficulty, we can only marvel that the infantry were able to win and to hold the ground.

The next day, September 15, was spent for the most part in making good the position gained and deepening the trenches to get some protection from the ever-growing artillery fire, which was the more intense as the great siege guns from Maubeuge were upon this day, for the first time, brought into action. At first the terrific explosions of these shells, the largest by far which had ever been brought into an actual line of battle, were exceedingly alarming, but after a time it became realised that, however omnipotent they might be against iron or concrete, they were comparatively harmless in soft soil, where their enormous excavations were soon used as convenient ready-made rifle-pits by the soldiers. This heavy fire led to a deepening of the trenches, which necessitated a general levy of picks and shovels from the country round, for a large portion of such equipment had been lost in the first week of the campaign.

Only two active movements were made in the course of the day, one being that Hamilton's Third Division advanced once more towards Aizy and established itself a mile or more to the north in a better tactical position. The 7th Brigade suffered considerable casualties in this change, including Colonel Hasted, of the 1st Wilts. The other was that Ferguson's Fifth Division fell back from Chivres, where it was exposed to a cross fire, and made its lines along the river bank, whence the Germans were never able to drive it, although they were only four hundred yards away in a position which was high above it. For the rest, it was a day of navvy's toil, though the men worked alternately with rifle and with pick, for there were continual German advances which withered away before the volleys which greeted them. By the 16th the position was fairly secure, and on the same day a welcome reinforcement arrived in the shape of the Sixth Division, forming the missing half of Pulteney's Third Corps.

Its composition is here appended :

DIVISION VI.—General KEIR.

16*th Infantry Brigade—General Ing. Williams.*
1st East Kent.
1st Leicester.
1st Shropshire Light Infantry.
2nd York and Lancaster.

17*th Infantry Brigade—General Walter Doran.*
1st Royal Fusiliers.
1st N. Stafford.
2nd Leinsters.
3rd Rifle Brigade.

18*th Infantry Brigade—General Congreve, V.C.*
1st W. York.
1st E. York.
2nd Notts and Derby (Sherwood Foresters).
2nd Durham Light Infantry.

Artillery.
2nd Brig. 21, 42, 53.
12th „ 43, 86, 87.
24th „ 110, 111, 112.
38th „ 24, 34, 72.
R.G.A. 24.

This division was kept in reserve upon the south side of the river. The French Commander-in-Chief had intimated that he intended to throw in reinforcements upon the left of the Sixth French Army, and so, as he hoped, to turn the German right. It was determined, therefore, that there should be no attempt at a British advance, but that the Allies should be content with holding the enemy to his positions. The two armies lay facing each other, therefore, at an average distance of about five hundred yards. The pressure was still most severe upon the 2nd Brigade on the extreme right. Bulfin's orders were to hold on at all costs, as he was the pivot of the whole line. He and his men responded nobly to the responsibility, although both they and their neighbours of Maxse's 1st Brigade had sustained a loss of over 1000 men each upon the 14th—25 per cent of their number. The shell-fire was incessant and from several converging directions. German infantry attacks were constant by night and by day, and the undrained trenches were deep in water. The men lay without overcoats and drenched to the skin, for the rain was incessant. Yet the sixth day found them on the exact ground upon which they had thrown their weary bodies after their attack. Nations desire from time to time to be reassured as to their own virility. Neither in endurance nor in courage have the British departed from the traditions of their ancestors. The unending strain of the trenches reached the limits of human resistance. But the line was always held.

On September 16 occurred an incident which may be taken as typical of the difference in the spirit with which the British and the Germans make war. Close to the lines of the Guards a barn which contained fifty wounded Germans was ignited by the enemy's shells. Under a terrific fire a rescue party rushed forward and got the unfortunate men to a place of safety.

Several of the British lost their lives in this exploit, including Dr. Huggan, the Scottish International footballer. The Germans mock at our respect for sport, and yet this is the type of man that sport breeds, and it is the want of them in their own ranks which will stand for ever between us.

September 17 was a day of incessant attacks upon the right of the line, continually repulsed and yet continually renewed. One can well sympathise with the feelings of the German commanders who, looking down from their heights, saw the British line in a most dangerous strategical position, overmatched by their artillery, with a deep river in their rear, and yet were unable to take advantage of it because of their failure to carry the one shallow line of extemporised trenches. Naturally, they came again and again, by night and by day, with admirable perseverance and daring to the attack, but were always forced to admit that nothing can be done against the magazine rifle in hands which know how to use it. They tried here and they tried there, these constant sudden outpourings of cheering, hurrying, grey-clad men. They were natural tactics, but expensive ones, for every new attack left a fresh fringe of stricken men in front of the British lines.

One incident upon the 17th stands out amid the somewhat monotonous record of trench attacks. On the extreme right of the British line a company of the 1st Northamptons occupied a most exposed position on the edge of the Chemin-des-dames. The men in a German trench which was some hundreds of yards in front hoisted a white flag and then advanced upon the British lines. It is well to be charitable in all these white flag incidents, since it is always possible

THE BATTLE OF THE AISNE 181

on either side that unauthorised men may hoist it and the officer in command very properly refuse to recognise it; but in this case the deception appears to have been a deliberate one. These are the facts. On seeing the flag, Captain Savage, of B Company Northamptons, got out of the trench and with Lieutenant Dimmer, of the Rifles, advanced to the Germans. He threw down his sword and revolver to show that he was unarmed. He found a difficulty in getting a direct answer from the Germans, so he saluted their officer, who returned his salute, and turned back to walk to his own trench. Dimmer, looking back, saw the Germans level their rifles, so he threw himself down, crying out, "For God's sake get down." Captain Savage stood erect and was riddled with bullets. Many of the Northamptons, including Lieutenant Gordon, were shot down by the same volley. The Germans then attempted an advance, which was stopped by the machine-guns of the 1st Queen's. Such deplorable actions must always destroy all the amenities of civilised warfare.

On the afternoon of the same day, September 17, a more serious attack was made upon the right flank of the advanced British position, the enemy reoccupying a line of trenches from which they had previously been driven. It was a dismal day of wind, rain, and mist, but the latter was not wholly an evil, as it enabled that hard-worked regiment, the 1st Northamptons, under their Colonel, Osborne Smith, to move swiftly forward and, with the help of the 1st Queen's, carry the place at the bayonet point. Half the Germans in the trench were put out of action, thirty-eight taken, and the rest fled. Pushing on after their success, they found the ridge beyond held by a considerable force of German infantry. The 2nd Rifles had come into the fight, and a dismounted squadron of the composite cavalry regiment put in some good work upon the flank. The action was continued briskly until dark, when both sides retained their ground with the exception of the captured line of trenches, which remained with the British. Seven officers and about 200 men were killed or wounded in this little affair.

The 18th found the enemy still acting upon the Napoleonic advice of *Tâtez toujours*. All day they were feeling for that weak place which could never be found. The constant attempts were carried on into the night with the same monotonous record of advance leading to repulse. At one time it was the line of the 1st Queen's—and no line in the Army would be less likely to give results. Then it was the left flank of the First Division, and then the front of the Second.

Now and again there were swift counters from the British, in one of which an enemy's trench was taken by the 1st Gloucesters with the two machine-guns therein. But there was no inducement for any general British advance. "We have nothing to lose by staying here," said a General, "whereas every day is of importance to the Germans, so the longer we can detain them here the better." So it seemed from the point of view of the Allies. There is a German point of view also, however, which is worthy of consideration. They were aware, and others were not, that great reserves of men were left in the Fatherland, even as there were in France and in Britain, but that, unlike France and Britain, they actually had the arms and equipment for them, so that a second host could rapidly be called into the field. If these legions were

THE BATTLE OF THE AISNE 183

in Belgium, they could ensure the fall of Antwerp, overrun the country, and seize the seaboard. All this could be effected while the Allies were held at the Aisne. Later, with these vast reinforcements, the German armies might burst the barrier which held them and make a second descent upon Paris, which was still only fifty miles away. So the Germans may have argued, and the history of the future was to show that there were some grounds for such a calculation. It was in truth a second war in which once again the Germans had the men and material ready, while the Allies had not.

Chapter VI.
The Battle of the Aisne.

This date, September 18, may be taken as the conclusion of the actual Battle of the Aisne, since from that time the operations defined themselves definitely as a mutual siege and gigantic artillery duel. The casualties of the British at the Aisne amounted, up to that date, to 10,000 officers and men, the great majority of which were suffered by Haig's First Army Corps. The action had lasted from the 13th, and its outstanding features, so far as our forces were concerned, may be said to have been the remarkable feat of crossing the river and the fine leadership of General Haig in the dangerous position in which he found himself. It has been suggested that the single unbroken bridge by which he crossed may have been a trap purposely laid by the Germans, whose plans miscarried owing to the simultaneous forcing of the river at many other points. As it was, the position of the First Corps was a very difficult one, and a reverse might have become an absolute disaster. It was impossible for General French to avoid this risk, for since the weather precluded all air reconnaissance, it was only by pushing his Army

The general position.

CHAPTER VI.

The Battle of the Aisne.

across that he could be sure of the enemy's dispositions. The net result was one more demonstration upon both sides that the defensive force has so great an advantage under modern conditions that if there be moderate equality of numbers, and if the flanks of each be guarded, a condition of stalemate will invariably ensue, until the campaign is decided by economic causes or by military movements in some other part of the field of operations.

There is ample evidence that for the time the German Army, though able with no great effort to hold the extraordinarily strong position which had been prepared for it, was actually in very bad condition. Large new drafts had been brought out, which had not yet been assimilated by the army. The resistance of Maubeuge had blocked one of their supply railroads, and for some time the commissariat had partially broken down. Above all, they were mentally depressed by meeting such resistance where they had been led to expect an easy victory, by their forced retreat when almost within sight of Paris, and by their losses, which had been enormous. In spite of their own great superiority in heavy guns, the French light field-pieces had controlled the battlefields. There is ample evidence in the letters which have been intercepted, apart from the statements and appearance of the prisoners, to show the want and depression which prevailed. This period, however, may be said to mark the nadir of the German fortunes in this year. The fall of Maubeuge improved their supplies of every sort, their reserves and Landwehr got broken in by the war of the trenches, and the eventual fall of Antwerp and invasion of Western Belgium gave them that moral stimulus which they badly needed.

THE BATTLE OF THE AISNE

CHAPTER VI.

The Battle of the Aisne.

Some wit amongst the officers has described the war as "months of boredom broken by moments of agony." It is the duty of the chronicler to record, even if he attempts to alleviate, the former, for the most monotonous procession of events form integral parts of the great whole. The perusal of a great number of diaries and experiences leaves a vague and disconnected recollection behind it of personal escapes, of the terror of high explosives, of the excellence of the rear services of the Army, of futile shellings—with an occasional tragic mishap, where some group of men far from the front were suddenly, by some freak of fate, blown to destruction,—of the discomforts of wet trenches, and the joys of an occasional relief in the villages at the rear. Here and there, however, in the monotony of what had now become a mutual siege, there stand out some episodes or developments of a more vital character, which will be recorded in their sequence.

It may be conjectured that, up to the period of the definite entrenchment of the two armies, the losses of the enemy were not greater than our own. It is in the attack that losses are incurred, and the attack had, for the most part, been with us. The heavier guns of the Germans had also been a factor in their favour. From the 18th onwards, however, the weekly losses of the enemy must have been very much greater than ours, since continually, night and day, they made onslaughts, which attained some partial and temporary success upon the 20th, but which on every other occasion were blown back by the rifle-fire with which they were met. So mechanical and half-hearted did they at last become that they gave the impression that those who made them had no hope of success, and that they were only done at the bidding of some imperious or imperial voice from the distance. In these attacks, though any one of them may have only furnished a few hundred casualties, the total effect spread over several weeks must have equalled that of a very great battle, and amounted, since no progress was ever made, to a considerable defeat.

Thus on September 19 there was a succession of attacks, made with considerable vivacity and proportional loss. About 4 P.M. one developed in front of the 4th and 6th Brigades of the First Corps, but was speedily stopped. An hour later another one burst forth upon the 7th and 9th Brigades of the Second Corps, with the same result. The artillery fire was very severe all day and the broad valley was arched from dawn to dusk by the flying shell. The weather was still detestable, and a good many were reported ill from the effects of constant wet and cold.

The 20th was the date of two separate attacks, one of which involved some hard fighting and considerable loss. The first, at eight in the morning, was upon Shaw's 9th Brigade and was driven off without great difficulty. The second was the more serious and demands some fuller detail.

On the arrival of the Sixth Division upon the 18th, Sir John French had determined to hold them in reserve and to use them to relieve, in turn, each of the brigades which had been so hard-worked during the previous week. Of these, there was none which needed and deserved a rest more than Bulfin's 2nd Brigade, which, after their attack upon the Chemin-des-dames upon the 14th, had made and held the trenches which formed both the extreme right and the advanced point of the British line. For nearly a

THE BATTLE OF THE AISNE

week these men of iron had lain where the battle had left them. With the object of relieving them, the 18th Brigade (Congreve's) of the Sixth Division was ordered to take their places. The transfer was successfully effected at night, but the newcomers, who had only arrived two days before from England, found themselves engaged at once in a very serious action. It may have been coincidence, or it may have been that with their remarkable system of espionage the Germans learned that new troops had taken the place of those whose mettle they had tested so often; but however this may be, they made a vigorous advance upon the afternoon of September 20, coming on so rapidly and in such numbers that they drove out the occupants both of the front British trenches—which were manned by three companies of the 1st West Yorkshires—and the adjoining French trench upon the right, which was held by the Turcos. The West Yorkshires were overwhelmed and enfiladed with machine-guns, a number were shot down, and others were taken prisoners.

Fortunately, the rest of the brigade were in immediate support, and orders were given by General Congreve to advance and to regain the ground that had been lost. The rush up the hill was carried out by the 2nd Notts and Derby Regiment (Sherwood Foresters) in the centre, with the remainder of the West Yorks upon their right, and the 2nd Durham Light Infantry upon their left. They were supported by the 1st East Yorks and by the 2nd Sussex, who had just been called out of the line for a rest. The 4th Irish Dragoon Guards at a gallop at first, and then dismounting with rifle and bayonet, were in the forefront of the fray. The advance was

CHAPTER VI.
The Battle of the Aisne.

over half a mile of ground, most of which was clear of any sort of cover, but it was magnificently carried out and irresistible in its impetus. All the regiments lost heavily, but all reached their goal. Officers were hit again and again, but staggered on with their men. Captain Popham, of the Sherwood Foresters, is said to have carried six wounds with him up the slope. Fifteen officers and 250 men were shot down, but the lost trench was carried at the point of the bayonet and the whole position re-established. The total casualties were 1364, more than half of which fell upon the West Yorkshires, while the majority of the others were Sherwood Foresters, East Yorkshires, and Durhams. Major Robb, of the latter regiment, was among those who fell. The Germans did not hold the trenches for an hour, and yet the engagement may be counted as a success for them, since our losses were certainly heavier than theirs. There was no gain, however, in ground. The action was more than a mere local attack, and the British line was in danger of being broken had it not been for the determined counter-attack of the 18th Brigade and of the Irish dragoons. To the north of this main attack there was another subsidiary movement on the Beaulne ridge, in which the 5th and 6th Brigades were sharply engaged. The 1st King's, the 2nd H.L.I., and the 2nd Worcesters all sustained some losses.

About this period both the British and the French armies began to strengthen themselves with those heavy guns in which they had been so completely overweighted by their enemy. On the 20th the French in the neighbourhood of our lines received twelve long-range cannon, firing a 35 lb. shell a distance of twelve kilometres. Three days later the

THE BATTLE OF THE AISNE 189

British opened fire with four new batteries of six-inch howitzers. From this time onwards there was no such great disparity in the heavy artillery, and the wounded from the monster shells of the enemy had at least the slight solace that their fate was not unavenged. The expenditure of shells, however, was still at the rate of ten German to one of the Allies. If the war was not won it was no fault of Krupp and the men of Essen. In two weeks the British lost nearly 3000 men from shell-fire.

It was at this time, September 20, that the Germans put a climax upon the long series of outrages and vandalisms of which their troops had been guilty by the bombardment of Rheims Cathedral, the Westminster Abbey of France. The act seems to have sprung from deliberate malice, for though it was asserted afterwards that the tower had been used as an artillery observation point, this is in the highest degree improbable, since the summit of the ridge upon the French side is available for such a purpose. The cathedral was occupied at the time by a number of German wounded, who were the sufferers by the barbarity of their fellow-countrymen. The incident will always remain as a permanent record of the value of that Kultur over which we have heard such frantic boasts. The records of the French, Belgian, and British Commissions upon the German atrocities, reinforced by the recollection of the burned University of Louvain and the shattered Cathedral of Rheims, will leave a stain upon the German armies which can never be erased. Their conduct is the more remarkable, since the invasion of 1870 was conducted with a stern but rigid discipline, which won the acknowledgment of the world. In

CHAPTER VI.

The Battle of the Aisne.

Rheims Cathedral.

190 THE BRITISH CAMPAIGN, 1914

CHAPTER VI.

The Battle of the Aisne.

spite of all the material progress and the superficial show of refinement, little more than a generation seems to have separated civilisation from primitive barbarity, which attained such a pitch that no arrangement could be made by which the wounded between the lines could be brought in. Such was the code of a nominally Christian nation in the year 1914.

Up to now the heavier end of the fighting had been borne by Haig's First Corps, but from the 20th onwards the Second and Third sustained the impact. The action just described, in which the West Yorkshires suffered so severely, was fought mainly by the 18th Brigade of Pulteney's Third Corps. On the 21st it was the turn of the Second Corps. During the night the 1st Wiltshire battalion of McCracken's 7th Brigade was attacked, and making a strong counter-attack in the morning they cleared a wood with the bayonet, and advanced the British line at that point. A subsequent attack upon the same brigade was repulsed. How heavy the losses had been in the wear and tear of six days' continual trench work is shown by the fact that when on this date the 9th Brigade (Shaw's) was taken back for a rest it had lost 30 officers and 860 men since crossing the Aisne.

The German heavy guns upon the 21st set fire to the village of Missy, but failed to dislodge the 1st East Surreys who held it. This battalion, in common with the rest of Ferguson's Division, were dominated night and day by a plunging fire from above. It is worth recording that in spite of the strain, the hardship, and the wet trenches, the percentage of serious sickness among the troops was lower than the normal rate of a garrison town. A few cases of

THE BATTLE OF THE AISNE

enteric appeared about this time, of which six were in one company of the Coldstream Guards. It is instructive to note that in each case the man belonged to the uninoculated minority.

A plague of spies infested the British and French lines at this period, and their elaborate telephone installations, leading from haystacks or from cellars, showed the foresight of the enemy. Some of these were German officers, who bravely took their lives in their hands from the patriotic motive of helping their country. Others, alas, were residents who had sold their souls for German gold. One such—a farmer—was found with a telephone within his house and no less a sum than a thousand pounds in specie. Many a battery concealed in a hollow, and many a convoy in a hidden road, were amazed by the accuracy of a fire which was really directed, not from the distant guns, but from some wayside hiding-place. Fifteen of these men were shot and the trouble abated.

The attacks upon the British trenches, which had died down for several days, were renewed with considerable vigour upon September 26. The first, directed against the 1st Queen's, was carried out by a force of about 1000 men, who advanced in close order, and, coming under machine-gun fire, were rapidly broken up. The second was made by a German battalion debouching from the woods in front of the 1st South Wales Borderers. This attack penetrated the line at one point, the left company of the regiment suffering severely, with all its officers down. The reserve company, with the help of the 2nd Welsh Regiment, retook the trenches after a hot fight, which ended by the wood being cleared.

CHAPTER VI.

The Battle of the Aisne.

Spies.

CHAPTER VI.

The Battle of the Aisne.

The Germans lost heavily in this struggle, 80 of them being picked up on the very edge of the trench. The Borderers also had numerous casualties, which totalled up to 7 officers and 182 men, half of whom were actually killed.

The Army was now in a very strong position, for the trenches were so well constructed that unless a shell by some miracle went right in, no harm would result. The weather had become fine once more, and the flying service relieved the anxieties of the commanders as to a massed attack. The heavy artillery of the Allies was also improving from day to day, especially the heavy British howitzers, aided by aeroplane observers with a wireless installation. On the other hand, the guns were frequently hit by the enemy's fire. The 22nd R.F.A. lost a gun, the 50th three guns, and other batteries had similar losses. Concealment had not yet been reduced to a science.

At this period the enemy seems to have realised that his attacks, whether against the British line or against the French armies which flanked it, and had fought throughout with equal tenacity, were a mere waste of life. The assaults died away or became mere demonstrations. Early in October the total losses of the Army upon the Aisne had been 561 officers and 12,980 men, a proportion which speaks well for the coolness and accuracy of the enemy's sharp-shooters, while it exhibits our own forgetfulness of the lessons of the African War, where we learned that the officer should be clad and armed so like the men as to be indistinguishable even at short ranges. Of this large total the Second Corps lost 136 officers and 3095 men, and the First Corps 348 officers and

THE BATTLE OF THE AISNE 193

6073 men, the remaining 77 officers and 3812 men being from the Third Corps and the cavalry.

It was at this period that a great change came over both the object and the locality of the operations. This change depended upon two events which had occurred far to the north, and reacted upon the great armies locked in the long grapple of the Aisne. The first of these controlling circumstances was that, by the movement of the old troops and the addition of new ones, each army had sought to turn the flank of the other in the north, until the whole centre of gravity of the war was transferred to that region. A new French army under General Castelnau, whose fine defence of Nancy had put him in the front of French leaders, had appeared on the extreme left wing of the Allies, only to be countered by fresh bodies of Germans, until the ever-extending line lengthened out to the manufacturing districts of Lens and Lille, where amid pit-shafts and slag-heaps the cavalry of the French and the Germans tried desperately to get round each other's flank. The other factor was the fall of Antwerp, which had released very large bodies of Germans, who were flooding over Western Belgium, and, with the help of great new levies from Germany, carrying the war to the sand-dunes of the coast. The operations which brought about this great change open up a new chapter in the history of the war. The actual events which culminated in the fall of Antwerp may be very briefly handled, since, important as they were, they were not primarily part of the British task, and hence hardly come within the scope of this narrative.

The Belgians, after the evacuation of Brussels in August, had withdrawn their army into the widespread fortress of Antwerp, from which they made frequent sallies upon the Germans who were garrisoning their country. Great activity was shown and several small successes were gained, which had the useful effect of detaining two corps which might have been employed upon the Aisne. Eventually, towards the end of September, the Germans turned their attention seriously to the reduction of the city, with a well-founded confidence that no modern forts could resist the impact of their enormous artillery. They drove the garrison within the lines, and early in October opened a bombardment upon the outer forts with such results that it was evidently only a matter of days before they would fall and the fine old city be faced with the alternative of surrender or destruction. The Spanish fury of Parma's pikemen would be a small thing compared to the *furor Teutonicus* working its evil deliberate will upon town-hall or cathedral, with the aid of fire-disc, petrol-spray, or other products of culture. The main problem before the Allies, if the town could not be saved, was to ensure that the Belgian army should be extricated and that nothing of military value which could be destroyed should be left to the invaders. No troops were available for a rescue, for the French and British old formations were already engaged, while the new ones were not yet ready for action. In these circumstances, a resolution was come to by the British leaders which was bold to the verge of rashness and so chivalrous as to be almost quixotic. It was determined to send out at the shortest notice a naval division, one brigade of which consisted of marines, troops who are second to none in the country's service, while the other two brigades were young

THE BATTLE OF THE AISNE 195

amateur sailor volunteers, most of whom had only been under arms for a few weeks. It was an extraordinary experiment, as testing how far the average sport-loving, healthy-minded young Briton needs only his equipment to turn him into a soldier who, in spite of all rawness and inefficiency, can still affect the course of a campaign. This strange force, one-third veterans and two-thirds practically civilians, was hurried across to do what it could for the failing town, and to demonstrate to Belgium how real was the sympathy which prompted us to send all that we had. A reinforcement of a very different quality was dispatched a few days later in the shape of the Seventh Division of the Regular Army, with the Third Division of Cavalry. These fine troops were too late, however, to save the city, and soon found themselves in a position where it needed all their hardihood to save themselves.

The Marine Brigade of the Naval Division under General Paris was dispatched from England in the early morning and reached Antwerp during the night of October 3. They were about 2000 in number. Early next morning they were out in the trenches, relieving some weary Belgians. The Germans were already within the outer enceinte and drawing close to the inner. For forty-eight hours they held the line in the face of heavy shelling. The cover was good and the losses were not heavy. At the end of that time the Belgian troops, who had been a good deal worn by their heroic exertions, were unable to sustain the German pressure, and evacuated the trenches on the flank of the British line. The brigade then fell back to a reserve position in front of the town.

On the night of the 5th the two other brigades of the division, numbering some 5000 amateur sailors, arrived in Antwerp, and the whole force assembled on the new line of defence. Mr. Winston Churchill showed his gallantry as a man, and his indiscretion as a high official, whose life was of great value to his country by accompanying the force from England. The bombardment was now very heavy, and the town was on fire in several places. The equipment of the British left much to be desired, and their trenches were as indifferent as their training. None the less they played the man and lived up to the traditions of that great service upon whose threshold they stood. For three days these men, who a few weeks before had been anything from schoolmasters to tram-conductors, held their perilous post. They were very raw, but they possessed a great asset in their officers, who were usually men of long service. But neither the lads of the naval brigades nor the war-worn and much-enduring Belgians could stop the mouths of those inexorable guns. On the 8th it was clear that the forts could no longer be held. The British task had been to maintain the trenches which connected the forts with each other, but if the forts went it was clear that the trenches must be outflanked and untenable. The situation, therefore, was hopeless, and all that remained was to save the garrison and leave as little as possible for the victors. Some thirty or forty German merchant ships in the harbour were sunk and the great petrol tanks were set on fire. By the light of the flames the Belgian and British forces made their way successfully out of the town, and the good service rendered later by our Allies upon the Yser and elsewhere is the best justification of the

THE BATTLE OF THE AISNE 197

policy which made us strain every nerve in order to do everything which could have a moral or material effect upon them in their darkest hour. Had the British been able to get away unscathed, the whole operation might have been reviewed with equanimity if not with satisfaction, but, unhappily, a grave misfortune, arising rather from bad luck than from the opposition of the enemy, came upon the retreating brigades, so that very many of our young sailors after their one week of crowded life came to the end of their active service for the war.

CHAPTER VI.

The Battle of the Aisne.

On leaving Antwerp it had been necessary to strike to the north in order to avoid a large detachment of the enemy who were said to be upon the line of the retreat. The boundary between Holland and Belgium is at this point very intricate, with no clear line of demarcation, and a long column of British somnambulists, staggering along in the dark after so many days in which they had for the most part never enjoyed two consecutive hours of sleep, wandered over the fatal line and found themselves in firm but kindly Dutch custody for the rest of the war. Some fell into the hands of the enemy, but the great majority were interned. These men belonged chiefly to three battalions of the 1st Brigade. The 2nd Brigade, with one battalion of the 1st, and the greater part of the Marines, made their way to the trains at St. Gilles-Waes, and were able to reach Ostend in safety. The remaining battalion of Marines, with a number of stragglers of the other brigades, were cut off at Morbede by the Germans, and about half of them were taken, while the rest fought their way through in the darkness and joined their comrades. The total losses of the British in the whole

CHAPTER VI.

The Battle of the Aisne.

misadventure from first to last were about 2500 men—a high price, and yet not too high when weighed against the results of their presence at Antwerp. On October 10 the Germans under General Von Beseler occupied the city. Mr. Powell, who was present, testifies that 60,000 marched into the town, and that they were all troops of the active army.

It has already been described how the northern ends of the two contending armies were endeavouring to outflank each other, and there seemed every possibility that this process would be carried out until each arrived at the coast. Early in October Sir John French represented to General Joffre that it would be well that the British Army should be withdrawn from the Aisne and take its position to the left of the French forces, a move which would shorten its line of communications very materially, and at the same time give it the task of defending the Channel coast. General Joffre agreed to the proposition, and the necessary steps were at once taken to put it into force. The Belgians had in the meanwhile made their way behind the line of the Yser, where a formidable position had been prepared. There, with hardly a day of rest, they were ready to renew the struggle with the ferocious ravagers of their country. The Belgian Government had been moved to France, and their splendid King, who will live in history as the most heroic and chivalrous figure of the war, continued by his brave words and noble example to animate the spirits of his countrymen.

From this time Germany was in temporary occupation of all Belgium, save only the one little corner, the defence of which will be recorded for ever. Little did she profit by her crime or by the excuses and forged documents by which she attempted to justify her action. She entered the land in dishonour and dishonoured will quit it. William, Germany, and Belgium are an association of words which will raise in the minds of posterity all that Parma, Spain, and the Lowlands have meant to us—an episode of oppression, cruelty, and rapacity, which fresh generations may atone for but can never efface.

CHAPTER VII

THE LA BASSÉE—ARMENTIÈRES OPERATIONS

(From October 11 to October 31, 1914)

The great battle line—Advance of Second Corps—Death of General Hamilton—The farthest point—Fate of the 2nd Royal Irish—The Third Corps—Exhausted troops—First fight of Neuve Chapelle—The Indians take over—The Lancers at Warneton—Pulteney's operations—Action of Le Gheir.

CHAPTER VII.

The La Bassée —Armentières operations.

IN accordance with the new plans, the great transference began upon October 3. It was an exceedingly difficult problem, since an army of more than 100,000 men had to be gradually extricated by night from trenches which were often not more than a hundred yards from the enemy, while a second army of equal numbers had to be substituted in its place. The line of retreat was down an open slope, across exposed bridges, and up the slope upon the southern bank. Any alarm to the Germans might have been fatal, since a vigorous night attack in the middle of the operation would have been difficult to resist, and even an artillery bombardment must have caused great loss of life. The work of the Staff in this campaign has been worthy of the regimental officers and of the men. Everything went without a hitch. The Second Cavalry Division (Gough's) went first, followed

LA BASSÉE—ARMENTIÈRES OPERATIONS 201

immediately by the First (De Lisle's). Then the infantry was withdrawn, the Second Corps being the vanguard; the Third Corps followed, and the First was the last to leave. The Second Corps began to clear from its trenches on October 3-4, and were ready for action on the Aire—Bethune line upon October 11. The Third Corps was very little behind it, and the First had reached the new battle-ground upon the 19th. Cavalry went by road; infantry marched part of the way, trained part of the way, and did the last lap very often in motor-buses. One way or another the men were got across, the Aisne trenches were left for ever, and a new phase of the war had begun. From the chalky uplands and the wooded slopes there was a sudden change to immense plains of clay, with slow, meandering, ditch-like streams, and all the hideous features of a great coal-field added to the drab monotony of Nature. No scenes could be more different, but the same great issue of history and the same old problem of trench and rifle were finding their slow solution upon each. The stalemate of the Aisne was for the moment set aside, and once again we had reverted to the old position where the ardent Germans declared, "This way we shall come," and the Allies, "Not a mile, save over our bodies."

The narrator is here faced with a considerable difficulty in his attempt to adhere closely to truth and yet to make his narrative intelligible to the lay reader. We stand upon the edge of a great battle. If all the operations which centred at Ypres, but which extend to the Yser Canal upon the north and to La Bassée at the south, be grouped into one episode, it becomes the greatest clash of arms ever seen up

Chapter VII.

The La Bassée —Armentières operations.

to that hour upon the globe, involving a casualty list—Belgian, French, British, and German—which could by no means be computed as under 250,000, and probably over 300,000 men. It was fought, however, over an irregular line, which is roughly forty miles from north to south, while it lasted, in its active form, from October 12 to November 20 before it settled down to the inevitable siege stage. Thus both in time and in space it presents difficulties which make a concentrated, connected, and intelligible narrative no easy task. In order to attempt this, it is necessary first to give a general idea of what the British Army, in conjunction with its Allies, was endeavouring to do, and, secondly, to show how the operations affected each corps in its turn.

During the operations of the Aisne the French had extended the Allied line far to the north in the hope of outflanking the Germans. The new Tenth French Army, under General Foch, formed the extreme left of this vast manœuvre, and it was supported on its left by the French cavalry. The German right had lengthened out, however, to meet every fresh extension of the French, and their cavalry had been sufficiently numerous and alert to prevent the French cavalry from getting round. Numerous skirmishes had ended in no definite result. It was at this period that it occurred, as already stated, to Sir John French that to bring the whole British Army round to the north of the line would both shorten very materially his communications and would prolong the line to an extent which might enable him to turn the German flank and make their whole position impossible. General Joffre having endorsed these views, Sir John took the steps which we have already seen.

LA BASSÉE—ARMENTIÈRES OPERATIONS 203

The British movement was, therefore, at the outset an aggressive one. How it became defensive as new factors intruded themselves, and as a result of the fall of Antwerp, will be shown at a later stage of this account.

CHAPTER VII.

The La Bassée —Armentières operations.

As the Second Corps arrived first upon the scene it will be proper to begin with some account of its doings from October 12, when it went into action, until the end of the month, when it found itself brought to a standstill by superior forces and placed upon the defensive. The doings of the Third Corps during the same period will be interwoven with those of the Second, since they were in close co-operation; and, finally, the fortunes of the First Corps will be followed and the relation shown between its doings and those of the newly arrived Seventh Division, which had fallen back from the vicinity of Antwerp and turned at bay near Ypres upon the pursuing Germans. Coming from different directions, all these various bodies were destined to be formed into one line, cemented together by their own dismounted cavalry and by French reinforcements, so as to lay an unbroken breakwater before the great German flood.

The task of the Second Corps was to get into touch with the left flank of the Tenth French Army in the vicinity of La Bassée, and then to wheel round its own left so as to turn the position of those Germans who were facing our Allies. The line of the Bethune—Lille road was to be the hinge, connecting the two armies and marking the turning-point for the British. On the 11th Gough's Second Cavalry Division was clearing the woods in front of the Aire—Bethune Canal, which marked the line of the Second Corps. By evening Gough had connected up the Third Division of the Second Corps with the Sixth Division of the Third Corps, which was already at Hazebrouck. On the 12th the Third Division crossed the canal, followed by the Fifth Division, with the exception of the 13th Brigade, which remained to the south of it. Both divisions advanced more or less north before swinging round to almost due east in their outflanking movement. The rough diagram gives an idea of the point from which they started and the positions reached at various dates before they came to an equilibrium. There were many weary stages, however, between the outset and the fulfilment, and the final results were destined to be barren as compared with the exertions and the losses involved. None the less it was, as it proved, an essential part of that great operation by which the British—with the help of their good allies—checked the German advance upon Calais in October and November, even as they had helped to head them off from Paris in August and September. During these four months the little British Army, far from being negligible, as some critics had foretold would be the case in a Continental war, was absolutely vital in holding the Allied line and taking the edge off the hacking German sword.

The Third Corps, which had detrained at St. Omer and moved to Hazebrouck, was intended to move in touch with the Second, prolonging its line to the north. The First and Second British Cavalry Divisions, now under the command of De Lisle and of Gough, with Allenby as chief, had a rôle of their own to play, and the space between the Second and Third Corps was now filled up by a French Cavalry Division under Conneau, a whole-hearted soldier always ready

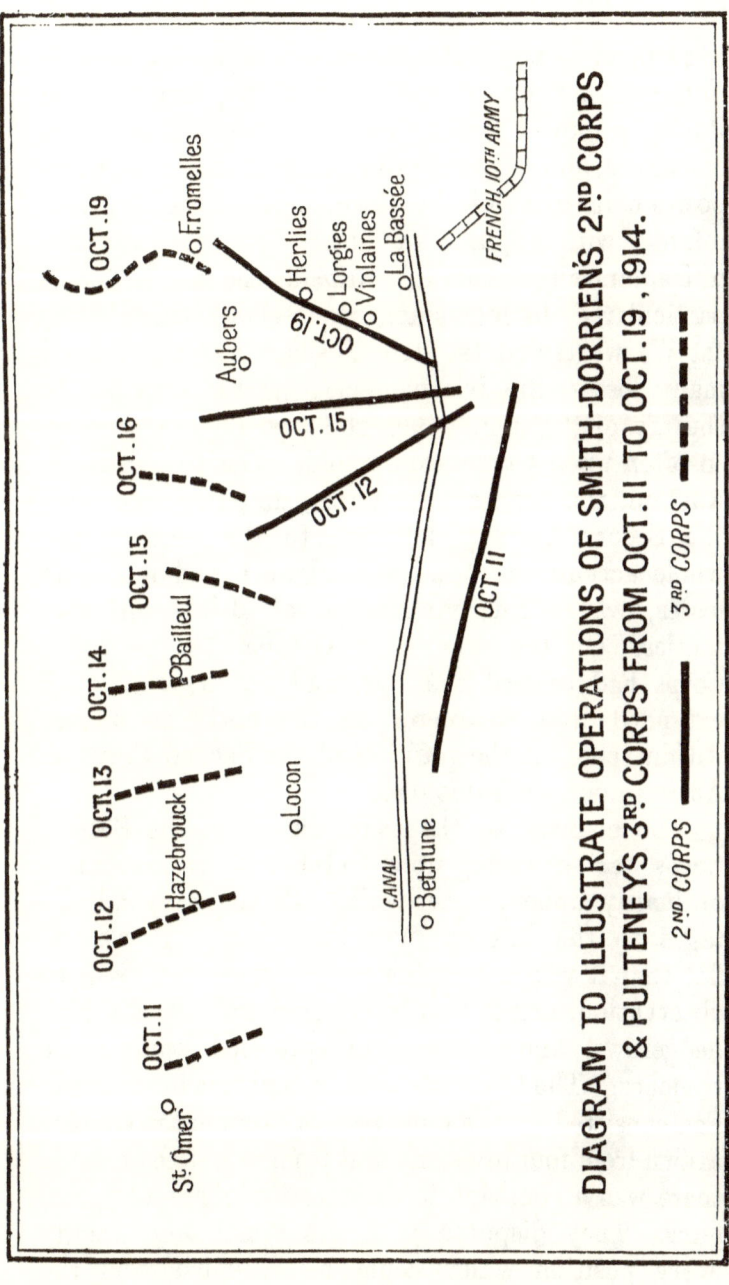

CHAPTER VII.

The La Bassée—Armentières operations.

to respond to any call. There was no strong opposition yet in front of the Third Corps, but General Pulteney moved rapidly forwards, brushed aside all resistance, and seized the town of Bailleul. A German position in front of the town, held by cavalry and infantry without guns, was rushed by a rapid advance of Haldane's 10th Infantry Brigade, the 2nd Seaforths particularly distinguishing themselves, though the 1st Warwicks and 1st Irish Fusiliers had also a good many losses, the Irishmen clearing the trenches to the cry of "Faugh-a-Ballagh!" which has sounded so often upon battlefields of old. The 10th Brigade was on the left of the corps, and in touch with the Second Cavalry Division to the north. The whole action, with its swift advance and moderate losses, was a fine vindication of British infantry tactics. On the evening of October 15 the Third Corps had crossed the Lys, and on the 18th they extended from Warneton in the north to almost within touch of the position of the Second Corps at Aubers upon the same date.

Advance of Second Corps.

The country to the south in which the Second Corps was advancing upon October 12 was an extraordinarily difficult one, which offered many advantages to the defence over the attack. It was so flat that it was impossible to find places for artillery observation, and it was intersected with canals, high hedgerows, and dykes, which formed ready-made trenches. The Germans were at first not in strength, and consisted for the most part of dismounted cavalry drawn from four divisions, but from this time onwards there was a constant fresh accession of infantry and guns. They disputed with great skill and energy every position which could be defended, and the

British advance during the day, though steady, was necessarily slow. Every hamlet, hedgerow, and stream meant a separate skirmish. The troops continually closed ranks, advanced, extended, and attacked from morning to night, sleeping where they had last fought. There was nothing that could be called a serious engagement, and yet the losses—almost entirely from the Third Division—amounted to 300 for the day, the heaviest sufferers being the 2nd Royal Scots.

On the next day, the 13th, the corps swung round its left so as to develop the turning movement already described. Its front of advance was about eight miles, and it met resistance which made all progress difficult. Again the 8th Brigade, especially the Royal Scots and 4th Middlesex, lost heavily. So desperate was the fighting that the Royal Scots had 400 casualties including 9 officers, and the Middlesex fared little better. The principal fighting, however, fell late in the evening upon the 15th Brigade (Gleichen's), who were on the right of the line and in touch with the Bethune Canal. The enemy, whose line of resistance had been considerably thickened by the addition of several battalions of Jaeger and part of the Fourteenth Corps, made a spirited counter-attack on this portion of the advance. The 1st Bedfords were roughly handled and driven back, with the result that the 1st Dorsets, who were stationed at a bridge over the canal near Givenchy, found their flanks exposed and sustained heavy losses, amounting to 400 men, including Major Roper. Colonel Bols, of the same regiment, enjoyed one crowded hour of glorious life, for he was wounded, captured, and escaped all on the same evening. It was in this

208 THE BRITISH CAMPAIGN, 1914

CHAPTER VII.

The La Bassée—Armentières operations.

action also that Major Vandeleur was wounded and captured.[1] A section of guns which was involved in the same dilemma as the Dorsets had to be abandoned after every gunner had fallen. The 15th Brigade was compelled to fall back for half a mile and entrench itself for the night. On the left the 7th Brigade (McCracken's) had some eighty casualties in crossing the Lys, and a detachment of Northumberland Fusiliers, who covered their left flank, came under machine-gun fire, which struck down their adjutant, Captain Herbert, and a number of men. Altogether the losses on this day amounted to about twelve hundred men.

Death of General Hamilton.

On the 14th the Second Corps continued its slow advance in the same direction. Upon this day the Third Division sustained a grievous loss in the shape of its commander, General Sir Hubert Hamilton, who was standing conversing with the quiet nonchalance which was characteristic of him, when a shell burst above him and a shrapnel bullet struck him on the temple, killing him at once. He was a grand commander, beloved by his men, and destined for the highest had he lived. He was buried that night after dark in a village churchyard. There was an artillery attack by the Germans during the service, and the group of silent officers, weary from the fighting line, who stood with bowed heads round the grave, could hardly hear the words of the chaplain for the whiz and crash of the shells. It was a proper ending for a soldier.

[1] Major Vandeleur was the officer who afterwards escaped from Crefeld and brought back with him a shocking account of the German treatment of our prisoners. Though a wounded man, the Major was kicked by the direct command of one German officer, and his overcoat was taken from him in bitter weather by another.

His division was temporarily taken over by General Colin Mackenzie. On this date the 13th Brigade, on the south of the canal, was relieved by French troops, so that henceforward all the British were to the north. For the three preceding days this brigade had done heavy work, the pressure of the enemy falling particularly upon the 2nd Scottish Borderers, who lost Major Allen and a number of other officers and men.

The 15th was a day of spirited advance, the Third Division offering sacrifice in the old warrior fashion to the shade of its dead leader. Guns were brought up into the infantry line and the enemy was smashed out of entrenched positions and loopholed villages in spite of a most manful resistance. The soldiers carried long planks with them and threw them over the dykes on their advance. Mile after mile the Germans were pushed back, until they were driven off the high road which connects Estaires with La Bassée. The 1st Northumberland and 4th Royal Fusiliers of the 9th Brigade, and the 2nd Royal Scots and 4th Middlesex of the 8th, particularly distinguished themselves in this day of hard fighting. By the night of the 15th the corps had lost 90 officers and 2500 men in the four days, the disproportionate number of officers being due to the broken nature of the fighting, which necessitated the constant leading of small detachments. The German resistance continued to be admirable.

On the 16th the slow wheeling movement of the Second Corps went steadily though slowly forward, meeting always the same stubborn resistance. The British were losing heavily by the incessant fighting, but so were the Germans, and it was becoming a

CHAPTER VII.

The La Bassée—Armentières operations.

question which could stand punishment longest. In the evening the Third Division was brought to a stand by the village of Aubers, which was found to be strongly held. The Fifth Division was instructed to mark time upon the right, so as to form the pivot upon which all the rest of the corps could swing round in their advance on La Bassée. At this date the Third Corps was no great distance to the north, and the First Corps was detraining from the Aisne. As the Seventh Division with Byng's Third Cavalry Division were reported to be in touch with the other forces in the north, the concentration of the British Army was approaching a successful issue. The weather up to now during all the operations which have been described was wet and misty, limiting the use of artillery and entirely preventing that of aircraft.

The farthest point.

On the 17th the advance was resumed and was destined to reach the extreme point which it attained for many a long laborious month. This was the village of Herlies, north-east of La Bassée, which was attacked in the evening by Shaw's 9th Brigade, and was carried in the dusk at the point of the bayonet by the 1st Lincolns and the 4th Royal Fusiliers. About the same time the Scots Fusiliers and Northumberlands had stormed Aubers. The 7th Brigade was less fortunate at the adjoining village of Illies, where they failed to make a lodgment, but the French cavalry on the extreme left, with the help of the 2nd Royal Irish, captured Fromelles. The Fifth Division also came forward a little, the right flank still on the canal, but the left bending round so as to get to the north of La Bassée. The 1st Devons, who had taken the place of the Dorsets,

LA BASSÉE—ARMENTIÈRES OPERATIONS

pushed forward with such fire that they were half a mile ahead of the Army and in great danger of being cut off, but by individual coolness and resource they managed to get back to safety.

On the 18th, Sir Charles Ferguson, who had done good work with the Army from the first gunshot of the war, was promoted to a higher rank and the command of the Fifth Division passed over to General Morland. Thus both divisions of the Second Corps changed their commanders within a week. On this date the infantry of the 14th Brigade, with some of the 13th Brigade, were within eight hundred yards of La Bassée, but found it so strongly held that it could not be entered, the Scottish Borderers losing heavily in a very gallant advance. The village of Illies also remained impregnable, being strongly entrenched and loopholed. Shaw's 9th Brigade took some of the trenches, but found their left flank exposed, so had to withdraw nearly half a mile and to entrench. In this little action the 1st Royal Scots Fusiliers bore the brunt of the fighting and the losses. Eight officers and nearly 200 men of this regiment were killed or wounded. A fresh German division came into action this day and their artillery was stronger, so that the prospects of future advance were not particularly encouraging. The British artillery was worked very hard, being overmatched and yet undefeatable. The strain both upon the men and the officers was constant, and the observation officers showed great daring and tenacity.

On the 19th neither the Third nor the Fifth Divisions made any appreciable progress, but one battalion was heavily engaged and added a fresh record to its ancient roll of valour. This was the

Chapter VII.

The La Bassée—Armentières operations.

Fate of the 2nd Royal Irish.

2nd Royal Irish under Major Daniell, who attacked the village of Le Pilly rather forward from the British left in co-operation with the French cavalry. The Irish infantry charged over eight hundred yards of clear ground, carried the village by storm, and entrenched themselves within it. This advance and charge, which was carried out with the precision of an Aldershot field day, although 130 men fell during the movement, is said by experienced spectators to have been a great feat of arms. The 20th saw a strong counter-attack of the Germans, and by the evening their two flanks had lapped round Le Pilly, pushing off on the one side the French cavalry of Conneau, and on the other a too small detachment of the Royal Fusiliers who were flanking the Irishmen. All day the defenders of Le Pilly were subjected to a terrific shell-fire, and all attempts to get messages to them were unavailing. In the evening they were surrounded, and only two or three men of the battalion were ever seen again. The gallant Daniell fell, and it is on record that his last audible words were a command to fix bayonets and fight to the end, the cartridges of the battalion being at that time exhausted. A German officer engaged in this attack and subsequently taken prisoner has deposed that three German battalions attacked the Royal Irish, one in front and one on each flank, after they had been heavily bombarded in enfilade. Several hundred Irish dead and wounded were taken out of the main trench.

There was now ample evidence that the Germans had received large reinforcements, and that their line was too strong to be forced. The whole object and character of the operations assumed, therefore, a

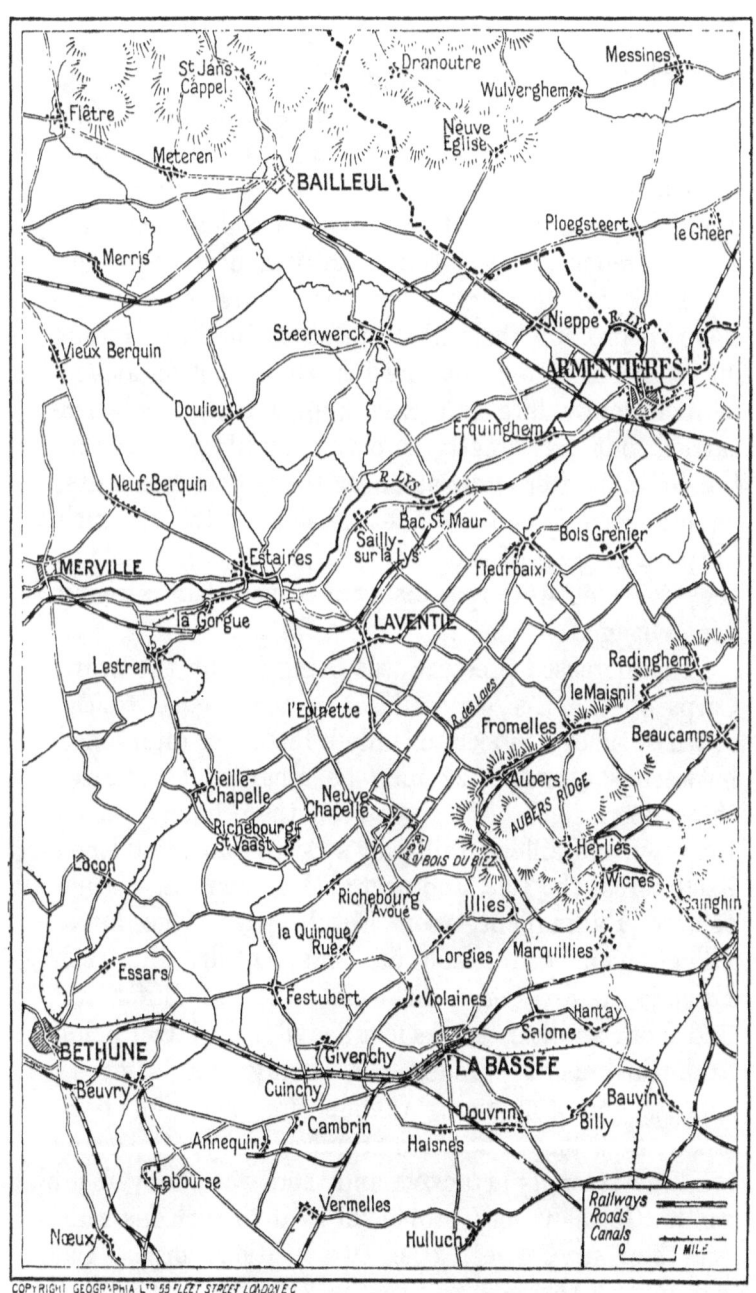

SOUTHERN END OF BRITISH LINE

CHAPTER VII.

The La Bassée —Armentières operations.

new aspect. The Second and Third Corps had swung round, describing an angle of ninety degrees, with its pivot upon the right at the La Bassée Canal, and by this movement it had succeeded in placing itself upon the flank of the German force which faced the Tenth French Army. But there was now no longer any flank, for the German reinforcements had enabled them to prolong their line and so to turn the action into a frontal attack by the British. Such an attack in modern warfare can only hope for success when carried out by greatly superior numbers, whereas the Germans were now stronger than their assailants, having been joined by one division of the Seventh Corps, a brigade of the Third Corps, and the whole of the Fourteenth Corps, part of which had already been engaged.

The Third Corps.

The increased pressure was being felt by the Third Corps on the Lys, as well as by the Second to the south of them; indeed, as only a few miles intervened between the two, they may be regarded as one for these operations. We have seen that, having taken the town of Bailleul, Pulteney's Corps had established itself across the Lys, and occupied a line from Warneton to Radinghem upon October 18. The latter village had been taken on that day by the 16th Brigade in an action in which the 1st Buffs and 2nd York and Lancasters lost heavily, the latter being ambushed as it pursued the enemy and losing 11 officers and 400 men. Colonel Cobbold fell back upon the village and held it successfully. Pulteney was now strongly attacked, and there was a movement of the Germans on October 20 as if to turn his right and slip in between the two British corps. The action was carried on into the 21st, the enemy still

LA BASSÉE—ARMENTIÈRES OPERATIONS 215

showing considerable energy and strength. The chief German advance during the day was north of La Bassée. It came upon the village of Lorgies, which was the point where the South Lancashires, of McCracken's 7th Brigade, forming the extreme right of the Third Division, were in touch with the East Surreys and Duke of Cornwall's of the 14th Brigade, forming the extreme left of the Fifth Division. It is necessary to join one's flats carefully in the presence of the Germans, for they are sharp critics of such matters. In this instance a sudden attack near Illies drove in a portion of the 2nd South Lancashires. This attack also destroyed the greater part of a company of the 1st Cornwalls in support. An ugly gap was left in the line, but the remainder of the Cornwalls, with the help of a company of the 1st West Kents and the ever-constant artillery, filled it up during the rest of the day, and the 2nd Yorkshire Light Infantry took it over the same night, the Cornishmen retiring with heavy losses but a great deal of compensating glory. The temporary gap in the line exposed the right flank of the 3rd Worcesters, who were next to the South Lancashires. They lost heavily in killed and wounded, their colonel, Stuart, being among the latter, though his injury did not prevent him from remaining in the battle line. Apart from this action at Lorgies, the 19th Brigade (Gordon's), upon the flank of Pulteney's Corps, sustained a very heavy attack, being driven back for some distance. It had been ordered to occupy Fromelles, and so close the gap which existed at that time between the left of the Second and the right of the Third Corps, situated respectively at Aubers and Radinghem. The chief fighting occurred

Chapter VII.

The La Bassée —Armentières operations.

216 THE BRITISH CAMPAIGN, 1914

CHAPTER VII.

The La Bassée —Armentières operations.

at the village of Le Maisnil, close to Fromelles. This village was occupied by the 2nd Argylls and half the 1st Middlesex, but they were driven out by a severe shell-fire followed by an infantry advance. The brigade fell back in good order, the regiments engaged having lost about 300 men. They took up a position on the right of the 16th Infantry Brigade at La Boutillerie, and there they remained until November 17, one severe attack falling upon them on October 29, which is described under that date.

On the morning of October 22 the Germans, still very numerous and full of fight, made a determined attack upon the Fifth Division, occupying the village of Violaines, close to La Bassée. The village was held by the 1st Cheshires, who, for the second time in this campaign, found themselves in a terribly difficult position. It is typical of the insolent high spirits of the men, in spite of all that they had endured, that upon the Germans charging forward with a war-cry which resembled, "Yip, Yip, Yip!" the British infantry joined in with "I-addy-ti-ay!" the whole forming the chorus of a once popular Gaiety song. The Cheshires inflicted heavy losses upon the stormers with rifle-fire, but were at last driven out, involving in their retirement the 1st Dorsets, who had left their own trenches in order to help them. Both regiments, but especially the Cheshires, had grievous losses, in casualties and prisoners. On advancing in pursuit the Germans were strongly counter-attacked by the 2nd Manchesters and the 1st Cornwalls, supported by the 3rd Worcesters, who, by their steady fire, brought them to a standstill, but were unable to recover the ground that had been lost, though the Cornwalls, who had

LA BASSÉE-ARMENTIÈRES OPERATIONS 217

been fighting with hardly a pause for forty-eight hours, succeeded in capturing one of their machine-guns. In the night the British withdrew their line in accordance with the general rearrangement to be described. Some rearguard stragglers at break of day had the amusing experience of seeing the Germans making a valiant and very noisy attack upon the abandoned and empty trenches.

Chapter VII.

The La Bassée—Armentières operations.

On this date, October 22, not only had Smith-Dorrien experienced this hold-up upon his right flank, but his left flank had become more vulnerable, because the French had been heavily attacked at Fromelles, and had been driven out of that village. An equilibrium had been established between attack and defence, and the position of the Aisne was beginning to appear once again upon the edge of Flanders. General Smith-Dorrien, feeling that any substantial advance was no longer to be hoped for under the existing conditions, marked down and occupied a strong defensive position, from Givenchy on the south to Fauquissart on the north. This involved a retirement of the whole corps during the night for a distance of from one to two miles, but it gave a connected position with a clear field of fire. At the same time the general situation was greatly strengthened by the arrival at the front of the Lahore Division of the Indian Army under General Watkis. These fine troops were placed in reserve behind the Second Corps in the neighbourhood of Locon.

It is well to remember at this point what Smith-Dorrien's troops had already endured during the two months that the campaign had lasted. Taking the strength of the corps at 37,000 men, they had lost, roughly, 10,000 men in August, 10,000 in

Exhausted troops.

> CHAPTER VII.
> The La Bassée —Armentières operations.

September, and 5000 up to date in these actions of October. It is certain that far less than 50 per cent of the original officers and men were still with the Colours, and drafts can never fully restore the unity and spirit of a homogeneous regiment, where every man knows his company leaders and his platoon. In addition to this they had now fought night and day for nearly a fortnight, with broken and insufficient sleep, laying down their rifles to pick up their spades, and then once again exchanging spade for rifle, while soaked to the skin with incessant fogs and rain, and exposed to that most harassing form of fighting, where every clump and hedgerow covers an enemy. They were so exhausted that they could hardly be woken up to fight. To say that they were now nearing the end of their strength and badly in need of a rest is but to say that they were mortal men and had reached the physical limits that mortality must impose.

The French cavalry divisions acting as links between Pulteney and Smith-Dorrien were now relieved by the 8th (Jullundur) Indian Infantry Brigade, containing the 1st Manchesters, 59th (Scinde) Rifles, 15th and 47th Sikhs. It may be remarked that each Indian brigade is made up of three Indian and one British battalion. This change was effected upon October 24, a date which was marked by no particular military event save that the Third Division lost for a time the services of General Beauchamp Doran, who returned to England. General Doran had done great service in leading what was perhaps the most hard-worked brigade in a hard-worked division. General Bowes took over the command of the 8th Infantry Brigade.

LA BASSÉE—ARMENTIÈRES OPERATIONS

On the night of October 24 determined attacks were made upon the trenches of the Second Corps at the Bois de Biez, near Neuve Chapelle, but were beaten off with heavy loss to the enemy, who had massed together twelve battalions in order to rush a particular part of the position. The main attack fell upon the 1st Wiltshires and the 2nd Royal Irish Rifles, belonging to McCracken's 7th Brigade, and also upon the 15th Sikhs, who seem to have been the first Indians to be seriously engaged, having nearly two hundred casualties. The 8th Brigade were also involved in the fight. The Germans had some temporary success in the centre of the trenches of the Third Division, where, in the darkness, they pushed back the 1st Gordon Highlanders, who lost very heavily. As the Highlanders fell back, the 2nd Royal Scots, upon their right, swung back its flank companies, covered the retirement, and then, straightening their ranks again, flung the Germans, at the point of their bayonets, out of the trenches. It was one of several remarkable feats which this fine battalion has performed in the war. Next morning the captured trenches were handed over to the care of the 4th Middlesex.

The pressure upon the exhausted troops was extreme upon this day, for a very severe attack was made also upon the Fifth Division, holding the right of the line. The soldiers, as already shown, were in no condition for great exertions, and yet, after their wont, they rose grandly to the occasion. The important village of Givenchy, destined for many a long month to form the advanced post upon the right of the Army, was held by the 1st Norfolks and 1st Devons, who defied all efforts of the enemy to dislodge them.

Chapter VII.

The La Bassée —Armentières operations.

Nevertheless, the situation was critical and difficult for both divisions, and the only available support, the 1st Manchesters from the Lahore Division, were pushed up into the fighting line and found themselves instantly engaged in the neighbourhood of Givenchy. It was dreadful weather, the trenches a quagmire, and the rifle-bolts often clogged with the mud. On the 26th Sir John French, realising how great was the task with which the weary corps was faced, sent up two batteries of 4·7 guns, which soon lessened the volume of the German artillery attack. At the same time General Maistre, of the Twenty-first French Corps, sent two of his batteries and two of his battalions. Thus strengthened, there was no further immediate anxiety as to the line being broken, especially as upon the 26th Marshal French, carefully playing card after card from his not over-strong hand, placed the Second Cavalry Division and three more Indian battalions in reserve to Smith-Dorrien's corps. The German advance had by no means spent itself, as on this day they came to close grips with the 2nd Irish Rifles and established themselves firmly in the village of Neuve Chapelle, near the centre of the British line, inflicting heavy loss upon the Royal Fusiliers, who tried to restore the position. A number of attacks were made to regain this village next day, in which as strange a medley of troops were employed as could ever before have found themselves as comrades in so minor an operation. There were South Lancashires, Royal Fusiliers, 9th Bhopal Infantry, 47th Sikhs, Chasseurs Alpins, and other units. In spite of—or possibly on account of—this international competition the village remained with the Germans, who were strongly reinforced, and

LA BASSÉE—ARMENTIÈRES OPERATIONS

managed by their shell-fire to clear some of the nearest trenches and gain some additional ground, hitting the 1st Wiltshires and 2nd Irish Rifles hard and making a number of prisoners, two or three hundred in all. Again the times had become critical, the more so as the 8th Indian Brigade to the north had also been attacked and roughly handled. The indomitable Smith-Dorrien was determined to have his village, however, and in the neighbouring French cavalry commander, General Conneau, he found a worthy colleague who was ready to throw his last man into the venture. The Second Cavalry, now under General Mullens, was also ready, as our cavalry has always been, to spring in as a makeweight when the balance trembled. The German losses were known to have been tremendous, and it was hoped that the force of their attack was spent. On the 28th the assault was renewed, prefaced by a strong artillery preparation, but again it was brought to a standstill. The 47th Sikhs fought magnificently from loopholed house to house, as did the Indian sappers and miners, while the cavalry showed themselves to be admirable infantry at a pinch, but the defence was still too strong and the losses too severe, though at one time Colonel McMahon, with his Fusiliers, had seized the whole north end of the village.

Some 60 officers and 1500 men had fallen in the day's venture, including 70 of the cavalry. The night fell with Neuve Chapelle still in the hands of the enemy, and the British troops to the north, east, and west of it in a semicircle. The 14th Brigade, coming up after dark, found the 1st West Kent Regiment reduced to 2 officers and 150 men, and the 2nd Yorkshire Light Infantry at about the same strength, still holding on to positions which had been committed to them three days before. The conduct of these two grand regiments upon that and the previous days excited the admiration of every one, for, isolated from their comrades, they had beaten off a long succession of infantry attacks and had been enfiladed by a most severe shell-fire. Second-Lieutenant White, with a still younger officer named Russell, formed the whole staff of officers of the West Kents. Major Buckle, Captain Legard, and many others having been killed or wounded, Penny and Crossley, the two sergeant-majors, did great work, and the men were splendid. These shire regiments, raised from the very soil of England, reflect most nearly her national qualities, and in their stolid invincibility form a fitting framework of a great national army. Speaking to the West Kents of this episode, General Smith-Dorrien said: " There is one part of the line which has never been retaken, because it was never lost. It was the particular trenches which your battalion held so grimly during those terrific ten days."

These determined efforts were not spent in vain, for the Germans would not bide the other brunt. Early on the 29th the British patrols found that Neuve Chapelle had been evacuated by the enemy, who must have lost several thousand men in its capture and fine subsequent defence. In this village fighting the British were much handicapped at this time by the want of high explosive shells to destroy the houses. The enemy's artillery made it impossible for the British to occupy it, and some time later it reverted to the Germans once more, being occupied by the Seventh Westphalian Corps. It was made an exceedingly strong advance position by the Germans,

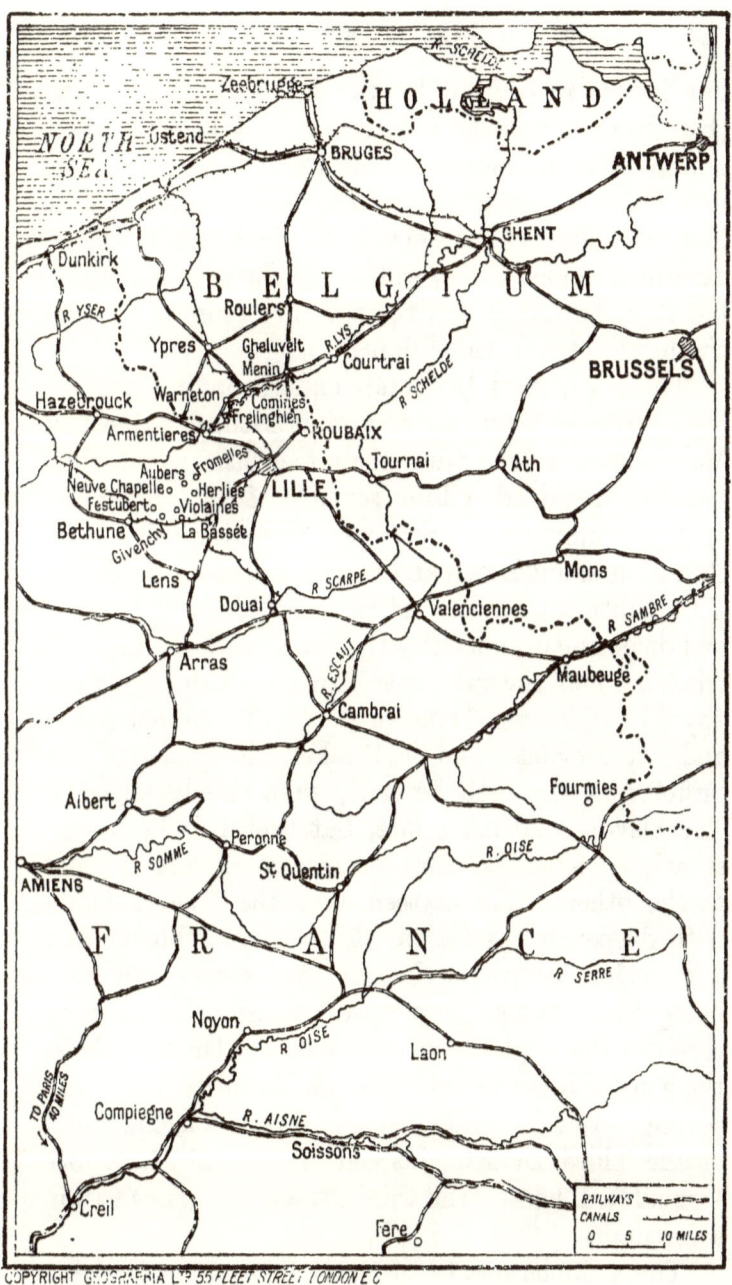

GENERAL VIEW OF SEAT OF OPERATIONS

CHAPTER VII.
The La Bassée —Armentières operations.

but it was reoccupied by the British Fourth Corps (Rawlinson's) and the Indian Corps (Willcocks') upon March 10 in an assault which lasted three days, and involved a loss of 12,000 men to the attackers and at least as many to the defenders. This battle will be described among the operations of the spring of 1915, but it is mentioned now to show how immutable were the lines between these dates.

The southern or La Bassée end of the line had also been attacked upon the 28th and 29th, and the 2nd Manchesters driven from their trenches, which they instantly regained, killing seventy of the enemy and taking a number of prisoners. It was in this action that Lieutenant Leach and Sergeant Hogan earned the V.C., capturing a trench at the head of ten volunteers and disposing of some fifty Germans. Morland's Fifth Division had several other skirmishes during these days, in which the Duke of Cornwall's, Manchesters, and 1st Devons, who had taken the place of the Suffolks in the 14th Brigade, were chiefly engaged. The Devons had come late, but they had been constantly engaged and their losses were already as great as the others. For sixteen days they had held on with desperate resolution, their Colonel Gloster and a considerable proportion of the officers and men being hit. When they were at last relieved they received the applause of the Army. On the whole, the general line was held, though the price was often severe. At this period General Wing took command of the Third Division instead of General Mackenzie—invalided home—the third divisional change within a fortnight.

The Indians take over.

The arduous month of October was now drawing to a close, and so it was hoped were the labours of the weary Second Corps. Already, on the top of all their previous casualties, they had lost 360 officers and 8200 men since on October 12 they had crossed the La Bassée Canal. The spirit of the men was unimpaired for the most part—indeed, it seemed often to rise with the emergency—but the thinning of the ranks, the incessant labour, and the want of sleep had produced extreme physical exhaustion. Upon October 29 it was determined to take them out of the front line and give them the rest which they so badly needed. With this end in view, Sir James Willcocks' Indian Corps was moved to the front, and it was gradually substituted for the attenuated regiments of the Second Corps in the first row of trenches. The greater part of the corps was drawn out of the line, leaving two brigades and most of the artillery behind to support the Indians. That the latter would have some hard work was speedily apparent, as upon this very day the 8th Gurkhas were driven out of their trenches. With the support of a British battalion, however, and of Vaughan's Indian Rifles they were soon recovered, though Colonel Venner of the latter corps fell in the attack. This warfare of unseen enemies and enormous explosions was new to the gallant Indians, but they soon accommodated themselves to it, and moderated the imprudent gallantry which exposed them at first to unnecessary loss.

Here, at the end of October, we may leave the Second Corps. It was speedily apparent that their services were too essential to be spared, and that their rest would be a very nominal one. The Third Corps will be treated presently. They did admirably all that came to them to do, but they were so placed that both flanks were covered by British troops, and they were less exposed to pressure than the others. The month closed with this corps and the Indians holding a line which extended north and south for about twenty miles from Givenchy and Festubert in the south to Warneton in the north. We will return to the operations in this region, but must turn back a fortnight or so in order to follow the very critical and important events which had been proceeding in the north. Before doing so it would be well to see what had befallen the cavalry, which, when last mentioned, had, upon October 11, cleared the woods in front of the Second Corps and connected it up with the right wing of the Third Corps. This was carried out by Gough's Second Cavalry Division, which was joined next day by De Lisle's First Division, the whole under General Allenby. This considerable force moved north upon October 12 and 13, pushing back a light fringe of the enemy and having one brisk skirmish at Mont des Cats, a small hill, crowned by a monastery, where the body of a Prince of Hesse was picked up after the action. Still fighting its way, the cavalry moved north to Berthen and then turned eastwards towards the Lys to explore the strength of the enemy and the passages of the river in that direction. Late at night upon the 14th General de Lisle, scouting northwards upon a motor-car, met Prince Alexander of Teck coming southwards, the first contact with the isolated Seventh Division.

On the night of the 16th an attempt was made upon Warneton, where the Germans had a bridge over the river, but the village was too strongly held. The 3rd Cavalry Brigade was engaged in the enterprise, and the 16th Lancers was the particular regiment upon whom it fell. The main street of the village was

LA BASSÉE—ARMENTIÈRES OPERATIONS

traversed by a barricade and the houses loopholed. The Germans were driven by the dismounted troopers, led by Major Campbell, from the first barricade, but took refuge behind a second one, where they were strongly reinforced. The village had been set on fire, and the fighting went on by the glare of the flames. When the order for retirement was at last given it was found that several wounded Lancers had been left close to the German barricade. The fire having died down, three of the Lancers—Sergeant Glasgow, Corporal Boyton, and Corporal Chapman—stole down the dark side of the street in their stockinged feet and carried some of their comrades off under the very noses of the Germans. Many, however, had to be left behind. It is impossible for cavalry to be pushful and efficient without taking constant risks which must occasionally materialise. The general effect of the cavalry operations was to reconnoitre thoroughly all the west side of the river and to show that the enemy were in firm possession of the eastern bank.

From this time onwards until the end of the month the cavalry were engaged in carrying on the north and south line of defensive trenches, which, beginning with the right of the Second Corps (now replaced by Indians) at Givenchy, was prolonged by the Third Corps as far as Frelingham. There the cavalry took it up and carried it through Comines to Wervicq, following the bend of the river. These lines were at once strongly attacked, but the dismounted troopers held their positions. On October 22 the 12th Lancers were heavily assaulted, but with the aid of an enfilading fire from the 5th Lancers drove off the enemy. That evening saw four more attacks, all of them repulsed, but so serious that Indian troops were brought up to support the cavalry. Every day brought its attack until they culminated in the great and critical fight from October 30 to November 2, which will be described later. The line was held, though with some loss of ground and occasional setbacks, until November 2, when considerable French reinforcements arrived upon the scene. It is a fact that for all these weeks the position which was held in the face of incessant attack by two weak cavalry divisions should have been, and eventually was, held by two army corps.

It is necessary now to briefly sketch the movements of the Third Corps (Pulteney's). Its presence upon the left flank of the Second Corps, and the fact that it held every attack that came against it, made it a vital factor in the operations. It is true that, having staunch British forces upon each flank, its position was always less precarious than either of the two corps which held the southern and northern extremities of the line, for without any disparagement to our Allies, who have shown themselves to be the bravest of the brave, it is evident that we can depend more upon troops who are under the same command, and whose movements can be certainly co-ordinated. At the same time, if the Third Corps had less to do, it can at least say that whatever did come to it was excellently well done, and that it preserved its line throughout. Its units were extended over some twelve miles of country, and it was partly astride of the River Lys, so that here as elsewhere there was constant demand upon the vigilance and staunchness of officers and men. On October 20 a very severe attack fell upon the 2nd Sherwood Foresters, who held the most advanced trenches of Congreve's 18th Brigade. They were nearly overwhelmed by the violence of the German artillery fire, and were enfiladed on each side by infantry and machine-guns. The 2nd Durhams came up in reinforcement, but the Foresters had already sustained grievous losses in casualties and prisoners, the battalion being reduced from 900 to 250 in a single day. The Durhams also lost heavily. On this same day, the 20th, the 2nd Leinsters, of the 17th Brigade, were also driven from their trenches and suffered severely.

On October 21 the Germans crossed the River Lys in considerable force, and upon the morning of the 22nd they succeeded in occupying the village of Le Gheir upon the western side, thus threatening to outflank the positions of the Second Cavalry Division to the north. In their advance in the early morning of the 22nd they stormed the trenches held by the 2nd Inniskilling Fusiliers, this regiment enduring considerable losses. The trenches on the right were held by the 1st Royal Lancasters and 2nd Lancashire Fusiliers. These two regiments were at once ordered by General Anley, of the 12th Brigade, to initiate a counter-attack under the lead of Colonel Butler. Anley himself, who is a hard-bitten soldier of much Egyptian fighting, moved forward his men, while General Hunter-Weston, the indefatigable blower-up of railway lines in South Africa, supported the counter-attack with the Somerset Light Infantry and the 1st East Lancashires. The latter regiment, under Colonel Lawrence, passed through a wood and reached such a position that they were able to enfilade the Germans in the open, causing them very heavy losses. The action was a brilliant success. The positions lost were reoccupied and the enemy severely punished, over a thousand Germans being killed or wounded, while 300 were taken prisoners. These belonged to the 104th and 179th Saxon regiments. It was a strange turn of fate which, after fifteen hundred years, brought tribesmen who had wandered up the course of the Elbe face to face in deadly strife with fellow-tribesmen who had passed over the sea to Britain. It is worth remarking and remembering that they are the one section of the German race who in this war have shown that bravery is not necessarily accompanied by coarseness and brutality.

On October 25 the attacks became most severe upon the line of Williams' 16th Brigade, and on that night the trenches of the 1st Leicesters were raked by so heavy a gunfire that they were found to be untenable, the regiment losing 350 men. The line both of the 16th and of the 18th Brigades was drawn back for some little distance. There was a lull after this, broken upon the 29th, when Gordon's 19th Brigade was attacked with great violence by six fresh battalions — heavy odds against the four weak battalions which composed the British Brigade. The 1st Middlesex Regiment was driven from part of its trenches, but came back with a rush, helped by their comrades of the 2nd Argyll and Sutherland Highlanders. The Germans were thrown out of the captured trenches, 40 were made prisoners, and 200 were slain. This attack was made by the 223rd and 224th Regiments of the XXIV. German Reserve Corps. It was not repeated.

On the 30th another sharp action occurred near St. Yves, when Hunter-Weston's 11th Brigade was momentarily pierced after dusk by a German rush, which broke through a gap in the Hampshires. The Somerset Light Infantry, under Major Prowse, came back upon them and the trenches were regained. In all such actions it is to be remembered that where a mass of men can suddenly be directed against scattered trenches which will only hold a few, it is no difficult matter to carry them, but at once the conditions reverse themselves and the defenders mass their supports, who can usually turn the intruders out once more.

This brings the general record of the doings of the Third Corps down to the end of October, the date on which we cease the account of the operations at the southern end of the British line. We turn from this diffuse and difficult story, with its ever-varying positions and units, to the great epic of the north, which will be inseparably united for ever with the name of Ypres.

CHAPTER VIII

THE FIRST BATTLE OF YPRES

(Up to the Action of Gheluvelt, October 31)

The Seventh Division—Its peculiar excellence—Its difficult position—A deadly ordeal—Desperate attacks on Seventh Division—Destruction of 2nd Wilts—Hard fight of 20th Brigade—Arrival of First Corps—Advance of Haig's Corps—Fight of Pilken Inn—Bravery of enemy—Advance of Second Division—Fight of Kruiseik cross-roads—Fight of Zandvoorde—Fight of Gheluvelt—Advance of Worcesters—German recoil—General result—A great crisis.

IT has already been seen that the Seventh Division (Capper's), being the first half of Rawlinson's Fourth Army Corps, had retired south and west after the unsuccessful attempt to relieve Antwerp. It was made up as follows :—

DIVISION VII.—General CAPPER.

20th Infantry Brigade—General Ruggles-Brise.
    1st Grenadier Guards.
    2nd Scots Guards.
    2nd Border Regiment.
    2nd Gordon Highlanders.

21st Infantry Brigade—General Watts.
    2nd Bedfords.
    2nd Yorks.
    2nd Wilts.
    2nd Scots Fusiliers.

THE FIRST BATTLE OF YPRES 233

CHAPTER VIII.

The first Battle of Ypres.

22nd *Infantry Brigade—General Lawford.*
1st South Staffords.
2nd Warwicks.
2nd Queen's West Surrey.
1st Welsh Fusiliers.

Artillery.
22nd Brigade R.F.A.
35th Brigade R.F.A.
3rd R.G.A.
111th R.G.A.
112th R.G.A.
14th Brigade R.H.A. C.F.

Engineers.
54, 55, F. Co.
7 Signal Co.
Divisional Cavalry.
Northumberland Yeomanry.

It is not too much to say that in an army where every division had done so well no single one was composed of such fine material as the Seventh. The reason was that the regiments composing it had all been drawn from foreign garrison duty, and consisted largely of soldiers of from three to seven years' standing, with a minimum of reservists. In less than a month from the day when this grand division of 18,000 men went into action its infantry had been nearly annihilated, but the details of its glorious destruction furnish one more vivid page of British military achievement. We lost a noble division and gained a glorious record.

Its peculiar excellence.

The Third Cavalry Division under General Byng was attached to the Seventh Division, and joined up with it at Roulers upon October 13. It consisted of—

6th *Cavalry Brigade—General Makings.*
3rd Dragoon Guards.   1st Royals.
10th Hussars.

7th *Cavalry Brigade—General Kavanagh.*
1st Life Guards.   1st Horse Guards.
2nd Life Guards.   K Battery, R.H.A.

234   THE BRITISH CAMPAIGN, 1914

CHAPTER VIII.

The first Battle of Ypres.

The First Army Corps not having yet come up from the Aisne, these troops were used to cover the British position from the north, the infantry lying from Zandvoorde through Gheluvelt to Zonnebeke, and the cavalry on their left from Zonnebeke to Langemarck from October 16 onwards. It was decided by Sir John French that it was necessary to get possession of the town of Menin, some distance to the east of the general British line, but very important because the chief bridge, by means of which the Germans were receiving their ever-growing reinforcements, was there. The Seventh Division was ordered accordingly to advance upon this town, its left flank being covered by the Third Cavalry Division.

Its difficult position.

The position was a dangerous one. It has already been stated that the pause on the Aisne may not have been unwelcome to the Germans, as they were preparing reserve formations which might be suddenly thrown against some chosen spot in the Allied line. They had the equipment and arms for at least another 250,000 men, and that number of drilled men were immediately available, some being Landwehr who had passed through the ranks, and others young formations which had been preparing when war broke out. Together they formed no less than five new army corps, available for the extreme western front, more numerous than the whole British and Belgian armies combined. This considerable force, secretly assembled and moving rapidly across Belgium, was now striking the north of the Allied line, debouching not only over the river at Menin, but also through Courtrai, Iseghem, and Roulers. It consisted of the 22nd, 23rd, 24th, 26th, and 27th reserve corps. Of these the 22nd, and later the 24th, followed the

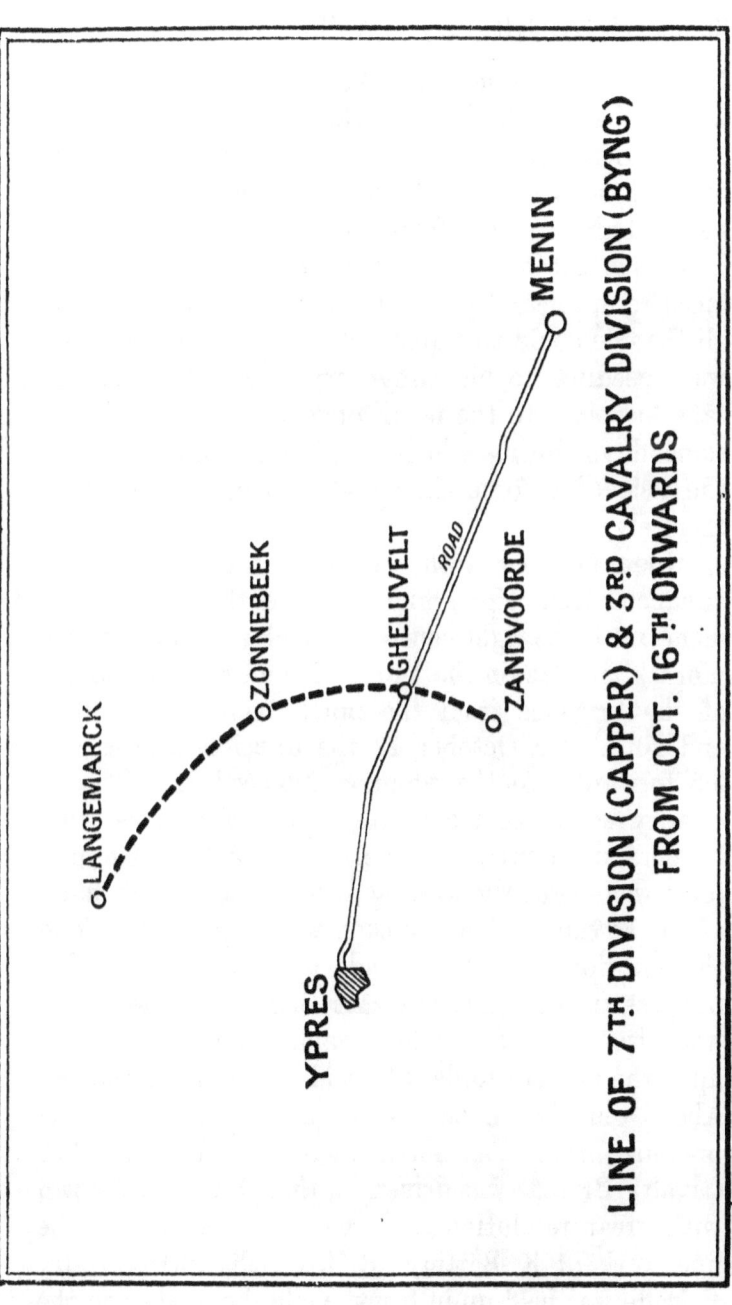

CHAPTER VIII.

The first Battle of Ypres.

Belgians to the line of the Yser, but the other corps were all available for an attack upon the flank of that British line which was faced by formidable opponents—a line which extended over thirty miles and had already been forced into a defensive attitude. That was the situation when the Seventh Division faced round near Ypres. Sir John French was doing all that he could to support it, and Sir Douglas Haig was speeding up his army corps from the Aisne to take his place to the north of Ypres, but there were some days during which Rawlinson's men were in the face of a force six or seven times larger than themselves.

Upon October 16th and 17th the division had advanced from Ypres and occupied the line already mentioned, the right centre of which rested about the ninth kilometre on the Ypres—Menin road, the order of the brigades from the north being 22nd, 21st, and 20th. On October 18 the division wheeled its left forward. As the infantry advanced, the covering cavalry soon became aware of grave menace from Roulers and Courtrai in the north. A large German force was evidently striking down on to the left flank of the advance. The division was engaged all along the line, for the 20th Brigade upon the right had a brisk skirmish, while the 21st Brigade in the centre was also under fire, which came especially heavily upon the 2nd Bedfords, who had numerous casualties. About ten o'clock on the morning of the 19th the pressure from the north increased, and the 7th Cavalry Brigade was driven in, though it held its own with great resolution for some time, helped by the fine work of K Battery, R.H.A. The 6th Cavalry Brigade was held up in front, while the danger on the

THE FIRST BATTLE OF YPRES 237

flank grew more apparent as the hours passed. In these circumstances General Rawlinson, fortified in his opinion by the precise reports of his airmen as to the strength of the enemy upon his left, came to the conclusion that a further advance would place him in a difficult position. He therefore dropped back to his original line. There can be little doubt that, if he had persevered in the original plan, his force would have been in extreme danger. As it was, before he could get it back the 1st Welsh Fusiliers were hard hit, this famous regiment losing a major, 5 captains, 3 lieutenants, and about 200 men. The order to retire had failed to reach it, and but for the able handling of Colonel Cadogan it might well have been destroyed.

On October 20, the situation being still obscure, the 20th Brigade carried out a reconnaissance towards Menin. The 2nd Wilts and 2nd Scots Fusiliers, of the 21st Brigade, covered their left flank. The enemy, however, made a vigorous attack upon the 22nd Brigade to the north, especially upon the Welsh Fusiliers, so the reconnaissance had to fall back again, the 1st Grenadier Guards sustaining some losses. The two covering regiments were also hard pressed, especially the Wiltshires, who were again attacked during the night, but repulsed their assailants.

From this time onwards the Seventh Division was to feel ever more and more the increasing pressure as the German army corps from day to day brought their weight to bear upon a thin extended line of positions held by a single division. It will be shown that they were speedily reinforced by the First Corps, but even after its advent the Germans were still able

238   THE BRITISH CAMPAIGN, 1914

CHAPTER VIII.

The first Battle of Ypres.

to greatly outnumber the British force. The story from this time onwards is one of incessant and desperate attacks by day and often by night. At first the division was holding the position alone, with the help of their attendant cavalry, and their instructions were to hold on to the last man until help could reach them. In the case of some units these instructions were literally fulfilled. One great advantage lay with the British. They were first-class trained soldiers, the flower of the Army, while their opponents, however numerous, were of the newly raised reserve corps, which showed no lack of bravery, but contained a large proportion of youths and elderly men in the ranks. Letters from the combatants have described the surprise and even pity which filled the minds of the British when they saw the stormers hesitate upon the edge of the trenches which they had so bravely approached, and stare down into them uncertain what they should do. But though the ascendancy of the British infantry was so great that they could afford to disregard the inequality of numbers, it was very different with the artillery. The German gunners were as good as ever, and their guns as powerful as they were numerous. The British had no howitzer batteries at all with this division, while the Germans had many. It was the batteries which caused the terrific losses. It may be that the Seventh Division, having had no previous experience in the campaign, had sited their trenches with less cunning than would have been shown by troops who had already faced the problem of how best to avoid high explosives. Either by sight or by aeroplane report the Germans got the absolute range of some portions of the British position, pitching their heavy shells exactly into the

THE FIRST BATTLE OF YPRES 239

trenches, and either blowing the inmates to pieces or else burying them alive, so that in a little time the straight line of the trench was entirely lost, and became a series of ragged pits and mounds. The head-cover for shrapnel was useless before such missiles, and there was nothing for it but either to evacuate the line or to hang on and suffer. The Seventh Division hung on and suffered, but no soldiers can ever have been exposed to a more deadly ordeal. When they were at last relieved by the arrival of reinforcements and the consequent contraction of the line, they were at the last pitch of exhaustion, indomitable in spirit, but so reduced by their losses and by the terrific nervous strain that they could hardly have held out much longer.

A short account has been given of what occurred to the division up to October 20. It will now be carried on for a few days, after which the narrative must turn to the First Corps, and show why and how they came into action to the north of the hard-pressed division. It is impossible to tell the two stories simultaneously, and so it may now be merely mentioned that from October 21 Haig's Corps was on the left, and that those operations which will shortly be described covered the left wing of the division, and took over a portion of that huge German attack which would undoubtedly have overwhelmed the smaller unit had it not been for this addition of strength. It is necessary to get a true view of the operations, for it is safe to say that they are destined for immortality, and will be recounted so long as British history is handed down from one generation to another.

On the 21st the enemy got a true conception of

the salient in front of the Seventh Division, and opened a vigorous attack, which lasted all day and assumed several different phases at different points. The feature of the morning of the 21st was the severe and, indeed, disastrous artillery fire upon Lawford's 22nd Brigade. The exact range of the British position seems to have been discovered with deadly results. Men, trenches, and machine-guns were all blown to pieces together. The 2nd Warwicks and the 1st Welsh Fusiliers were the two battalions upon which the storm beat hardest, and each of them had some hundreds of casualties. In three days the Welsh Fusiliers, who were on the exposed left flank, lost three-quarters of their effectives, including twenty-three of their officers, and yet preserved their military spirit. It became clearer as experience accumulated that the best trenches, if they are once fairly located, can be made untenable or turned into the graves of their occupants by the use of high explosives. The German fire was so severe that it was reckoned that one hundred and twenty shells an hour into or round a trench was a not uncommon rate of fall. The 2nd Queen's also lost seven officers and many men in this day's fighting. In spite of the heavy losses from gunfire the German infantry could make no progress, being held up by a flanking fire of the South Staffords.

In the afternoon of October 21 a strong attack was made upon the 21st Brigade in the centre of the line. The brigade was holding a front of two and a half miles, and, although the attack was generally beaten back, a certain number of stormers got through between the trenches and into the woods beyond. Here they lurked for a couple of days, during which time the 2nd Yorkshire Regiment, behind whose

THE FIRST BATTLE OF YPRES 241

line they were lying, were often compelled to have each alternate man facing a different way to keep down the fire. The battalion sent itself reinforcements by hurrying its right company over to help to clear its left. This movement was successful, but was attended with heavy losses, including several officers. Some of the Royal Scots Fusiliers had been forced out of their trenches on the right, and made, under Major Ian Forbes, a gallant attempt to re-establish them, in which Captain Fairlie and many men were lost. The Wiltshires also endured a very severe attack, which they repulsed with great loss to the enemy. On this same eventful day, the 21st, the Second Cavalry Division had been pushed back at Holbeke, and the Germans got round the right flank of the hard-pressed infantry. It was then that General Rawlinson brought his Third Cavalry Division round and established it upon his right instead of his left flank. From this time until October 30 this cavalry division was holding Zandvoorde Ridge, sharing day by day in all the perils and the glories of their comrades of the Seventh Division. There was no more dangerous point than that which was held by the cavalry, and their losses, especially those of the 10th Hussars, were in proportion to the danger. In the course of a few days the Hussars lost Colonel Barnes, Majors Mitford and Crichton and many officers and men.

On October 22 the Second Division of Haig's First Corps, which had been fully occupied to the north with operations which will presently be described, moved down to cover the ground vacated by the Third Cavalry Division and to relieve the pressure upon the infantry of the Seventh Division. The 4th Guards Brigade took its position upon their immediate left. It was time. For four days they had covered the enormous front of eight miles against at least four times their own number, with more than six times their weight of artillery. It was touch and go. They were nearly submerged. It was indeed a vision of joy when the worn and desperate men, looking over their shoulders down the Ypres—Menin road, saw the head of a British column coming swiftly to the rescue. It was the 2nd Highland Light Infantry and the 2nd Worcesters, dispatched from the 5th Brigade, and never was reinforcement more needed. Shortly afterwards further help in the shape of a detachment of the Munster Fusiliers, two troops of the ever-helpful Irish Horse, and one section of artillery appeared upon the scene.

Upon this date (October 22) the 22nd Infantry Brigade of the Seventh Division had fallen back to the railway crossings near Zonnebeke. Thus the salient which the Germans had been attacking was straightened out. Unhappily, the change caused another smaller salient farther south, at the point which was held by the 2nd Wiltshires. On the 22nd and 23rd there was a tremendous shelling of this sector, which was followed on the 24th by an infantry advance, in which the Wiltshires, who had been previously much reduced, were utterly overwhelmed and practically destroyed. The disastrous attack broke upon the British line just after daybreak. The enemy pushed through behind each flank of the Wiltshires, elbowing off the Scots Fusiliers on one side and the Scots Guards on the other. The Germans got in force into the Polygon Woods behind. There were no reserves available save the Northumberland Hussars, a corps which has the honour of being the

THE FIRST BATTLE OF YPRES 243

first British territorial corps to fight for its country. With the aid of some divisional cyclists, this handful of men held back the Germans until the 2nd Warwicks from the north were brought to stem the advance. The Warwicks charged through the wood, their gallant Colonel Loring riding his horse beside them without boot or legging, having been wounded some days before. "Where my men go I go as well," was his answer to medical remonstrance. He was killed by a bullet, but he died at a moment of victory, for his last earthly vision was that of his infantry driving the last Germans out of the wood. Besides their colonel, the regiment lost many officers and men in this fine advance, which was most vigorously supported by the 2nd Worcesters, the only reinforcement within reach. The Worcesters lost 6 officers and 160 men, but did much execution and took a number of prisoners.

At this time the 20th Brigade, being the extreme right of the Seventh Division, held an extended line from Kruiseik cross-roads, about a mile east of Gheluvelt village, to near Zandvoorde, with a salient at the village of Kruiseik. On the night of the 25th the Germans planned a furious attack upon the whole salient. The assailants, who were mostly Saxons, broke through the 2nd Scots Guards just north of Kruiseik and got behind the line, which was pushed back for some distance, though Captain Paynter, with the right-hand company, held his position. A counter-attack by the Guards retook the line, together with 200 prisoners, including 7 officers. On the morning of the 26th the Germans were back on them, however, and began by blowing in the trenches of the Border Regiment south of Kruiseik. The German

Chapter VIII.

The first Battle of Ypres.

Hard fight of 20th Brigade.

CHAPTER VIII.

The first Battle of Ypres.

guns had found the exact range of the trenches, and the defenders had the same terrible and intolerable experience which had befallen some of their comrades two days before. It was simply impossible to stand up against the incessant shower of shattering shells. So great was the concussion and the nervous strain that many of the men exposed to it got completely dazed or even became delirious. Grenadiers, Scots Guards, and South Staffords, of the 20th Brigade, held the line until the front trenches were carried by the Germans and many of the occupants made prisoners. It was pitch dark, and it was impossible to tell friend from foe. Major Fraser of the Scots Guards, going forward to reconnoitre, was shot dead and his party was destroyed. A house in a field taken by the Guards yielded no fewer than 200 prisoners, but in the confused fighting in the darkness our losses were greater than our gains. It was in this night-fighting that Lord Dalrymple, Colonel Bolton, and other officers, with some hundreds of men, fell into the hands of the enemy after a most heroic resistance to overpowering numbers and to a weight of artillery which was crushing in its effect. The King's Company of the 1st Grenadiers was isolated and in great danger, but managed to link up with the British line. The 1st South Staffords also lost some hundreds of men, and was only saved by fine handling on the part of Colonel Ovens. Kruiseik was abandoned, and a new line taken up half a mile farther back. It was a critical night, during which the energy and firmness of General Capper were splendidly employed in re-forming and stiffening his sorely tried division. On the 26th the 20th Brigade, which had been so heavily

THE FIRST BATTLE OF YPRES

hit the day before, was drawn out of the line for a rest, and the two other brigades closed up to cover a shorter line. The work of the 20th at Kruiseik had been magnificent, but their losses were appalling, including their Brigadier, Ruggles-Brise, who was wounded. Here, for the instant, we shall leave the Seventh Division, though their ordeal was by no means done, and we shall turn to those other forces which had been forming in the northern or Ypres section of the long battle line.

The reader will remember, if he casts his mind back, that the whole British line, as it extended from the south about October 18, consisted of the Second Corps and the advance guard of the Indians near La Bassée; then, in succession, the Third Corps in the Armentières district, the First Cavalry and Second Cavalry near Messines and Wytschaete, the Seventh Division near Gheluvelt, and finally the Third Cavalry on their left, joining up with the French, who carried the line to where the Belgians were reforming on the Yser. The First Corps had detrained from the Aisne, and was concentrated between St. Omer and Hazebrouck upon October 18 and 19. They represented a last British reserve of about thirty-five thousand men to set against the large new armies who were advancing from the north. The urgent question to be decided was where they should be placed, since there were so many points which needed reinforcement.

Sir John French has explained in his dispatch the reasons which swayed him in deciding this question. "I knew," he said, "that the enemy were by this time in greatly superior strength upon the Lys and that the Second and Third Cavalry and Fourth Corps

(Seventh Division) were holding a much wider front than their strength and numbers warranted. Taking these facts alone into consideration, it would have appeared wise to throw the First Corps in to strengthen the line, but this would have left the country north and east of Ypres and the Ypres Canal open to a wide turning movement by the Third Reserve Corps and at least one Landwehr Division which I knew to be operating in that region. I was also aware that the enemy was bringing large reinforcements up from the east, which could only be opposed for several days by two or three French cavalry divisions, some French Territorials, and the Belgian Army."

He proceeds to state his opinion that the Belgian Army was in no condition to withstand unsupported such an attack, and that if it were allowed to sweep past us it was very likely to wash away all opposition before it, and get into the Channel ports in our rear. With this consideration in his mind, Sir John French took the bold and dangerous, but absolutely necessary, step of leaving the long, thin, thirty-mile line to do the best it could, and prolonging it by another ten or twelve miles by forming up the First Corps on the same alignment, so as to present as long a British breakwater as possible to the oncoming flood. There was nothing else to be done, and the stronger the flood the more need there was to do it, but it is safe to say that seldom in history has so frail a barrier stood in the direct track of so terrible a storm.

In accordance with this resolution, Haig's First Corps moved, on October 20, through Poperinghe and Ypres and took their place upon the north or left side of the Seventh Division. On their own left in this position was the French cavalry corps of

General de Mitry, while the Third Division of British cavalry was on their right. As the movement commenced Sir John French had a personal interview with General Haig, in which he held out hopes that the greater part of the new German levies had been deflected to hold our southern advance, and that he would only find the Third Reserve Corps and some Landwehr in front of him to the north of Ypres. His object was to advance upon the line of Bruges and drive the enemy towards Ghent. Meanwhile the gallant little Belgian army, which was proving itself a glutton at fighting, was entrenched along the line of the Ypres Canal and the Yser River, where they held their own manfully in spite of all that they had endured.

The first large landmark in the direction of Bruges was Thorout, and towards this the First Corps, with the Third Cavalry Division upon its right, took its first steps, little thinking that it was butting forward against an approaching army of at least double its own strength. It was very quickly made to realise its position, however, and any dreams of a victorious entry into Bruges were speedily dispelled. Only too fortunate would it be if it could hold its own line without retreat and disaster. Upon the 21st Haig's men attacked Poel-Chapelle and Passchendaale, French cavalry and Territorials (the Eighty-seventh and Eighty-ninth Divisions) under General Bidon advancing on their left, while the Seventh Division, as already described, kept pace upon its right. There was strong opposition from the first, but the corps advanced in spite of it until the pressure from the north became too severe for the French, whose flank was exposed to the full force of it.

CHAPTER VIII.

The first Battle of Ypres.

The British attack upon the morning in question was planned as follows. The Second Division was to advance upon Passchendaale. The First had orders to take Poel-Chapelle. The latter movement was headed by the 3rd Brigade, who were directed by General Landon to go forward about nine o'clock, the 1st Queen's having the station for their objective while the 1st South Wales Borderers attacked the village. The 1st Gloucesters were in reserve. The enemy met the attack with shell-fire, which it was difficult to locate, as the country was flat and enclosed. The progress of the movement, however, was steady though slow. About ten o'clock there were signs of a considerable hostile infantry advance from the north. The attack, however, made good progress up to midday, when there was a general retirement of the French Territorials, followed later by the French cavalry upon the British left. They moved back towards Bixschote. The Gloucester Regiment, who had been thrown out to reinforce that flank, were also driven back, and were in turn reinforced by the Coldstream Guards. This battalion executed a bayonet charge in clearing the small village of Koekuit, but later on had to retire, finding their flank exposed. It should be mentioned that one French corps, the Seventh Cavalry Division, kept its position upon the British left, and it is also only fair to point out that as the German advance was mainly from the north, it was upon the left flank, covered by the French, that it would fall. The 1st Camerons were now dispatched to the flank to stiffen the French resistance, taking up their position near the inn which is midway upon the road between Steenstraate and Langemarck, north of the village

THE FIRST BATTLE OF YPRES 249

of Pilken—an inn with which they were destined to have stirring associations. With the support of the 46th Battery, the Highlanders held up a German brigade which was thrusting through behind our main line; but farther west, in the Steenstraate direction, the defence against a northern advance was miserably thin, consisting only of one company of the Sussex Regiment and the 116th Battery. In the circumstances the more success Haig's troops attained in front, and the more they advanced, the more dangerous was their position upon the flank.

About 2.30 the German advance from the north became more formidable, and the 1st South Welsh Borderers, between Langemarck and Poel-Chapelle, were heavily counter-attacked and suffered considerable loss, between two and three hundred in all. Two companies of the 2nd Welsh were pushed up to their help. It was clear, however, that the advance could not be continued. The 1st Brigade was therefore ordered to hold the line between Steenstraate and Langemarck, with their centre at the inn north of Pilken, so as to face the German advance from the north. Then from Langemarck the British line turned southwards, being carried on for two miles by the 3rd Brigade to hold the enemy who were coming from the east. The 2nd Brigade was in reserve at Boesinghe. During this long and difficult day the Second Division, operating upon the right of the First, was not subjected to the same anxiety about its flank. It advanced upon its objective in the face of severe opposition, ending more than once in a brief bayonet encounter. Several counter-attacks were made by the Germans, but they were all beaten back with loss. About two o'clock, however,

CHAPTER VIII.

The first Battle of Ypres.

the Second Division learned of the flank pressure which was holding up the First Division, and also of the extreme need for help experienced by the 22nd Brigade of the Seventh Division on their right. In these circumstances it was necessary to abandon the idea of further advance and to send south those reinforcements, the opportune arrival of which has been already described.

As a net result of the two days' operations General Haig was not able to attain the line of Passchendaale—Poel-Chapelle, as originally planned, but he gained sufficient ground to establish himself from Langemarck to Zonnebeke, more than half-way to his objective. The whole character of the operations during these days was more of the familiar British type, being conducted upon the surface of the earth rather than under it, and cavalry making its last appearance for many a long day. Many fine deeds of valour were done. In one of these Captain Rising, of the Gloucester Regiment, with ninety men, defended some point with such heroic tenacity that when, some days afterwards, the Brigadier attempted to get the names of the survivors for commendation not one could be found. Quaintly valorous also is the picture of Major Powell, of the North Lancashires, leading his wing with a badly-sprained ankle, and using a cottage chair for a crutch, upon which he sat down between rushes. It is hopeless, however, and even invidious to pick instances where the same spirit animated all. The result was definite. It had been clearly shown that the enemy were in considerably greater strength than had been imagined, and instead of a rearguard action from weak forces the British found themselves in the presence of a strong German

THE FIRST BATTLE OF YPRES

advance. All day large forces of the enemy were advancing from Roulers and were impinging upon different points of the Franco-British line. These troops were composed of partially-trained men, volunteers and reservists, but they attacked with the utmost determination, and endured heavy losses with great bravery. It is a remarkable proof of the elaborate preparations for war made by Germany that, behind all their original gigantic array, they still had ready within the country sufficient arms and uniforms to fit out these five new army corps. He who plans finds it easy to prepare, and whoever will compare this profusion of munitions in Germany with the absolute lack of them in the Allied countries will have no further doubt as to which Government conspired against the peace of the world.

On October 21, Sir John French began to feel that there were new factors in his front. In the evening, at a meeting with Haig and Rawlinson, he discussed the unexpected strength of the German reinforcements and admitted that the scheme of an advance upon Bruges would become impossible in the face of such numbers. Intelligence reports indicated that there was already a German army corps in front of each British division. General Joffre had promised considerable French reinforcements upon October 24, and all that could be done was for the British troops to hold their ground to the last man and to resist every pressure until the equality of the forces could be restored. Could they hold the line till then? That was the all-important question.

October 22 was the first day of that long ordeal of incessant attacks which the First Corps was called

CHAPTER VIII.

The first Battle of Ypres.

upon to endure, until by constant attrition it had become almost as worn as the Seventh Division to the south. On this day the German attack, which had not yet attained the full volume of later days, spent itself here and there along the extended lines. Only at one point did the enemy have some success, which, however, was the prelude to disaster.

Fight of Pilken Inn.

The line from Steenstraate to Langemarck, defending the British left flank, was held by the 1st Brigade, the Scots Guards upon the extreme left, then the Cameron Highlanders, and the Black Watch in reserve. In the middle of the line north of Pilken was a solitary inn, already mentioned, round which trenches had been cut in horse-shoe fashion, the concavity of the shoe pointing southwards. This point marked the junction between the Camerons and the Scots Guards. About 3 P.M. this position was driven in and captured by a sudden and determined advance of the enemy. The German charge was a fine feat of arms, for it was carried out largely by *Einjahrige*, who may be roughly compared to the Officers' Training Corps of our British system. These high-spirited lads advanced singing patriotic songs, and succeeded in carrying the trenches in the face of soldiers who are second to none in the British Army—soldiers, too, who had seen much service, while the German cadets were new to the work. The performance was much appreciated by British officers and men.

The Black Watch endeavoured without success to restore the line, and the 1st Northamptons were called upon from divisional reserve, while from all parts troops converged towards the gap. On the arrival of the Northamptons they pushed up towards

THE FIRST BATTLE OF YPRES 253

the interval which now existed between the Scots Guards and the remains of the Camerons, but found the gap broader than had been thought, and strongly occupied. It was then evening, and it was thought best to delay the counter-attack until morning and so have time to bring up reinforcements. The 1st North Lancashires and the 2nd South Staffords were accordingly ordered up, together with the 1st Queen's Surrey and the 2nd Rifles, the whole operation being under the immediate command of General Bulfin. The advance began at six in the morning, over very difficult ground which had been barb-wired during the night. The progress was slow but steady, and at eleven o'clock an assault upon the inn was ordered. The position was critical, since the enemy was now firmly lodged in the very centre of the flank of the British position, and was able to enfilade all the trenches of the First Division. The Queen's Surrey, the 2nd King's Royal Rifles, and the 1st North Lancashires charged home with splendid energy, capturing the trenches round the inn, besides releasing sixty Camerons and taking over five hundred prisoners. The trenches were carried by the North Lancashires, led by Major Carter. It was the second time within six weeks that this battalion had made a decisive bayonet charge. The price paid was six officers and 150 men. The inn itself was rushed by Captain Creek's company of the Queen's, while Major Watson, of the same regiment, organised the final advance. The fighting at this point was not finished for the day. In the late evening the enemy, with fine tenacity of purpose, attacked the inn once more and drove the Queen's out of a salient. The line was then straightened on each side

CHAPTER VIII.

The first Battle of Ypres.

254 THE BRITISH CAMPAIGN, 1914

<small>CHAPTER VIII.
The first Battle of Ypres.</small>

of the inn and remained firm. Both the attack on the inn and the defence of the line were splendidly supported by the field artillery.

Whilst the 1st Brigade had in this fashion got into and out of a dangerous position, there had been a severe attack upon two regiments of Landon's 3rd Brigade stationed at Langemarck. The defending units were the 2nd Welsh Regiment and the 1st Gloucesters. Aided by a strong artillery backing, they beat off these attacks and inflicted a very heavy loss upon the enemy. The Allied line to the north was solid and unbroken.

<small>Bravery of enemy.</small>

The British losses during these operations of the First Corps amounted to 1500 men, while those of the Germans were exceedingly heavy. These inexperienced troops advanced with an indiscriminating enthusiasm which exposed them to severe retaliation. It is doubtful if at any time in the campaign the British fire found so easy a mark. One thousand five hundred dead were counted in the vicinity of Langemarck, and the total loss (including over six hundred prisoners) could not have been less than 10,000 men. Correspondence afterwards captured showed that the Twenty-third Reserve Corps sustained such losses that for a time at least it was out of action. The Twenty-seventh Reserve Corps was also hard hit. A letter from a soldier in the 246th Regiment mentions that only eighty men were left of his battalion after the action of the 24th.

On October 24 and 25 the arrival of French reinforcements allowed the British to shorten up their defensive line, which had been unduly extended. The Seventeenth Division of the Ninth French Army Corps took over the line of the Second Division, which

THE FIRST BATTLE OF YPRES 255

was drawn back to St. Jean, and in turn took over part of the front of the Seventh Division. French territorial troops, under General de Mitry, relieved the First British Division on the line Hannebeke—Langemarck—Steenstraate. The First Division was drawn back to Zillebeke.

CHAPTER VIII.

The first Battle of Ypres.

Meantime the Second Division, having the French Ninth Corps upon its left and the Seventh Division upon its right, made an attack towards Bacelaer, taking two guns and some prisoners. This advance was renewed upon the 26th, this being the day upon which, as already described, the Germans pushed back the 20th Brigade of the Seventh Division at the Kruiseik salient, creating a situation which brought the Second Division to a standstill.

Advance of Second Division.

In this movement forward of the Second Division from October 24 to 26, the Guards' 4th Brigade were on the right, the 6th Brigade on the left, with the French to the left of them. The 5th Brigade were in reserve. Two small villages were taken by storm, the Germans being driven out of loopholed houses, though at a considerable cost of officers and men. It was in this operation that Colonel Bannatyne, the gallant leader of the 1st King's Liverpool, was killed. Ten other officers and several hundred men of this corps were killed or wounded. The 1st Berkshires, fighting to the left of the King's, shared in its losses and in its success. The Irish Guards were held up before Reutel and separated from the rest of the force, but managed to extricate themselves after some anxious hours.

On October 27, Sir John French came in person to Hooge, at the rear of the fighting line, and inquired into the state of the hard-pressed troops. He found

CHAPTER VIII.

The first Battle of Ypres.

the Seventh to be now such a skeleton division that it was thought best to join it with Haig's First Corps, forming one single command.

The attendant Third Cavalry Division was also attached to the First Corps. These readjustments took place upon October 27. They were, of course, of a temporary character until the eagerly awaited Eighth Division should arrive and so give General Rawlinson a complete Fourth Corps. At present there was a very immediate prospect that half of it might be annihilated before the second half appeared. The general arrangement of this section of the battlefield was now as depicted, the Seventh Division being entirely south of the Ypres—Menin roadway.

This date, the 27th, was memorable only for an advance of the 6th Brigade. These continual advances against odds were wonderful examples of the aggressive spirit of the British soldiers. In this instance ground was gained, but at the cost of some casualties, especially to the 1st Rifles, who lost Prince Maurice of Battenberg and a number of officers and men.

Fight of Kruiseik crossroads.

And now the great epic of the first Battle of Ypres was rising to its climax, and the three days of supreme trial for the British Army were to begin. Early upon October 29, a very heavy attack developed upon the line of the Ypres—Menin road. There is a village named Gheluvelt, which is roughly half-way upon this tragic highway. It lay now immediately behind the centre of the British line. About half a mile in front of it the position ran through the important cross-roads which lead to the village of Kruiseik, still in the British possession. The line through the

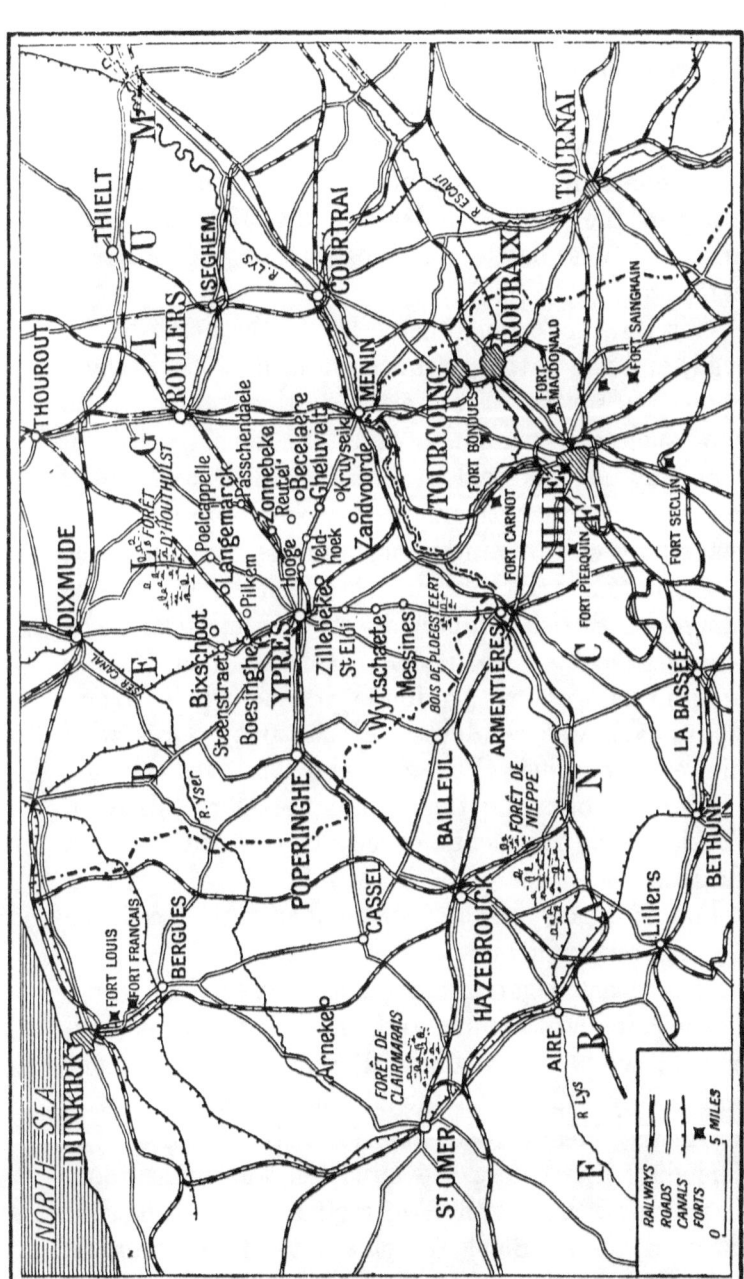

GENERAL SCENE OF OPERATIONS

Chapter VIII.
The first Battle of Ypres.

Kruiseik cross-roads was that which was furiously assailed upon this morning, and the attack marked the beginning of a great movement to drive in the front continuing throughout the 30th and culminating in the terrible ordeal of the 31st, the crisis of the Ypres battle and possibly of the Western campaign.

FitzClarence's 1st Brigade lay to the north of the road, and the battered, much-enduring 20th Brigade upon the south. They were destined together to give such an example of military tenacity during that day as has seldom been equalled and never exceeded, so that the fight for the Kruiseik cross-roads may well live in history amongst those actions, like Albuera and Inkermann, which have put the powers of British infantry to an extreme test. The line was held by about five thousand men, but no finer units were to be found in the whole Army. The attack was conducted by an army corps with the eyes of their Emperor and an overpowering artillery encouraging them from the rear. Many of the defending regiments, especially those of the 20th Brigade, had already been terribly wasted. It was a line of weary and desperate men who faced the German onslaught.

The attack began in the mists of the early morning. The opening was adverse to the British, for the enemy, pushing very boldly forward upon a narrow front and taking full advantage of the fog, broke a way down the Menin road and actually got past the defending line before the situation was understood. The result was that the two regiments which flanked the road, the 1st Black Watch and the 1st Grenadiers, were fired into from behind and endured terrible

THE FIRST BATTLE OF YPRES 259

losses. Among the Grenadiers Colonel Earle, Majors Forrester and Stucley, Lord Richard Wellesley, and a number of other officers fell, while out of 650 privates only 150 were eventually left standing. The 2nd Gordons, upon the right of the Grenadiers, suffered nearly as heavily, while the 1st Coldstream, upon the left of the Black Watch, was perhaps the hardest hit of all, for at the end of that dreadful day it had not a single officer fit for duty. The right company of the 1st Scots Guards shared the fate of the Coldstream. The line was pushed back for a quarter of a mile and Kruiseik was evacuated, but the dead and wounded who remained in the trenches far exceeded in numbers those who were able to withdraw.

Two small bodies who were cut off by the German advance did not fall back with their comrades, and each of them made a splendid and successful resistance. The one near Kruiseik was a mixed party under Major Bottomley of the 2nd Queen's West Surrey. The other was C Company of the 2nd Gordons under Captain B. G. R. Gordon and Lieutenant Laurence Carr. These small islands of khaki, in the midst of a broad stream of grey, lay so tight and fired so straight that they inflicted very great damage upon the enemy, and were able to hold their own, in ever-diminishing numbers, until under the protection of darkness the survivors regained the British line.

In the meantime, a number of small dashing counter-attacks by the indomitable infantry was bringing the British line forward again. South of the road the Gordons, under Colonel Uniacke, dashed themselves again and again against the huge host which faced them, driving them back, and then in their turn recoiling before the ponderous advance of the army corps. They were maddened by the sound of the rolling fire ahead of them, which showed that their own C Company was dying hard. In one of these counter-attacks Captain Brooke brought every straggler into the fray, and died while trying to cut his way through to his comrades. To the north of the road Captain Stephen, with the remains of the 1st Scots Guards, threw themselves upon the German flank and staggered it by their fire. The Germans, who had almost reached Gheluvelt, were now worried in this way on either flank, while the 2nd Border battalion and the Welsh Borderers with the rallied remains of the broken regiments were still facing them in front. The enemy was held, was stricken front and flank with a murderous fire, and recoiled back down the Menin road. Imperial eyes and overmastering guns were equally powerless to drive them through that iron defence. Five thousand British soldiers had driven back an army corps, but had left more than half their number upon the scene of victory.

The Second Division, to the north of the road in the direction of Reutel, had been ordered to counter-attack, and the other brigades of the Seventh Division to the south did the same. While Haig had a man standing he was ready to hit back. Between these two flanking forces there was a movement in the centre to follow the Germans back and to recover some of the lost ground. Landon's Third Brigade, less the Gloucester Regiment, was pushed forward. These troops moved past Gheluvelt and advanced along the line of the road, the 1st Queen's, their right-hand unit, linking up by a happy chance with their own 2nd Battalion, who were now on the left of the 22nd Brigade of the Seventh Division. Left

THE FIRST BATTLE OF YPRES

of the Queen's were the 2nd Welsh to the immediate south of the main road, while to their left again lay the 1st South Wales Borderers, in front of the village of Gheluvelt. By evening these troops had recovered some of the ground, but the village of Kruiseik, which had always constituted a salient, was now abandoned. The cross-roads also remained in the hands of the enemy. Landon's Brigade continued to bar the further German advance preparing in stern resignation for the renewed and heavier blow which all knew to be in readiness, and which was destined two days later to bring them a glorious annihilation.

It was clear upon the evening of the 29th that serious mischief was afoot, for there were great signs of movement on the German side, and all night the continual rattle of wheels was heard to the eastward. These menacing sounds were actually caused by a very strong reinforcement, the Fifteenth German Corps (Strasburg) of the regular army, which, followed by the Thirteenth Corps and the Second Bavarian Corps, were coming into the battle line with the declared intention of smashing their way through to Ypres. Correspondence, afterwards captured, showed that the German Emperor had issued a special appeal to these troops, declaring that the movement was one which would be of decisive importance to the war. It was, of course, not the venerable town of Ypres which had assumed such a place in the mind both of the Emperor and his people, but it was Calais and the Channel coast to which it was the door. Once in the possession of these points, it seemed to their perfervid minds that they would be in a position to constrain Great Britain to an ignominious peace, a course which would surely have ruined the cause of the Allies and placed the whole world under the German heel. No less was the issue at stake. The British Army from Langemarck in the north to La Bassée in the south were resolutely determined that the road was barred, while to left and to right they had stout-hearted comrades of Belgium and of France.

At half-past six upon October 30 a very heavy attack developed, which involved the whole line of the First Corps and also the French Ninth Corps upon its left. This attack upon the left was carried out by the Reserve Corps 26 and 27, with whom we had had previous dealings, and it was repulsed with considerable loss by the French and the 6th British Brigade. To the south, however, the British were very violently engaged down the whole line of trenches from the position of the Seventh Division near the Ypres—Menin road, through Zandvoorde, where the Third Cavalry Division was holding on under great difficulties, and on southward still, past the position of the Second Cavalry down to Messines, where the First Cavalry Division was also heavily engaged. The front of battle was not less than twelve miles in length, with one continuous long-drawn rattle of small arms and roar of guns from end to end.

The British may have anticipated that the chief blow would fall at the same spot as had been attacked the day before. As a matter of fact, it was directed farther south, at Zandvoorde, on the immediate right of the Seventh Division.

The first sign of success for the strenuous German efforts upon October 30 was the driving in of Kavanagh's 7th Guards' Cavalry Brigade from their trenches at the Zandvoorde Ridge. On this ridge,

THE FIRST BATTLE OF YPRES 263

which is not more than a hundred and twenty feet high, the Germans concentrated so tremendous and accurate a fire that the trenches were in many places demolished and became entirely untenable. The survivors of the Life Guards and Blues who made up this brigade withdrew steadily through the reserve trenches, which were held by the 6th cavalry Brigade, and reformed at Klein Zillebeke in the rear. Two squadrons, however, and Lord Worsley's machine-gun section were killed or taken by the assailants. The unoccupied trenches were seized by the Sixth Bavarian Reserve Division, who advanced rapidly in order to improve their advantage, while their artillery began to pound the reserves. The cavalry had been strengthened, however, by the Greys and 3rd Hussars upon the left, while the 4th Hussars lined up on the right, and C, I, and K Horse Artillery batteries vigorously supported. In spite of great pressure, the position was held. Farther south the First Cavalry Division was also at very close grips with the Twenty-sixth Division of the Thirteenth German Army Corps, and was hard put to it to hold its own. Along the whole cavalry position there was extreme strain. A squadron of the 1st Royals were forced to evacuate the château of Holebeke, and the line in this quarter was pushed back as far as St. Eloi, thus flattening a considerable salient.

The danger of a position which consists of so long a line with few reserves is that any retirement at any point immediately exposes the flanks of the neighbouring units to right and left. Thus the evacuation of Zandvoorde threw open the right flank of the Seventh Division, even as its left had been in the air upon the day before. On getting through, the Germans were

CHAPTER VIII.

The first Battle of Ypres.

on the right rear of the 1st Welsh Fusiliers and enfiladed them badly, destroying all the officers and a considerable proportion of the regiment, which had already been greatly reduced. Colonel Cadogan was among those who fell. The 22nd Brigade was forced to fall back, and the 2nd Yorkshires and 2nd Scots Fusiliers, of the 21st Brigade, being left in a salient, suffered heavily, especially the latter battalion, the conduct of which from first to last was remarkable even among such men as fought beside them. These two regiments held on with the greatest determination until orders to retire reached them, which were somewhat belated, as several orderlies were killed in bringing them. The 2nd Bedfords, who had themselves sustained very severe losses from the German artillery fire, covered the retirement of the remains of these two gallant units. The Seventh Division then covered the line from the canal through Klein Zillebeke and along the front of the woods to near Gheluvelt.

The position was now most critical. The Germans were in possession of Zandvoorde Ridge on the British right flank, a most important position whence guns could command a considerable area. Ypres was only four miles distant. There was nothing but a line of weary and partially broken infantry to protect the flank from being entirely pierced. The whole of a German active army corps was attacking upon this line. The order was given to hold the new positions at all costs, but on the evening of the 30th the situation was full of menace for the morrow. The German flood was still thundering against the barrier, and the barrier seemed to be giving. At about 2 P.M. on October 30 the 1st Irish Guards and the 2nd Grenadiers, who were in reserve to two battalions of the Cold-

THE FIRST BATTLE OF YPRES

stream in trenches in the Polygon Wood, near Reutel Village, were ordered to help the Seventh Division. General Capper subsequently directed them to take the place of the cavalry on the right of his division. The Irish Guards were accordingly on the right of the Seventh Division from now onwards, and the Grenadiers were on their right, extending down to the canal in front of Klein Zillebeke. The commander of the Ninth French Corps also, with that fine loyalty which his comrades have shown again and again during the war, easing many a difficult and perhaps saving some impossible situations, put three battalions and some cavalry at the disposal of the British. Two regiments of Bulfin's 2nd Brigade were also brought across and thrust into the gap. But the outlook that evening was not cheering. The troops had been fighting hard for two days without a break. The losses had been heavy. The line had been driven back and was greatly strained. It was known that the Germans were in great strength and that the attack would be renewed on the morrow. The troops and their leaders faced the immediate future in a spirit of sombre determination.

During the 30th Landon's Brigade had strengthened their position near Gheluvelt, and General Haig, realising that this was the key of his line, moved up the 2nd King's Royal Rifles and the 1st North Lancashires to form a reserve under the orders of General Landon. These regiments took a position south-west of Gheluvelt and connected up more closely between the Seventh Division and the 3rd Brigade of the First Division. It was well that a closely-knitted line had been formed, for at the dawn of day upon the 31st a most terrific attack was made,

Chapter VIII.

The first Battle of Ypres.

Fight of Gheluvelt

which was pushed with unexampled fierceness during the whole day, falling chiefly upon the centre and left of the Seventh Division and upon the 1st Queen's and 2nd Welsh of the Third Brigade.

A weak point developed, unfortunately, in the front line, for the Seventh Division in its enfeebled condition was further weakened by forming somewhat of a salient in the Kruiseik direction. They behaved with all their usual magnificent gallantry, but they were not numerous enough to hold the ground. The line was broken and the remains of the 2nd Royal Scots Fusiliers, after being exposed to heavy fire from 5.30 A.M., were outflanked and surrounded in the early afternoon. The bulk of the survivors of this battalion had been sent to reinforce the line elsewhere, but the remainder, some sixty in number, were killed, wounded, or taken, including their gallant colonel, Baird Smith, who had been hit the day before. The Picton tradition which disregards wounds unless they are absolutely crippling was continually observed by these stern soldiers. On the left of the Scots Fusiliers the 2nd Bedfords were also involved in the catastrophe, but drew off with heavy losses.

The left wing of the Seventh Division began to retire, and the 1st Queen's upon the right of the 3rd Brigade had both their flanks turned and were reduced to a handful under Major Watson and Lieutenant Boyd, who still held together as a unit. It was a great morning in the history of this regiment, as the two battalions had fought side by side, and their colonels, Pell and Coles, had both fallen in the action.

The line of the 3rd Brigade had been drawn up across the Menin road some four hundred yards to the east of the village. The road itself was held by

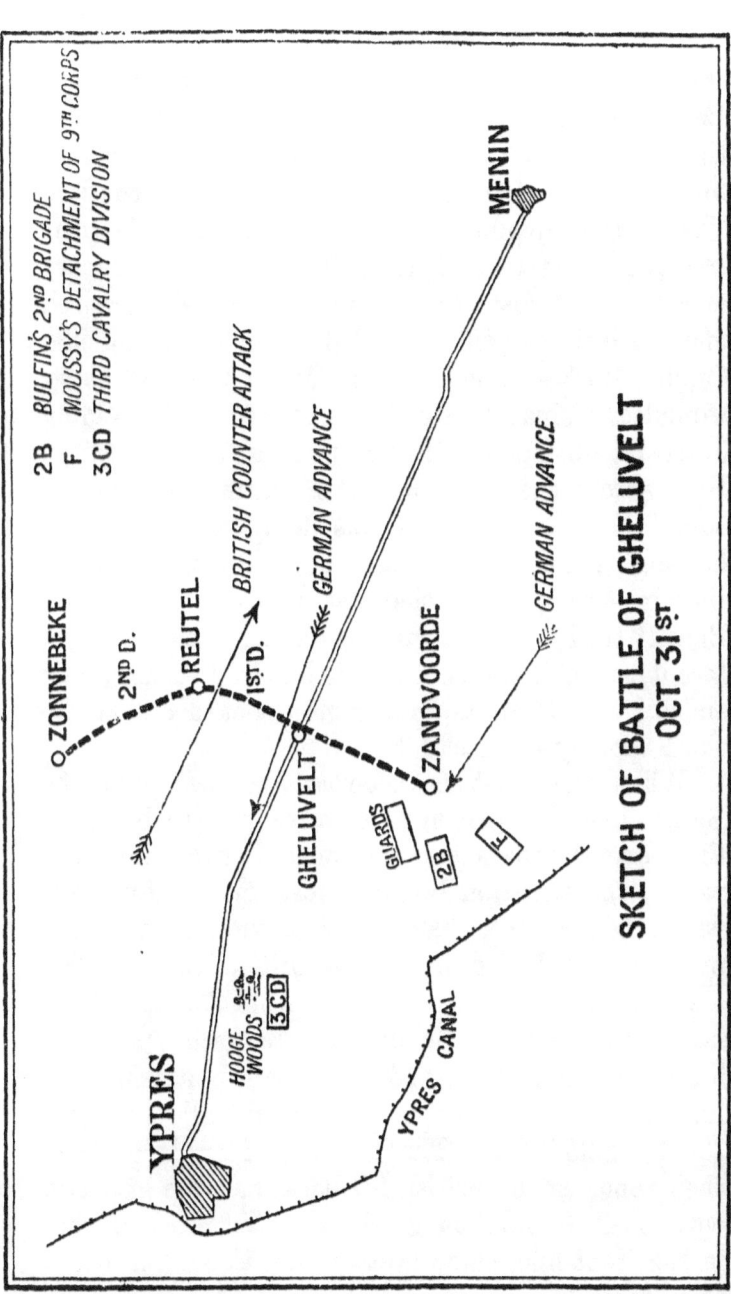

the 2nd Welsh Regiment, supported by the 54th Battery (Major Peel), which was immediately behind the village. Both the battalion and the battery fought desperately in a most exposed situation. The Welsh Regiment were driven out of their trenches by a terrific shell-fire followed by an infantry attack. They lost during the day nearly six hundred men, with sixteen officers, killed, wounded, or missing. Colonel Morland was killed and Major Prichard badly wounded. Finally, after being pushed back, holding every possible point, they formed up under Captain Rees across the open in a thin skirmishing line to cover the battery, which was doing great work by holding back the German advance. One German gun was in action upon the Menin road. Lieutenant Blewitt took a British gun out on to the bare road to face it, and a duel ensued at five hundred yards, which ended by the German gun being knocked out at the third shot by a direct hit.

When the First Division at the centre of the British line were driven in, as already described, and the Seventh Division were pushed back into the woods, the situation became most critical, for there was a general retirement, with a victorious enemy pressing swiftly on upon the British centre. The men behaved splendidly, and the officers kept their heads, taking every opportunity to form up a new line. The 2nd Rifles and 1st North Lancashires in immediate support of the centre did all that men could to hold it firm. The German artillery lengthened their range as the British fell back, and the infantry, with their murderous quick-firers scattered thickly in the front line, came rapidly on. Communications were difficult, and everything for a time was chaos and confusion. It looked for an hour or two as if Von Deimling, the German leader, might really carry out his War Lord's command and break his road to the sea. It was one of the decisive moments of the world's history, for if the Germans at that period had seized the Channel ports, it is difficult to say how disastrous the result might have been both to France and to the British Empire. At that moment of darkness and doubt a fresh misfortune, which might well have proved overwhelming, came upon the hard-pressed forces. About 1.30 a shell exploded in the headquarters at the château of Hooge, and both General Lomax, of the First Division, and General Munro, of the Second, were put out of action, the first being wounded and the second rendered unconscious by the shock. It was a brain injury to the Army, and a desperately serious one, for besides the two divisional commanders the single shell had killed or wounded Colonels Kerr and Perceval, Major Paley, Captains Ommany and Trench, and Lieutenant Giffard. General Landon, of the 3rd Brigade, took the command of the First Division at a moment's notice, and the battle went forward. A line was hurriedly formed, men digging as for their lives, whilst broken units threw themselves down to hold off the rolling grey wave that thundered behind. The new position was three-quarters of a mile back and about four hundred yards in advance of Veldhoek, which is the next village down the Ypres road. The Seventh Division had also been rolled back, but the fiery Capper, their divisional chief, who has been described as a British Samurai, was everywhere among his regiments, reforming and bracing them. The British soldiers, with their incomparable regimental officers, rose to the crisis, whilst General Haig was behind the line at Hooge, directing and controlling, like a great engineer who seeks to hold a dam which carries an overpowering head of water. By three o'clock the new line was firmly held.

Now General Haig, seeking round for some means of making a counter-attack, perceived that on his left flank he had some reserve troops who had been somewhat clear of the storm and might be employed. The 2nd Worcesters were ordered to advance upon Gheluvelt, the initiative in this vital movement coming from General Fitz-Clarence of the 1st Brigade. On that flank the troops had not joined in the retirement, and, including the South Wales Borderers of the 3rd Brigade, were still in their original trenches, being just north of the swathe that had been cut in the British line, and just south of where the Second Division, extended to cracking point, with one man often for every eight or nine feet, and no supports, were defending the left flank of the Army.

When the village of Gheluvelt and the trenches to the north of it had been captured by the enemy, a gap had been left of about five hundred yards between the northern edge of the village and these South Wales Borderers. This gap the 2nd Worcesters were ordered to fill. They were in reserve at the time in the south-west corner of the Polygon Wood, but on being called upon they made a brilliant advance under Major Hankey. One company (A) was detached to guard the right flank of the advance. The other three companies came on for a thousand yards. At one point they had to cross two hundred and twenty yards of open under heavy shrapnel-fire. One hundred men fell, but the momentum of the charge

THE FIRST BATTLE OF YPRES 271

was never diminished. Their rapid and accurate fire drove back the German infantry, while their open order formation diminished their own losses. Finally they dashed into the trenches and connected up the village with the line of the Welsh Borderers. Their right platoons, under Captain Williams, held the village until nearly midnight. Altogether the advance cost the battalion 187 casualties, including 3 officers, out of 550 who were in the ranks that day. Up to dusk the Worcesters were exposed to heavy shrapnel-fire, and small detached parties of the enemy came round their right flank, but their position was strengthened and strongly held until the final readjustment of the line. It was a fine advance at a critical moment, and did much to save the situation. The whole movement was strongly supported by the guns of the 42nd Battery, and by some of the 1st Scots Guards upon the left of the Welsh Borderers.

It has been stated that a line had been formed near Veldhoek, but this difficult operation was not performed in an instant, and was rather the final equilibrium established after a succession of oscillations. The British were worn to a shadow. The 2nd Queen's had 2 officers and 60 men left that night, the 2nd Welsh had 3 officers and 93 men. Little groups, who might have been fitted into a large-sized drawing-room, were settling a contention upon which the fate of the world might depend. But the Germans also had spent all their force. The rattle of musketry behind their advance was enough to tell them that the British were still in their trenches, and the guns were for ever playing on them with deadly effect. Gradually they began to dissolve away among the thick woods which flank the road. They were

CHAPTER VIII.

The first Battle of Ypres.

learning that to penetrate the line of a resolute adversary is not necessarily the prelude to victory. It may mean that the farther you advance the more your flanks are exposed. So it was now, when the infantry to the north on one side and the Third Cavalry Division on the other were closing in on them. That long tentacle which was pushing its way towards Ypres had to be swiftly withdrawn once more, and withdrawn under a heavy fire from the 29th, 41st, and 45th field batteries.

German recoil.

The scattered German infantry who had taken refuge in the woods of Hooge, which lie to the south of the road, were followed up by mounted and dismounted men of the Royals, 10th Hussars, and 3rd Dragoon Guards, aided by some French cavalry. These troops advanced through the woods, killing or taking a number of the enemy. By nightfall the Germans had fallen back along the whole debated line; the various British units, though much disorganised, were in close touch with each other, and the original trenches had in the main been occupied, the Berkshire Regiment helping to close the gap in the centre. The flood had slowly ebbed away, and the shaken barrier was steady once more, thanks to the master-hands which had so skilfully held it firm. The village of Gheluvelt remained in the hands of the Germans, but the British trenches were formed to the west of it, and the road to the sea was barred as effectually as ever. These are the main facts of the action of Gheluvelt, which may well be given a name of its own, though it was only one supremely important episode in that huge contention which will be known as the First Battle of Ypres.

In the southern portion of the Ypres area at

THE FIRST BATTLE OF YPRES 273

Klein Zillebeke a very sharp engagement was going on, which swung and swayed with as much violence and change as the main battle on the Menin road. The German attack here was hardly inferior in intensity to that in the north. Having pushed back Lawford's weak brigade (22nd) it struck full upon part of Bulfin's 2nd Brigade, which had been detached from the First Division and sent to cover the right of the Seventh Division. Its own flank was now exposed, and its situation for a time was critical. The German advance was sudden and impetuous, coming through a wood which brought the dense mass of the enemy's leading formation almost unseen right up to the British line. The position of the 2nd Brigade was pierced, and the two regiments present, the 2nd Sussex and the 1st Northamptons, were driven back with loss. Their brigadier rallied them some hundreds of yards to the rear, where they formed up into a skirmish line in the open, and, though unable to advance, kept back the Germans with their rifle-fire. The losses still continued, however, and the enemy came on again and again with numbers which seemed inexhaustible. Suddenly there was a charging yell from behind a low slope covering the rear, and over the brow there appeared some three hundred survivors of the 2nd Gordons, rushing at full speed with fixed bayonets. At the same moment the dismounted troopers of the 6th Cavalry Brigade and a company of sappers ran forward to join in the charge. The whole British force was not one to three of its opponents, but as the reinforcing line swept on, cheering with all its might, the survivors of the hard-pressed brigade sprang up with a shout and the united wave burst over the Germans. Next moment they had

CHAPTER VIII.

The first Battle of Ypres.

T

274   THE BRITISH CAMPAIGN, 1914

CHAPTER VIII.
The first Battle of Ypres.
General result.

broken and were flying for their lives through the Zwartelen Wood. The pursuit lasted for some distance, and a great number of the enemy were bayoneted, while several hundreds were taken prisoners.

There have been few more critical occasions in the British operations than this action upon October 31, when the Germans so nearly forced their way to Ypres. It is the peculiarity of modern warfare that, although vast armies are locked in a close struggle, the number of men who can come into actual contact at any one point is usually far more limited than in the old days, when each host could view the other from wing to wing. Thus the losses in such an action are small as compared with the terrific death-roll of a Napoleonic battle. On the other hand, when the operations are viewed broadly and one groups a series of actions into one prolonged battle, like the Aisne or Ypres, then the resulting losses become enormous. The old battle was a local conflagration, short and violent. The new one is a widespread smoulder, breaking here and there into flame. In this affair of Gheluvelt the casualties of the British did not exceed 2000 or 3000, while those of the Germans, who were more numerous and who incurred the extra loss which falls upon the attack, could not have been less than twice that figure. One thousand five hundred dead were actually picked up and six hundred prisoners were taken. Some hundreds of prisoners were also taken by the enemy. The British artillery, which worked desperately hard all day, had many losses both upon the 30th and the 31st. The 12th Battery had all its guns silenced but one, and many others were equally hard hit.

On the night of the 31st considerable French

THE FIRST BATTLE OF YPRES 275

reinforcements began to arrive, and it was high time that they did so, for the First Corps, including the Seventh Division, were likely to bleed to death upon the ground that they were holding. It had stood the successive attacks of four German corps, and it had held its line against each of them. But its own ranks had been grievously thinned and the men were weary to death. The strain, it should be added, was equally great upon the Ninth French Corps to the north, which had its own set of assailants to contend with. Now that the line of the Yser, so splendidly guarded by the Belgians, had proved to be impregnable, and that the French from Dixmude in the north had repulsed all attacks, the whole German advance upon Calais, for which Berlin was screaming, was centred upon the Ypres lines. It was time, then, that some relief should come to the hard-pressed troops. For several days the French on the right and the left took the weight of the attack upon themselves, and although the front was never free from fighting, there was a short period of comparative rest for Haig's tired men. In successive days they had lost Kruiseik, Zandvoorde, and Gheluvelt, but so long as they held the semicircle of higher ground which covers Ypres these small German gains availed them nothing.

CHAPTER VIII.

The first Battle of Ypres.

Looking back at the three actions of the 29th, 30th, and especially of the 31st of October, one can clearly perceive that it was the closest thing to a really serious defeat which the Army had had since Le Cateau. If the Germans had been able to push home their attack once again, it is probable that they would have taken Ypres, and that the results would have been most serious. Sir John French is reported

A great crisis.

CHAPTER VIII.

The first Battle of Ypres.

as having said that there was no time in the Mons retreat when he did not see his way, great as were his difficulties, but that there was a moment upon October 31 when he seemed to be at the end of his resources. To Sir John at Ypres converged all the cries for succour, and from him radiated the words of hope and encouragement which stiffened the breaking lines. To him and to his untiring lieutenant, Douglas Haig, the Empire owed more that day than has ever been generally realised. The latter was up to the firing line again and again rallying the troops. The sudden removal of the two divisional commanders of the First Corps was a dreadful blow at such a moment, and the manner in which General Landon, of the 3rd Brigade, took over the command of the First Division at a moment's notice was a most noteworthy performance. The fact that three divisions of infantry with brigades which resembled battalions, and battalions which were anything from companies to platoons, destitute of reserves save for a few dismounted cavalry, barred the path to a powerful German army, is one of the greatest feats of military history. It was a very near thing. There was a time, it is said, when the breech-blocks had actually been taken from the heavy guns in order to disable them, and some of the artillery had been passed back through Ypres. But the line held against all odds, as it has done so often in the past. The struggle was not over. For a fortnight still to come it was close and desperate. But never again would it be quite so perilous as on that immortal last day of October, when over the green Flemish meadows, beside the sluggish water-courses, on the fringes of the old-world villages, and in the heart of

THE FIRST BATTLE OF YPRES

the autumn-tinted woods, two great Empires fought for the mastery.

Such was the British epic. There was another to the north which was no less wonderful, and which will be celebrated by the poets and historians of the lands to which the victors belong. It will tell of the glorious stand during this critical ten days of the Belgians, so weary, so battered, and yet so indomitable. It will tell how they made head against the hosts of the Duke of Würtemberg, and how in the end they flooded their own best land with the salt water which would sterilise it in order to cover their front. It will tell also of the splendid Frenchmen who fought at Dixmude, of Ronarch with his invincible marines, and of Grossetti, the fat and debonair, seated in an armchair in the village street and pointing the road to victory with his cane. Not least, perhaps, in that epic will be the tale of the British monitors who, with the deadly submarines upon one side of them and the heavy German batteries upon the other, ran into the Flemish coast and poured their fire upon the right flank of the attacking Germans. Ten days the great battle swung and swayed, and then here as at Ypres the wave of the invaders ebbed, or reached its definite flood. It would be an ungenerous foe who would not admit that they had fought bravely and well. Not all our hatred of their national ideals nor our contempt for their crafty misleaders can prevent us from saluting those German officers and soldiers who poured out their blood like water in the attempt to do that which was impossible.

Chapter VIII.

The first Battle of Ypres.

CHAPTER IX

THE FIRST BATTLE OF YPRES (*continued*)

(From the Action of Gheluvelt to the Winter Lull)

Attack upon the cavalry—The struggle at Messines—The London Scots in action—Rally to the north—Terrible losses—Action of Zillebeke—Record of the Seventh Division—Situation at Ypres—Attack of the Prussian Guard—Confused fighting—End of the First Battle of Ypres—Death of Lord Roberts—The Eighth Division.

CHAPTER IX.

The first Battle of Ypres.

Attack upon the cavalry.

WHILST this severe fighting had been going on to the north of the British position, the centre, where the dismounted cavalry were holding the line of trenches, was so terribly pressed that it is an extraordinary thing that they were able to hold their own. The Second Corps, which at that time had just been withdrawn for a rest from the La Bassée lines, were the only available reinforcements. When news was flashed south as to the serious state of affairs, two regiments, the 2nd Yorkshire Light Infantry and the 2nd Scottish Borderers from the 13th Infantry Brigade, were sent up in motor-buses by road to the relief. Strange indeed was the sight of these vehicles flying along the Flemish roads, plastered outside with the homely names of London suburbs and crammed with the grimy, much-enduring infantry. The lines at Messines were in trouble, and so also were those at Wytschaete farther to the north. To this latter place

THE FIRST BATTLE OF YPRES 279

went two battalions of Shaw's 9th Brigade, the 1st Northumberland Fusiliers and the 1st Lincolns. Hard work awaited the infantry at Messines and at Wytschaete, for in both places Allenby's troopers were nearly rushed off their feet.

It has already been shown that on October 30 a severe assault was made upon the Third Cavalry Division, when the 7th Brigade (Kavanagh's) was forced out of Zandvoorde by the Fifteenth German Army Corps. Upon this same date a most strenuous attack, made in great force and supported by a terrific shell-fire, was directed along the whole line of the cavalry from Wytschaete to Messines. No British troops have been exposed to a more severe ordeal than these brave troopers, for they were enormously outnumbered at every point, and their line was so thin that it was absolutely impossible for them to prevent it from being pierced by the masses of infantry, from the Twenty-fourth Corps and Second Bavarian Corps, which were hurled against them. From the extreme left of the Second Cavalry Division near Wytschaete to the right of the First Cavalry Division south of Messines the same reports came in to the anxious General, of trenches overwhelmed or enfiladed, and of little isolated groups of men struggling most desperately to keep a footing against an ever-surging grey tide which was beating up against them and flowing through every gap. In the north Gough's men were nearly overwhelmed, the 5th Irish Lancers were shelled out of a farmhouse position, and the 16th Lancers, shelled from in front and decimated by rifles and machine-guns from the flank, were driven back for half a mile until three French battalions helped the line to reform. The pressure, however,

CHAPTER IX.

The first Battle of Ypres.

280   THE BRITISH CAMPAIGN, 1914

CHAPTER IX.

The first Battle of Ypres.

was still extreme, the Germans fighting with admirable energy and coming forward in never-ending numbers. An Indian regiment of the 7th (Ferozepore) Brigade, the 129th Baluchis, had been helping the cavalry in this region since October 23, but their ranks were now much decimated, and they were fought almost to a standstill. Two more British regiments from the Second Corps, the 1st Lincolns and the 1st Northumberland Fusiliers of the 9th Brigade, together with their Brigadier, Shaw, who was a reinforcement in himself, were, as already stated, hurried off from the south in motor-buses to strengthen Gough's line. Advancing into what was to them an entirely strange position these two veteran regiments sustained very heavy losses, which they bore with extreme fortitude. They were surprised by the Germans on the road between Kemmel and Wytschaete on the night of October 31, the same night upon which the London Scottish to the south of them were so heavily engaged. Colonel Smith succeeded in extricating the Lincolns from what was a most perilous position, but only after a loss of 16 officers and 400 men. The Fusiliers were almost as hard hit. For forty-eight hours the battle swung backwards and forwards in front of Wytschaete, and in the end the village itself was lost, but the defensive lines to the west of it were firmly established. By November the second strong French reinforcements had appeared, and it was clear that this desperate attempt to break through the very centre of the British position had definitely failed.

The struggle at Messines.

The struggle at Messines, some five miles to the south, had been even more severe and sanguinary than at Wytschaete. In the early morning of the 31st the Bays and the 5th Dragoon Guards upon the left of the

THE FIRST BATTLE OF YPRES 281

Messines position, after a heavy shell-fire, were driven out of their trenches by a sudden furious advance of the German infantry. The front of the village of Messines was held by Wild's 57th Rifles, who were driven in by the same attack, every officer engaged being killed or wounded. A reserve company of Wild's Rifles and a squadron of the 5th Dragoon Guards endeavoured to restore the fight, but could not hold the torrent. The 9th Lancers, also in front of the village and to the right of the Indians, held on for a long time, repulsing the infantry attacks, until they were driven back by the deadly shell-fire. At one time they were enfiladed on both sides and heard the Germans roaring their war-songs in the dark all round them; but they were able, owing to the coolness of Colonel Campbell and the discipline of his veteran troopers, to fall back and to reform upon the western side of the village. Lance-Corporal Seaton distinguished himself by covering the retreat of his whole squadron, remaining single-handed in his trench until his maxim was destroyed, after he had poured a thousand shots into the close ranks of his assailants.

The situation was so serious after dawn upon the 31st that General De Lisle had to call for help from Wilson's Fourth Infantry Division, holding the line upon his right. The Inniskilling Fusiliers were extended so as to relieve his right flank. The struggle within Messines was still going forward with fighting from house to house, but the Germans, who were coming on with overpowering numbers and great valour, were gradually winning their way forward. The Oxfordshire Hussars, fresh from the base, were thrown into the combat. A second line of defence

CHAPTER IX.

The first Battle of Ypres.

had been arranged a mile or so to the west, near Wulverghem, but if Messines must go the victors should at least pay the price down to the last drop of blood which could be wrung from them. Reinforcements were within sight, both French and British, but they were scanty in quantity though superb in quality. It was a most critical position, and one cannot but marvel at the load of responsibility which Sir John French had to bear upon this day, for from the left of Haig's First Corps in the north down to Neuve Chapelle in the south, a stretch of twenty-five miles, there was hardly a point which was not strained to the verge of cracking. Cool and alert, he controlled the situation from his central post and threw in such reinforcements as he could find, though, indeed, they could only be got by taking them from places where they were wanted and hurrying them to places where they were needed even more urgently. He was strengthened always by the knowledge that General Joffre behind him was doing all that a loyal colleague could to find fresh columns of his splendid infantrymen to buttress up the hard-pressed line.

For the moment, however, none of these were available, and Messines was still partly in British, partly in German hands. Briggs's 1st Brigade—Bays, 5th Dragoon Guards, and 11th Hussars—with the Oxfords, held on to the western edge of the town. To their left, linking up with Gough's men in the Wytschaete sector, was the 4th Dragoon Guards. Late in the afternoon the 2nd Scots Borderers and the 2nd Yorkshire Light Infantry, the joint detachment under Major Coke, arrived from the south, and were at once advanced upon Messines to stiffen the defence.

THE FIRST BATTLE OF YPRES

Under heavy fire they established themselves in the village. Evening fell with desperate street fighting and the relative position unchanged. Twice the Bavarians stormed into the central square, and twice they fell back after littering it with their bodies. It seemed hopeless to hold the village against the ever-growing pressure of the Germans, and yet the loss of the village entailed the loss of the ridge, which would leave a commanding position in the hands of the enemy. Village and ridge were mutually dependent, for if either were lost the other could not be held.

As it proved, it was the ridge and not the village which could no longer sustain the pressure. On the night of October 31 Mullen's 2nd Cavalry Brigade—9th Lancers, 4th Dragoon Guards, and 11th Hussars—took over the defence from Briggs. Of these, the 4th Dragoon Guards were to the left of the village upon the ridge. The London Scottish had been brought up, and they were placed upon the left of the 4th Dragoon Guards, forming a link of the defence which connected up the Second Cavalry Division with the First. The right-hand regiment of the latter, the 6th Carbineers, of Bingham's 4th Brigade, were upon the left of the London Scottish. These two regiments held the centre of the ridge. The London Scottish had already suffered considerable losses. Hurried up from the lines of communication to St. Eloi, they were pushed forward at once into action, and were exposed for hours to all the nerve-racking horrors of a heavy shell-fire endured in most insufficient trenches. A more severe ordeal was in store for them, however, during the grim night which lay before them. The admirable behaviour of Colonel Malcolm's men excited the more attention as they were the first Territorial infantry to come into action, and they set a standard which has been grandly sustained by the quarter-million of their comrades who have from first to last come into the line.

On the early morning of November 1 there had been a strong attempt within the village to improve the British position, and some ground was actually gained by the cavalrymen, the Yorkshire Light Infantry, and the Scots Borderers. What occurred, however, on the ridge to the north made all further effort a useless waste of life. The Bavarian infantry had come with an irresistible rush against the thin British line. The order to hold their ground at all costs was given, and the London Scots answered it in a way which gained the highest praise from the many soldiers who saw it. It is not claimed that they did better than their Regular comrades. That would be impossible. The most that can be said is that they proved themselves worthy to fight in line with them. After being exposed for several hours to heavy shell-fire, it was no light task for any troops to be called upon to resist a direct assault. From nine in the evening of October 31 to two in the morning, under the red glare of burning houses, Colonel Malcolm's Scottish and Colonel Annesley's Carbineers held back the Bavarian advance, an advance which would have meant the piercing of the British line. At two o'clock the Bavarians in greatly predominant force were all round the Scots, and even the reserve companies found work for their bayonets, preventing the enemy from encircling their companions. The losses were very heavy—400 men and 9 officers, including their gallant doctor, M'Nab, who was villainously stabbed as he bandaged a patient. In spite of the great pressure,

THE FIRST BATTLE OF YPRES

the ground was held all night, and it was not till dawn, when the regiment found that it was outflanked on both sides and nearly surrounded, that, under cover of the fire of E Battery R.H.A., it fell back. The Carbineers and the Scots were close together, and the Germans, with their usual quick ingenuity, approached the former with a cry of "We are the London Scots." A disaster might have occurred in the darkness but for the quickness and bravery of a young officer, Lieutenant Hope Hawkins, who rushed forward, discovered the identity of the Germans, and fell, riddled with bullets, even while he gave warning to his comrades.

The Germans had won the ridge, but the British line was still intact and growing stronger every hour. The village was held by the Scots Borderers and Yorkshiremen until nearly ten o'clock, when they were ordered to fall back and help to man the new line. The shock had been a rude one, but the danger-hour was past here as in the north.

The fateful November 1 had come and gone. The villages of Messines and Wytschaete were, it is true, in German hands, but French reinforcements of the Sixteenth Corps were streaming up from the south, the line, though torn and broken, still held firm, and the road to Calais was for ever blocked. There was still pressure, and on November 2 the 11th Hussars were badly cut up by shell-fire, but the line was impregnable. Sir John French summed up in a few terse words the true meaning of the operations just described, when he said afterwards, in addressing the 9th Lancers, "Particularly I would refer to the period, October 31, when for forty-eight hours the Cavalry Corps held at bay two German army corps.

During this period you were supported by only three or four battalions, shattered and worn by previous fighting, and in so doing you rendered inestimable service." There have been few episodes in the war which have been at the same time so splendid and so absolutely vital. The First Cavalry Division lost 50 per cent of its numbers between October 30 and November 2, and the Second Division was hardly in better case, but never did men give their lives to better purpose. Their heroism saved the Army.

Meanwhile the current of operations was evidently running strongly towards the northern end of the British line, where help was badly needed, as Haig's men had been fought almost to exhaustion. There was no British reinforcement available save only the weary Second Corps, the remains of which from this date began to be drafted northwards. It was already known that the German Emperor had appeared in person in that region, and that a great concentration of his troops was taking place. At the same time the French were making splendid exertions in order to stiffen their own line and help us in those parts, like Messines, Wytschaete, and Ploegsteert, where the attack was most formidable. It was a great gathering towards the north, and clearly some hard blows were to be struck. Northwards then went General Morland, of the Fifth Division, taking with him four more weak battalions. The whole line had moved upwards towards the danger spot, and these troops now found themselves east of Bailleul, close to the village of Neuve Eglise. For the moment General Smith-Dorrien was without an army, for half his men were now supporting General Willcocks in the south

THE FIRST BATTLE OF YPRES

and half General Allenby or General Haig in the north. The British leaders all along the line were, as usual, desperately endeavouring to make one man do the work of three, but they were buoyed up by the knowledge that good Father Joffre, like some beneficent earthly Providence, was watching over them from the distance, and that fresh trainfuls of his brave little men were ever steaming into the danger zone. Day by day the line was thickening and the task of the Kaiser becoming more difficult. It was hoped that the crisis was past. If our troops were exhausted so also, it was thought, were those of the enemy. We could feel elated by the knowledge that we had held our ground, while they could hardly fail to be depressed by the reflection that they had made little progress in spite of so many heroic efforts, and that Calais was as far from them as ever.

The narrative must now return to the defenders of the Ypres approaches, who were left in a state of extreme exhaustion by the critical action of October 31. On November 1 the First Corps was not in a condition to do more than to hold its line. This line was now near to Veldhoek, to the west of Gheluvelt village, and to that extent the Germans had profited by their desperate fighting, but this was a detail of small consequence so long as an unbroken British Army covered the town that was still the objective of the enemy. The Ninth French Corps to the north of the British had lost heavily, but to the south of the canal lay the Sixteenth French Corps, which was in comparatively good condition. This corps now made an advance to take some of the pressure off the British line, while Moussy's regiments to the north of the canal were to co-operate with Bulfin's men upon their left. Upon the left of Bulfin's 2nd Brigade were two battalions of the 4th Brigade of Guards.

One of these battalions had a terrible experience upon this morning. For some reason the trenches of the Irish Guards were exposed to an enfilading fire from the high explosives of the Germans, which wrought even more than their customary damage. For hours the Guardsmen lay under a terrific fire, to which they could make no reply, and from which they could obtain no protection. When at last, in the afternoon, they were compelled to fall back, their losses had been great, including their colonel, Lord Ardee, 7 other officers, and over 300 men. It is the hard fate of the side which is weaker in artillery to endure such buffetings with no possibility of return.

The French attack of the Sixteenth Corps had been brought to a speedy standstill, and a severe counter-attack, preceded by a heavy shell-fire, had fallen upon General Moussy's men and upon the half of the 2nd Brigade. Help was urgently needed, so the remains of the 7th Brigade from the Third Cavalry Division were hurried forward. The Germans were now surging up against the whole right and right-centre of the line. It seems to have been their system to attack upon alternate days on the right and on the centre, for it will be remembered that it was on October 29 that they gained the Gheluvelt cross-roads, and on October 31 Gheluvelt village, both in the centre, while on October 30 they captured the Zandvoorde ridge upon the British right, and now, on November 1, were pressing hard upon the right once more.

That morning the Army sustained a loss in the person of General Bulfin, who was wounded in the

THE FIRST BATTLE OF YPRES 289

head by shrapnel. Fortunately his recovery was not a lengthy one, and he was able to return in January as commander of the Twenty-eighth Division. Upon his fall, Lord Cavan, of the 4th Brigade, took over the command upon the hard-pressed right wing. At half-past one the hundred survivors of the 2nd Gordons, on the right of the Seventh Division, and the 2nd Oxford and Bucks, were desperately hard pressed by a strong German infantry advance, and so were the remains of the Sussex and Northamptons. The only available help lay in the 23rd Field Company of Royal Engineers. Our sappers proved, as they have so often done before, that their hearts are as sound as their heads. They pushed off the enemy, but incurred heavy losses. The situation was still critical when at the summons of Lord Cavan the 2nd Grenadiers advanced and cleared the Germans from the woods in the front and flank, while the 10th Hussars supported their advance. A gap had been left in the trenches from which the Irish Guards had been pushed, but this was now filled up by cavalry, who connected up with the French on their right and with the Guards upon their left. The general effect of the whole day's fighting was to drive the British line farther westward, but to contract it, so that it required a smaller force. Two battalions—the Gordons and the Sussex—could be taken out and brought into reserve. The centre of the line had a day's rest and dug itself into its new positions, but the units were greatly mixed and confused.

November 2 brought no surcease from the constant fighting, though the disturbance of these days, severe as it was, may be looked upon as a mere ground swell after the terrific storm of the last days of October.

CHAPTER IX.

The first Battle of Ypres.

On the morning of the 2nd the Ninth French Corps upon the British left, under General Vidal, sent eight battalions forward to the south and east in the direction of Gheluvelt. Part of this village was actually occupied by them. The Germans meanwhile, with their usual courage and energy, were driving a fresh attack down that Menin road which had so often been reddened by their blood. It was the day for a centre attack on their stereotyped system of alternate pushes, and it came duly to hand. An initial success awaited them as, getting round a trench occupied by the Rifles, they succeeded in cutting off a number of them. The 3rd Brigade was hurried up by General Landon to the point of danger, and a French Zouave regiment helped to restore the situation. A spirited bayonet charge, in which the Gloucesters led, was beaten back by the enemy's fire. After a day of confused and desultory fighting the situation in the evening was very much as it had been in the morning. Both that night and the next day there was a series of local and sporadic attacks, first on the front of the Second Division and then of the Seventh, all of which were driven back. The Germans began to show their despair of ever gaining possession of Ypres by elevating their guns and dropping shells upon the old Cloth Hall of that historic city, a senseless act of spiteful vandalism which exactly corresponds with their action when the Allied Army held them in front of Rheims.

November 4 was a day of menaces rather than of attacks. On this day, units which had become greatly mixed during the incessant and confused fighting of the last fortnight were rearranged and counted. The losses were terrible. The actual

THE FIRST BATTLE OF YPRES 291

strength of the infantry of the First Division upon that date was: 1st Brigade, 22 officers, 1206 men; 2nd Brigade, 43 officers, 1315 men; 3rd Brigade, 27 officers, 970 men; which make the losses of the whole division about 75 per cent. Those of the Second Division were very little lighter. And now for the 25 per cent remainder of this gallant corps there was not a moment of breathing space or rest, but yet another fortnight of unremitting work, during which their thin ranks were destined to hold the German army, and even the Emperor's own Guard, from passing the few short miles which separated them from their objective. Great was the " will to conquer " of the Kaiser's troops, but greater still the iron resolve not to be conquered which hardened the war-worn lines of the soldiers of the King.

Chapter IX. The first Battle of Ypres.

November 5 was a day of incessant shell-fire, from which the Seventh Division, the 4th and the 6th Brigades were the chief sufferers. On this day the Seventh Division, which had now been reduced from 12,000 infantry to 2333, was withdrawn from the line. In their place were substituted those reinforcements from the south which have already been mentioned. These consisted of eleven battalions of the Second Corps under General McCracken; this corps, however, was greatly worn, and the eleven battalions only represented 3500 rifles. The Seventh Division was withdrawn to Bailleul in the south, but Lawford's 22nd Brigade was retained in corps reserve, and was destined to have one more trial before it could be spared for rest. The day was memorable also for a vigorous advance of the Gloucester Regiment, which was pushed with such hardihood that they

Terrible losses.

292   THE BRITISH CAMPAIGN, 1914

CHAPTER IX.

The first Battle of Ypres.

sustained losses of nearly half their numbers before admitting that they could not gain their objective. A description has been given here of the events of the north of the line and of the cavalry positions, but it is not to be supposed that peace reigned on the south of this point. On the contrary, during the whole period under discussion, while the great fight raged at Ypres, there had been constant shelling and occasional advances against the Third Corps in the Armentières section, and also against the Indians and the Second Corps down to the La Bassée Canal.

The most serious of these occurred upon November 9. Upon this date the Germans, who had knocked so loudly at Messines and at Wytschaete without finding that any opening through our lines was open to them, thought that they might find better luck at Ploegsteert, which is a village on the same line as the other two. Wytschaete is to the north, Messines in the middle, and Ploegsteert in the south, each on the main road from Ypres to Armentières, with about four miles interval between each. The German attack was a very strong one, but the hundredfold drama was played once more. On the 3rd Worcesters fell the brunt, and no more solid fighters have been found in the Army than those Midland men from the very heart of England. A temporary set-back was retrieved and the line restored. Major Milward, of the Worcesters, a very gallant officer, was grievously wounded in this affair. The counter-attack which restored the situation was carried out mainly by the 1st East Lancashires, who lost Major Lambert and a number of men in the venture.

Action of Zillebeke.

Upon November 6, about 2 P.M., a strong German advance drove in those French troops who were on

THE FIRST BATTLE OF YPRES

the right of Lord Cavan's Brigade — 4th — which occupied the extreme right of Haig's position. The point was between Klein Zillebeke and the canal, where a German lodgment would have been most serious. The retirement of the French exposed the right flank of the 1st Irish Guards. This flank was strongly attacked, and for the second time in a week this brave regiment endured very heavy losses. No. 2 company was driven back to the support trenches, and No. 1 company, being isolated, was destroyed. Their neighbours on the left, the 2nd Grenadiers stood fast, but a great and dangerous alley-way was left for the Germans round the British right wing. The situation was splendidly saved by Kavanagh's 7th Cavalry Brigade, who galloped furiously down the road to the place where they were so badly needed. This hard-worked *corps d'élite*, consisting of the 1st and 2nd Life Guards supported by the Blues, now dismounted and flung themselves into the gap, a grimy line of weather-stained infantry with nothing left save their giant physique and their spurs to recall the men who are the pride of our London streets. The retiring French rallied at the sight of the sons of Anak. An instant later the Germans were into them, and there was a terrific *mêlée* of British, French, and Prussians, which swung and swayed over the marshland and across the road. Men drove their bayonets through each other or fired point-blank into each other's bodies in a most desperate fight, the Germans slowly but surely recoiling, until at last they broke. It was this prompt and vigorous stroke by Kavanagh's Brigade which saved a delicate situation. Of the three cavalry regiments engaged, two lost their colonels—Wilson of the Blues and Dawnay

CHAPTER IX.

The first Battle of Ypres.

of the 2nd Life Guards. Sixteen officers fell in half an hour. The losses in rank and file were also heavy, but the results were great and indeed vital. The whole performance was an extraordinarily fine one.

Early on the morning of November 7 Lawford's 22nd Brigade, which was now reduced to 1100 men, with 7 officers, was called upon to retake a line of trenches which the enemy had wrested from a neighbouring unit. Unbroken in nerve or spirit by their own terrific losses, they rushed forward, led by Lawford himself, a cudgel in his hand, carried the trench, captured three machine-guns, held the trench till evening, and then retired for a time from the line. Captains Vallentin and Alleyne, who led the two regiments into which the skeleton brigade had been divided, both fell in this feat of arms. After this action there remained standing the brigadier, 3 officers, and 700 men. The losses of the brigade work out at 97 per cent of the officers and 80 per cent of the men, figures which can seldom have been matched in the warfare of any age, and yet were little in excess of the other brigades, as is shown by the fact that the whole division on November 7 numbered 44 officers and 2336 men. It is true that many British regiments found themselves in this campaign with not one single officer or man left who had started from England, but these were usually the effects of months of campaigning. In the case of the Seventh Division, all these deadly losses had been sustained in less than three weeks. Britain's soldiers have indeed been faithful to the death. Their record is the last word in endurance and military virtue.

The division was now finally withdrawn from the fighting line. It has already been stated that there

THE FIRST BATTLE OF YPRES

were reasons which made its units exceptionally fine ones. In General Capper they possessed a leader of enormous energy and fire, whilst his three brigadiers —Watts, Lawford, and Ruggles-Brise—could not be surpassed by any in the Army. Yet with every advantage of officers and men there will always be wonder as well as admiration for what they accomplished. For three days, before the First Corps had come thoroughly into line, they held up the whole German advance, leaving the impression upon the enemy that they were faced by two army corps. Then for twelve more days they held the ground in the very storm-centre of the attack upon Ypres. When at last the survivors staggered from the line, they had made a name which will never die.

The bulk of Smith-Dorrien's Corps had now been brought north, so that from this date (November 7) onwards the story of the First and Second Corps is intimately connected. When we last saw this corps it will be remembered that it had been withdrawn from the front, having lost some twelve thousand men in three weeks of La Bassée operations, and that the Indian Corps had taken over their line of trenches. Such fighting men could not, however, be spared in the midst of such a fight. The hospital was the only rest that any British soldier could be afforded. Whilst they had still strength to stand they must line up to the German flood or be content to see it thunder past them to the coast. They were brought north, save only Bowes' 8th Brigade and Maude's 14th, which remained with the Indians in the south. Although the Seventh Division had been drawn out of the line, its attendant cavalry division still remained to give its very efficient help to General Haig.

296 THE BRITISH CAMPAIGN, 1914

CHAPTER IX.

The first Battle of Ypres.

The British position, though by no means secure, was getting stronger day by day, for General d'Urbal of the Eighth French Army to the north, and General Maud'huy to the south, had both been strongly reinforced, and with their usual good comradeship did all they could to strengthen the flanks and shorten the front of the British line.

The men of the Second Corps who had come north from the La Bassée district were not left long unmolested in their new sphere of operations. On the afternoon of November 7 there was a hot German attack upon that portion of the line which had just been vacated by the Seventh Division. The trenches were now held by the Fifth Division (Morland's).

The enemy may have hoped for some advantage from a change which they may well have observed, but they found that, though the units might be different, the same old breed still barred their path. On this occasion, after the early rush had spent itself upon the 1st Lincolns, it was the 2nd West Ridings who led the counter-charge. The line, however, was never fully re-established. A number of smaller attacks broke upon the front of the Second Division on the same day, leaving a few score of prisoners behind them as they ebbed. On the same day, November 7, the enemy got into the trenches of the 2nd Highland Light Infantry and remained in them, for all of them were bayoneted or taken. Upon this day the London Scottish were brought up into the Ypres line—a sign, if one were needed, that after the action described they were accepted as the peers of their comrades of the Regular Army, for no empty compliments are passed when the breaking of a unit may mean the enfilading of a line.

November 8 was a quiet day, but it was well known from every report of spy, scout, and aeroplane to be the lull before the storm. One German brigade came down the Menin road, and went up it again leaving a hundred dead on or beside the causeway. This attack inflicted some loss upon the 1st North Lancashires and on the 1st Scots Guards. The 1st Bedfords captured a trench that night. The 9th and the 10th were uneventful, and the tired troops rested on their arms, though never free for an hour from the endless pelting of shells. To the north and east the Eagles were known to be gathering. There were the Emperor, the Emperor's Guard, and a great fresh battle of the Germans ready for one grand final dash for Calais, with every rifle in the firing line and every cannon to support it. Grave messages came from headquarters, warning words were passed to anxious brigadiers, who took counsel with their colonels as to fire-fields and supports. Batteries were redistributed, depleted limbers refilled, and observation posts pushed to the front, while the untiring sappers gave the last touches to traverse and to trench. All was ready for the fray. So close were the lines that at many points the conversations of the enemy could be heard.

The Germans had already concentrated a large number of troops against this part of the British line, and they were now secretly reinforced by a division of the Prussian Guard. Documents found afterwards upon the dead show that the Guard had had special orders from the Emperor to break the line at all costs. The brigades which attacked were made up of the 1st and 2nd Foot Guards, the Kaiser Franz Grenadiers No. 2, the Königin Augusta Grenadiers No. 4, and

CHAPTER IX.

The first Battle of Ypres.

the battalion of Garde Jäger—13,000 men in all. It was to be victory or death with the *corps d'élite* of the German army, but it was no less victory or death with the men who opposed them. After an artillery preparation of appalling intensity for three hours along the line of both the First and Second Divisions, the infantry advance began about 9.30 on the morning of November 11 amid a storm of wind and rain. They are gregarious fighters, the Germans, finding comfort and strength in the rush of serried ranks. Even now the advance was made in a close formation, but it was carried out with magnificent dash, amazing valour, and a pedantic precision which caused, for example, the leading officers to hold their swords at the carry. The Prussian Guardsmen seemed to have lost nothing, and also to have learned nothing, since their famous predecessors lay dead in their ranks before St. Privat, forty-four years before. The attack was directed against the front of the two divisions of the First British Army Corps, but especially on the 1st Brigade, so that Guardsman faced Guardsman, as at Fontenoy. There were none of the chivalrous greetings of 1745, however, and a stern hatred hardened the hearts of either side. The German Guard charged on the north of the Menin road, while a second advance by troops of the line was made upon the south, which withered away before the British fire. Nothing could stop the Guards, however. With trenches blazing and crackling upon their flank, for the advance was somewhat diagonal, they poured over the British position and penetrated it at three different points where the heavy shells had overwhelmed the trenches and buried the occupants, who, in some cases, were bayoneted as they struggled out from under the earth. It was a terrific moment. The yells of the stormers and the shrill whistles of their officers rose above the crash of the musketry-fire and roar of the guns. The British fought in their customary earnest silence, save for the short, sharp directions of their leaders. "They did not seem angry—only business-like," said a hostile observer. The troops to the immediate north of the Menin road, who had been shelled out of their trenches by the bombardment, were forced back and brushed aside into the woods to the north, while the Germans poured through the gap. The 4th Royal Fusiliers of the 9th Brigade, upon the right of the point where the enemy had penetrated, were enfiladed and lost their gallant colonel, MacMahon, a soldier who had done great service from the day of Mons, and had just been appointed to a brigade. The regiment, which has worked as hard and endured as great losses as any in the campaign, was reduced to 2 officers and 100 men.

The German Guard poured on into the woods which lay in the immediate rear of the British position, but their formation was broken and the individualism of the Briton began to tell. Next to MacMahon's regiment lay the 1st Scots Fusiliers, sister battalion to that which had been destroyed upon October 31. With fierce joy they poured volleys into the flank of the Guard as the grey figures rushed past them into the woods. Four hundred dead Germans were afterwards picked out from the underwood at this point. The Scots Fusiliers were also hard hit by the German fire.

At this period the Germans who had come through the line had skirted the south of a large wood of half-grown trees, called the Polygon Wood, and had advanced into the farther one, named Nonnebusch. At this point they were close to the British artillery, which they threatened to overwhelm. The 41st Brigade R.F.A., and especially the 16th Field Battery, were in the immediate line of their advance, and the gunners looking up saw the grey uniforms advancing amid the trees. Colonel Lushington, who commanded the artillery brigade, hurriedly formed up a firing line under his adjutant, composed partly of his own spare gunners and partly of a number of Engineers, reinforced by cooks, officers' servants, and other odd hands who are to be found in the rear of the army, but seldom expect to find themselves in the van of the fight. It was a somewhat grotesque array, but it filled the gap and brought the advance to a halt, though the leading Germans were picked up afterwards within seventy yards of the guns.

Whilst the position was critical at this point of the front, it was no less so upon the extreme right, where the French detachment, who still formed a link between the canal on the south and the British right flank, were shelled out of their trenches and driven back. Lord Cavan's 4th Brigade, their nearest neighbours, were too hard pressed to be able to help them. To the north of the Menin road a number of British units were intact, and these held up the German flood in that region. There are two considerable woods—the Polygon to the north and the Nonnebusch to the south-west of the Polygon—the edges of which have defined the British position, while their depths have harboured their artillery. Now the 1st King's Liverpool Regiment held firm to the south of the Polygon Wood, while north of them were

THE FIRST BATTLE OF YPRES 301

the 2nd Highland Light Infantry, with a field company of Engineers. Farther to the south-west were the 1st Connaught Rangers, while on the other side of the Nonnebusch road was the 7th Cavalry Brigade. In the afternoon of this day the enemy, skirting the south of the Polygon Wood, had actually entered the Nonnebusch Wood, in which it faced the artillery as already described. In the Polygon Wood, when they penetrated the trenches of the 1st Brigade, they had the King's Liverpool Regiment on their right, which refused to move, so that for a long time the Prussian Guard and the King's lay side by side with a traverse between them. "Our right is supported by the Prussian Guard," said the humorous adjutant of the famous Lancashire regiment. While the main body of the Guard passed on, some remained all day in this trench.

The German Guardsmen had been prevented from submerging the 41st Brigade of Artillery, and also the 35th Heavy Battery, by the resistance of an improvised firing line. But a more substantial defence was at hand. The 2nd Oxford and Bucks Light Infantry, which had been in divisional reserve near Ypres, had been brought forward and found itself at Westhoek, near the threatened guns. This regiment is the old 52nd, of the Peninsular Light Division, a famous corps which threw itself upon the flank of Napoleon's Guard at Waterloo and broke it in the crisis of the battle. Once again within a century an Imperial Guard was to recoil before its disciplined rush. Under Colonel Davies the regiment swept through the wood from north-west to south-east, driving the Germans, who had already been badly shaken by the artillery fire, in a headlong rout.

Many threw down their arms. The loss to the Oxfords was surprisingly small, well under fifty in all. As they emerged from the wood they were joined by some of the 1st Northamptons from the 2nd Brigade upon the right, while on the left there was a rush of Connaughts and Highland Light Infantry from their own (Haking's) brigade and of Engineers of the 25th Field Company, who showed extraordinary initiative and gallantry, pushing on rapidly, and losing all their officers save one and a number of their men without flinching for an instant. A party of the Gloucesters, too, charged with the Northamptons upon the right, for by this time units were badly mixed up, as will always happen in woodland fighting. "It was all a confused nightmare," said one who tried to control it. The line of infantry dashed forward, a company of the Oxfords under Captain H. M. Dillon in the lead, and the khaki wave broke over a line of trenches which the Germans had taken, submerging all the occupants. There was another line in front, but as the victorious infantry pushed forward to this it was struck in the flank by a fire from French batteries, which had been unable to believe that so much progress could have been made in so short a time.

It was now nearly dark, and the troops were in the last stage of exhaustion. Of the 1st Brigade something less than 400 with 4 officers could be collected. It was impossible to do more than hold the line as it then existed. Two brave attempts were made in the darkness to win back the original front trenches, but it could not be done, for there were no men to do it. Save for one small corner of the Polygon Wood, the Germans had been completely

THE FIRST BATTLE OF YPRES 303

cleared out from the main position. At twelve and at four, during the night, the British made a forward movement to regain the advanced trenches, but in each case the advance could make no progress. At the very beginning of the second attempt General FitzClarence, commanding the 1st Brigade, was killed, and the movement fizzled out. Besides General FitzClarence, the Army sustained a severe loss in General Shaw of the 9th Brigade, who was struck by a shell splinter, though happily the wound was not mortal. The German losses were exceedingly severe: 700 of their dead were picked up within a single section of the British line, but the main loss was probably sustained in the advance before they reached the trenches. Killed, wounded, and prisoners, their casualties cannot have been less than 10,000 men.[1] It was a fine attack, bravely delivered by fresh troops against weary men, but it showed the German leaders once for all that it was impossible to force a passage through the lines. The Emperor's Guard, driven on by the Emperor's own personal impetus, had recoiled broken, even as the Guard of a greater Emperor had done a century before from the indomitable resistance of the British infantry. The constant fighting had reduced British brigades to the strength of battalions, battalions to companies, and companies to weak platoons, but the position was still held. They had, it is true, lost about five hundred yards of ground in the battle, but a shorter line was at once dug, organised, and manned. The barrier to Ypres was as strong as ever.

The strain upon the men, however, had been terrific. "Bearded, unwashed, sometimes plagued

---

[1] The German returns for the Guard alone at this battle are reported at 1170 dead, 3991 wounded, 1719 missing.

with vermin, the few who remained in the front line were a terrible crew," says the American, Coleman. "They were like fierce, wild beasts," says another observer. They had given their all, almost to their humanity, to save Britain. May the day never come when Britain will refuse to save them.

Glancing for a moment down the line to the south, there had been continuous confused contention during this time, but no great attack such as distinguished the operations in the north. Upon November 7 two brisk assaults were made by the Germans in the Armentières area, one upon the Fourth Division of the Third Corps and the other upon the Seaforth Highlanders, who were brigaded with the Indians. In each case the first German rush carried some trenches, and in each the swift return of the British regained them. There were moderate losses upon both sides. On the same date the 13th Infantry Brigade lost the services of Colonel Martyn of the 1st West Kents, who was seriously wounded the very day after he had been appointed to a brigade.

This attack upon November 11 represents the absolute high-water mark of the German efforts in this battle, and the ebb was a rapid one. Upon November 12 and the remainder of the week, half-hearted attempts were made upon the British front, which were repulsed without difficulty. To the north of the line, where the French had held their positions with much the same fluctuations which had been experienced by their Allies, the German assault was more violent and met with occasional success, though it was finally repelled with very great loss. The 14th was to the French what the 11th had been to the British—the culmination of violence and the prelude of rest. The weather throughout this period was cold and tempestuous, which much increased the strain upon the weary troops. Along the whole line from Ypres to Bethune there were desultory shellings with an occasional dash by one side or the other, which usually ended in the capture of a trench and its recapture by the supports in the rear. It was in one of these sporadic German attacks in the Klein Zillebeke section that the 2nd King's Royal Rifles held their trench against heavy odds, and their machine-gun officer, Lieutenant Dimmer, thrice wounded and still fighting, won the coveted Cross by his valour. Each gallant advance and capture of the Germans was countered by an equally gallant counter-attack and recapture by the British. The long line sagged and swayed, but never bent or broke. The era of battles had passed, but for thirty miles the skirmishes were incessant. So mixed and incessant had been the fighting that it was a very difficult task during these days to tidy up the line and get each scattered group of men back to its own platoon, company, and battalion.

On Tuesday, November 17, the fighting suddenly assumed a more important character. The attack was again in the Ypres section and fell chiefly upon the battalions of the Second Corps, if so dignified a name as "battalion" can be given to bodies of men which consisted very often of less than a normal company, commanded, perhaps, by two junior officers. The 4th Brigade of Guards was also heavily engaged this day, and so were the cavalry of the Third Division. The general locale of the action was the same as that which had been so often fought over before, the Second Corps being to the south of the Ypres—Menin

306 THE BRITISH CAMPAIGN, 1914

Chapter IX.

The first Battle of Ypres.

road, with Lord Cavan's Guardsmen upon their right and the cavalry upon the right of the Guards. After a severe shelling there was a serious infantry advance, about one o'clock, which took some trenches, but was finally driven back and chased for a quarter of a mile. McCracken's 7th Brigade bore a chief part in this fighting, and the 1st Wiltshires particularly distinguished themselves by a fine charge led by Captain Cary-Barnard. The 2nd Grenadiers did great work during the day.

An even heavier advance was made in the afternoon to the south of that which was broken in the morning. This involved an oblique advance across the British front, which was stopped and destroyed before it reached the trenches by the deadly fire of rifles and machine-guns. Over a thousand dead were left as a proof of the energy of the attack and the solidity of the resistance. Farther to the south a similar attack was beaten back by the cavalry after a preliminary shelling in which the 3rd Dragoon Guards suffered severely. This attack was repelled by the Third Cavalry Division, to which the Leicestershire and North Somerset Yeomanry were now attached. The latter did fine service in this action. Altogether, November 17 was a good day for the British arms and a most expensive one for the Germans.

End of the first Battle of Ypres.

We have now reached the end of the Battle of Ypres, which attained its maximum fury, so far as the British line was concerned, from October 29 to November 11. This great contest raged from the sand dunes of the north, where the Belgians fought so well, through the French Marine Brigade at Dixmude, and the Ninth French Corps, to General Haig's Corps, which was buttressed on the right towards

THE FIRST BATTLE OF YPRES

the latter part of the battle by the Sixteenth French Corps. Farther south yet another French corps supported and eventually took the place of the British cavalry opposite the lost villages of Wytschaete and Messines. From there ran the unbroken lines of the imperturbable Third Corps, which ended to the south in the trenches originally held by the Second British Corps, and later by the Indians. Across the La Bassée Canal the French once again took up the defence.

It is not an action, therefore, which can be set down to the exclusive credit of any one nation. Our Allies fought gloriously, and if their deeds are not set down here, it is from want of space and of precise information, not from want of appreciation. But, turning to the merely British aspect of the fight—and beyond all doubt the heavier share fell upon the British, who bore the brunt from the start to the end,—it may be said that the battle lasted a clear month, from October 12, when Smith-Dorrien crossed the La Bassée Canal, to November 11, when the German Guard reeled out of the Nonnebusch Wood. We are so near these great events that it is hard to get their true proportion, but it is abundantly clear that the battle, in its duration, the space covered, the numbers engaged, and the losses endured, was far the greatest ever fought up to that time by a British Army. At Waterloo the losses were under 10,000. In this great fight they were little short of 50,000. The fact that the enemy did not recoil and that there was no sensational capture of prisoners and guns has obscured the completeness of the victory. In these days of nations in arms a beaten army is buttressed up or reabsorbed by the huge forces of

CHAPTER IX.

The first Battle of Ypres.

which it is part. One judges victory or defeat by the question whether an army has or has not reached its objective. In this particular case, taking a broad view of the whole action, a German force of at least 600,000 men set forth to reach the coast, and was opposed by a force of less than half its numbers who barred its way. The Germans did not advance five miles in a month of fighting, and they lost not less than 150,000 men without any military advantage whatever, for the possession of such villages as Gheluvelt, Wytschaete, or Messines availed them not at all. If this is not a great victory, I do not know what military achievement would deserve the term. Ypres was a Plevna—but a Plevna which remained for ever untaken.

Death of Lord Roberts.

On November 15 Lord Roberts died whilst visiting the Army, having such an end as he would have chosen, within earshot of the guns and within the lines of those Indian soldiers whom he loved and had so often led. The last words of his greatest speech to his fellow-countrymen before the outbreak of that war which he had foreseen, and for which he had incessantly tried to prepare, were that they should quit themselves like men. He lived to see them do so, and though he was not spared to see the final outcome, his spirit must at least have been at rest as to the general trend of the campaign. The tradition of his fascinating character, with its knightly qualities of gentleness, bravery, and devotion to duty, will remain as a national possession.

The Eighth Division.

About this time, though too late for the severe fighting, there arrived the Eighth Division, which would enable Sir Henry Rawlinson to complete his Fourth Corps.

THE FIRST BATTLE OF YPRES

The Eighth Division was composed as follows :—

DIVISIONAL GENERAL—General DAVIES.
  23rd *Infantry Brigade—General Penny.*
    2nd Scots Rifles.
    2nd Middlesex.
    2nd West Yorkshires.
    2nd Devons.
  24th *Infantry Brigade—General Carter.*
    1st Worcesters.
    2nd East Lancashires.
    1st Notts and Derby.
    2nd Northamptons.
  25th *Infantry Brigade—General Lowry Cole.*
    2nd Lincolns.
    2nd Berkshires.
    1st Irish Rifles.
    2nd Rifle Brigade.
    13th London (Kensingtons).
    Artillery.
    5th Brigade R.H.A., G.O.Z.
    45th Brigade R.F.A.
    33rd Brigade R.F.A.
    Heavy Batteries 118, 119.
    2, 5, F. Cos. R.E.
    8 Signal Co.
    Divisional Cavalry.
    Northampton Yeomanry.
    8th Cyclists.

We have now arrived at what may be called the great winter lull, when the continuation of active operations was made impossible by the weather conditions, which were of the most atrocious description. It was the season which in a more classic age of warfare was spent in comfortable winter quarters. There was no such surcease of hardship for the contending lines, who were left in their trenches face to face, often not more than fifty yards apart, and each always keenly alert for any devilry upon the part of the other. The ashes of war were always redly smouldering, and sometimes, as will be seen, burst up into sudden furious flame. It was a period of rain-storms and of frost-bites, of trench mortars and of

CHAPTER IX.

The first Battle of Ypres.

hand grenades, of weary, muddy, goat-skinned men shivering in narrow trenches, and of depleted brigades resting and recruiting in the rearward towns. Such was the position at the Front. But hundreds of miles to the westward the real future of the war was being fought out in the rifle factories of Birmingham, the great gun works of Woolwich, Coventry, Newcastle, and Sheffield, the cloth looms of Yorkshire, and the boot centres of Northampton. In these and many other places oversea the tools for victory were forged night and day through one of the blackest and most strenuous winters that Britain has ever known. And always on green and waste and common, from Cromarty to Brighton, wherever soldiers could find billets or a village of log huts could be put together, the soldier citizens who were to take up the burden of the war, the men of the Territorials and the men of the new armies, endured every hardship and discomfort without a murmur, whilst they prepared themselves for that great and glorious task which the future would bring. Even those who were too old or too young for service formed themselves into volunteer bands, who armed and clothed themselves at their own expense. This movement, which sprang first from the small Sussex village of Crowborough, was co-ordinated and controlled by a central body of which Lord Desborough was the head. In spite of discouragement, or at the best cold neutrality from Government, it increased and prospered until no fewer than a quarter of a million of men were mustered and ready entirely at their own expense and by private enterprise — one of the most remarkable phenomena of the war.

CHAPTER X

A RETROSPECT AND GENERAL SUMMARY

Position of Italy—Fall of German colonies—Sea affairs—Our Allies.

THERE has been no opportunity during this somewhat breathless narrative of the great events which will ever be associated with the names of Mons, the Marne, the Aisne, and Ypres to indicate those factors which were influencing the course of the war in other regions. They do not come properly within the scope of this narrative, nor does the author profess to have any special information concerning them, but they cannot be absolutely omitted without interfering with a correct view of the general situation. They will therefore be briefly summarised in retrospect before the reader is carried on into a more particular account of the trench warfare of the early winter of 1914.

The most important European event at the outbreak of the war, outside the movement of the combatants, was the secession of Italy from the Central Powers on the grounds that her treaty applied only to wars of defence whilst this was manifestly one of aggression. Italian statesmen could speak with the more decision upon the point since the plot had been unfolded before their eyes. A year previously they had been asked to join in an unprovoked

CHAPTER X.

A retrospect and general summary.

Fall of German colonies.

attack upon Serbia, and in refusing had given clear warning to their allies how such an outrage would be viewed. The Central Powers, however, puffed up by their vainglory and by the knowledge of their own secret preparations, were persuaded that they had ample strength to carry out their intentions without aid from their southern ally. Italy, having denounced the treaty, remained a neutral, but it was always clear that she would sooner or later throw in her strength with those who were at war with Austria, her secular enemy. It was not, however, until May 1915 that she was in a position to take a definite step. It should be remembered to her eternal honour that the time at which she did eventually come in was one which was very overcast for the Allies, and that far from fulfilling the cynical German prophecy that she would "hasten to the assistance of the conqueror," she took grave risks in ranging herself upon the side of her Latin sister. Upon August 24 Japan also declared war, and by November 7 had completed her share of the common task, for Tsingtau, the only German colony in Eastern Asia, was captured by a Japanese expeditionary force aided by a British contingent. Already the vast Colonial erection of Germany, those numerous places in the sun which she had annexed all over the globe, were beginning to crumble. The little Togoland colony fell upon August 26. New Zealand took over German Samoa upon August 31. The Australians occupied the Bismarck Archipelago upon September 7, and New Guinea upon the 25th. These smaller twigs were easily lopped, but the main boughs were made of tougher stuff. A premature attack upon German East Africa by an expeditionary force from India met with a severe check immediately after landing. In South Africa the Germans succeeded in blowing into a small flame the smouldering ashes of the old Boer War. De Wet and others broke their oaths and took up arms, but the majority remained splendidly loyal, and by the beginning of December Botha had brought the insurrection to an end, and was able henceforth to devote his grand powers of leadership and organisation to the extinction of the enemy's south-western colony.

Chapter X.

A retrospect and general summary.

A word, too, about sea affairs before we turn to the further detailed account of the British winter upon the Continent. In good time the Fleet had been ordered to her war-stations at the north and east of Scotland, with the result that German ocean commerce was brought to an immediate and absolute stop. The German ships *Goeben* and *Breslau*, which were cut off at the outbreak of the war in the Mediterranean, succeeded in a very clever fashion in reaching the Dardanelles and safety. Having taken refuge at Constantinople, these ships played a prominent part in determining Turkey to take action against the Allies on October 31, a most disastrous decision both for Turkey, which met her ruin, and for the Allies, who found their task greatly increased through the excellent fighting power of the Turkish forces.

Sea affairs.

A brisk action was fought upon August 28 in the Heligoland Bight, when Admiral Beatty with his cruiser-squadron and a number of light craft visited the enemy in his own waters, sinking three German warships and sustaining no losses himself. Among the prisoners was the son of Chief Admiral Von Tirpitz. Numerous minor actions led to no noteworthy result, but the power of the submarine, already prophesied before the war, speedily made itself manifest. Several small British cruisers were destroyed by these craft, and finally a considerable disaster occurred through the sinking of the three cruisers, *Hogue*, *Aboukir*, and *Cressy*, upon September 22. This dashing and cool-headed exploit was brought off by a young lieutenant named Weddigen. Much as we suffered from his action, it was recognised in Britain as having been a remarkable deed of arms upon a very different plane to those execrable murders of civilians with which the German submarine service was afterwards associated. Some months later Weddigen's submarine rose amongst the Grand Fleet whilst it was in motion, and was rammed and destroyed by the *Dreadnought*.

The outbreak of war had seen a considerable number of German cruisers at large, and these would undoubtedly have been strongly reinforced had it not been for the speed with which the British Fleet took up its war-stations. As it was, the amount of damage to commerce was not serious, and by the New Year all the wanderers had been rounded up. The most successful raider was the *Emden*, under Captain Müller, which captured and destroyed numerous British merchant-ships, bombarded the Madras gas-works, and sank by a surprise attack a small Russian cruiser and a French destroyer before it was finally cornered and sunk by the Australian cruiser *Sydney* off Cocos Island upon November 10. Captain Müller, though forced by circumstances to adopt certain measures not recognised in honourable naval warfare, behaved on the whole in the manner which one associates with the term naval officer. The

Karlsruhe had also considerable success as a naval raider, but met her end through an unexplained explosion some little time after her consort the *Emden*. On the whole, the damage inflicted by German commerce destroyers was very much less than had been anticipated.

On November 1, Admiral Craddock's squadron, consisting of the *Monmouth*, the *Good Hope*, and two small vessels, was engaged by a superior squadron under Admiral von Spee at Coronel off the coast of Chili. The result was a British defeat, the two cruisers being sunk by gun-fire with all hands. This disaster was dramatically revenged, as within six weeks, upon December 8, a special cruiser-squadron dispatched from England under Admiral Sturdee entirely destroyed the fleet of Von Spee in the Battle of the Falkland Islands. The British Fleet was considerably stronger, and little credit can be claimed save for the admirable strategy which enabled Sturdee to find the enemy in that vast waste of waters as promptly and directly as if the meeting had been by appointment.

There were no other outstanding naval events in 1914 save a raid upon Cuxhaven by aeroplanes, escorted by light cruisers, which probably did little harm as the weather was misty. This occurred upon Christmas Day 1914. It had been preceded by an attack by German cruisers on December 16 upon West Hartlepool, Scarborough, and Whitby. As the two latter towns were open watering-places, and as numerous civilians were the victims of the raid, it was recognised from this time onwards that the German Navy was as little trammelled by international law or by the feelings of humanity as the German

CHAPTER X.

A retrospect and general summary.

CHAPTER X.

A retrospect and general summary.

Our Allies

Army had shown itself to be in France, Belgium, and Russia.

The general movement of the French armies has been touched upon in recording the experiences of the British, for after their glorious victory at the Marne and the hold-up at the Aisne, it was at Ypres that the real fighting was done, the rest of the long line down to the Swiss frontier playing a subsidiary part. The Russians, however, had experienced both extremities of fortune, for their victory at Lemberg over the Austrians upon September 2 was of a very glorious character, while their defeat by the Germans at Tannenberg in East Prussia was no less decisive. All the events of the outset of the war were inglorious for Austria, who received rapidly the punishment which she deserved for her wanton disturbance of the world's peace. Apart from the blows which she received from Russia, she was severely defeated by the Serbians on August 17, and her invading army was driven out of the country which she had wronged. At the end of the year she had lost the whole of Galicia to the Russians, who in turn had been pushed out of East Prussia by the German armies under Von Hindenburg. An invasion of Poland by the Germans was held up after very severe fighting, failing to reach Warsaw, which was its objective.

These were the main incidents of the world's war during the months which have been under review. As those months passed the terrific nature of the task which they had undertaken became more and more clear to the British, but further reflection had confirmed them in their opinion that the alternative course of abandoning their friends and breaking their pledge to Belgium was an absolutely unthinkable

A RETROSPECT

one, so that however great the trials and sacrifices in blood and treasure, they were not further embittered by the reflection that they could possibly have been avoided. Very greatly were they cheered in that dark hour by the splendid, whole-hearted help from India, Canada, Australia, and New Zealand, help which was even more valuable from a moral than from a material standpoint. With this brief synopsis we will now return to those operations which are the proper subject of this volume.

Chapter X.
A retrospect and general summary.

CHAPTER XI

THE WINTER LULL OF 1914

Increase of the Army—Formation of the Fifth Corps—The visit of the King—Third Division at Petit Bois—The fight at Givenchy—Heavy losses of the Indians—Fine advance of 1st Manchesters—Advance of the First Division—Singular scenes at Christmas.

Chapter XI.
The winter lull of 1914.

THE winter lull may be said to have extended from the great combats at Ypres of the middle of November 1914 to the opening of the spring campaign in March 1915; but we will only follow it here up to the end of the year. It was a period of alternate rest and discomfort for the troops with an ever-present salt of danger. For days they found themselves billeted with some approach to comfort in the farmhouses and villages of Flanders, but such brief intervals of peace were broken by the routine of the trenches, when, in mud or water with a clay cutting before their faces and another at their backs, they waited through the long hours, listening to the crack of the sniper's rifle, or the crash of the bursting shell, with an indifference which bordered upon thankfulness for anything that would break the drab monotony of their task. It was a scene of warfare which was new to military experience. The vast plain of battle lay in front of the observer as a flat and lonely wilderness, dotted with ruined houses from which no homely wreath of smoke

THE WINTER LULL OF 1914

rose into the wintry air. Here and there was an untidy litter of wire; here and there also a clump of bleak and tattered woodland; but nowhere was there any sign of man. And yet from the elevation of an aeroplane it might be seen that the population of a large city was lurking upon that motionless waste. Everywhere the airman would have distinguished the thin brown slits of the advance trenches, the broader ditches of the supports and the long zigzags of the communications, and he would have detected that they were stuffed with men—grey men and khaki, in every weird garment that ingenuity could suggest for dryness and for warmth—all cowering within their shelters with the ever-present double design of screening themselves and of attacking their enemy. As the German pressure became less, and as more regiments of the Territorials began to arrive, taking some of the work from their comrades of the Regulars, it was possible to mitigate something of the discomforts of warfare, to ensure that no regiments should be left for too long a period in the trenches, and even to arrange for week-end visits to England for a certain number of officers and men. The streets of London got a glimpse of rugged, war-hardened faces, and of uniforms caked with the brown mud of Flanders, or supplemented by strange Robinson Crusoe goatskins from the trenches, which brought home to the least imaginative the nature and the nearness of the struggle.

<small>CHAPTER XI.

The winter lull of 1914.</small>

Before noting those occasional spasms of activity —epileptic, sometimes, in their sudden intensity— which broke out from the German trenches, it may be well to take some note of the general development of those preparations which meant so much for the

<small>Increase of the Army.</small>

320   THE BRITISH CAMPAIGN, 1914

CHAPTER XI.

The winter lull of 1914.

future. The Army was growing steadily in strength. Not only were the old regiments reinforced by fresh drafts, but two new divisions of Regulars were brought over before the end of January. These formed the Twenty-seventh and Twenty-eighth Divisions under Generals Snow and Bulfin, two officers who had won a name in the first phase of the war. The two Divisions together formed the Fifth Army Corps under General Plumer, the officer who had worked so hard for the relief of Mafeking in 1900. The Divisions, composed of splendid troops who needed some hardening after tropical service, were constituted as follows, the list including territorial battalions attached, but excluding the artillery as well as the four original regular units in each brigade :

Formation of the Fifth Corps.

FIFTH ARMY CORPS
GENERAL PLUMER.

TWENTY-SEVENTH DIVISION.—General SNOW.

80th Brigade—General Fortescue.
Princess Pat. Canadians.
4th Rifle Brigade.
3rd King's Royal Rifles.
4th King's Royal Rifles.
2nd Shrop. Light Infantry.

81st Brigade—General MacFarlane.
9th Royal Scots (T.F.).
2nd Cameron Highlanders.
1st Argyll and Sutherlands.
1st Royal Scots.
2nd Gloucesters.
9th Argyll and Sutherlands (T.F.).

82nd Brigade—General Longley.
1st Leinsters.
2nd Royal Irish Fusiliers.
2nd Duke of Cornwall's Light Infantry.
1st Royal Irish.
1st Cambridge (T.F.).
Army Troops, 6th Cheshires.

THE WINTER LULL OF 1914

TWENTY-EIGHTH DIVISION.—General BULFIN.

83rd Brigade—General Boyle.

2nd E. Yorkshire.
1st King's Own York. Light Infantry.
1st Yorks. and Lancasters.
2nd Royal Lancasters.
3rd Monmouths (T.F.).
5th Royal Lancasters (T.F.).

84th Brigade—General Winter.

2nd Northumberland Fusiliers.
1st Suffolks.
1st Welsh.
2nd Cheshires.
12th London Rangers (T.F.).
1st Monmouths (T.F.).

85th Brigade—General Chapman.

2nd East Kent.
2nd East Surrey.
3rd Middlesex.
3rd Royal Fusiliers.
8th Middlesex (T.F.).

CHAPTER XI.

The winter lull of 1914.

Besides this new Fifth Army Corps, there had been a constant dribble of other territorial units to the front, where they were incorporated with various regular brigades. The London Scottish, which had done so well, was honoured by admission to the 1st Brigade of Guards. The Artists' Rifles, 28th London, had the unique distinction of being set aside as an officers' training corps, from which officers were actually drawn at the rate of a hundred a month. The Honourable Artillery Company, brigaded with the 7th Brigade, was among the first to arrive. Conspicuous among the newcomers were the London Rifle Brigade, the 4th Suffolk, the Liverpool Scottish, the 5th and 6th Cheshires, the 1st Herts, the 2nd Monmouthshires, Queen Victoria Rifles, and Queen's Westminsters. These were among the earlier arrivals, though it seems invidious to mention names where the spirit of all was equally good. Among the yeomanry, many had already seen considerable service—notably the North and South Irish Horse, who had served from the beginning, the Northumberland Hussars, the North Somersets, the Oxford Hussars, and the Essex Yeomanry. Most of the troops named above shared the discomfort of the winter campaign before the great arrival of the new armies from England in the spring. There can be no better earned bar upon a medal than that which stands for this great effort of endurance against nature and man combined.

To take events in their order: beyond numerous gallant affairs of outposts, there was no incident of importance until the evening of November 23, when the Germans, who had seemed stunned for a week or so, showed signs of returning animation. On this day, some eight hundred yards of trench held by Indian troops in the neighbourhood of Armentières were made untenable by the German artillery, especially by the *minen-werfer* — small mortars which threw enormous bombs by an ingenious arrangement whereby the actual shell never entered the bore but was on the end of a rod outside the muzzle. Some of these terrible missiles, which came through the air as slowly as a punted football, were 200 lbs. in weight and shattering in their effects. There was an advance of the 112th Regiment of the Fourteenth German Corps, and the empty trenches were strongly occupied by them—so strongly that the first attempt to retake them was unsuccessful in the face of the rifle and machine-gun fire of the defenders. A second more powerful counter-attack was organised by General Anderson of the Meerut Division, and this time the Germans were swept out of their position and the line

THE WINTER LULL OF 1914

re-established. The fighting lasted all night, and the Ghurkas with their formidable knives proved to be invaluable for such close work, while a party of Engineers with hand-bombs did great execution—a strange combination of the Asiatic with the most primitive of weapons and the scientific European with the most recent. It was a substantial victory as such affairs go, for the British were left with a hundred prisoners, including three officers, three machine-guns, and two mortars.

The first week of December was rendered memorable by a visit of the King to the Army. King George reviewed a great number of his devoted soldiers, who showed by their fervent enthusiasm that one need not be an autocratic War-lord in order to command the fierce loyalty of the legions. After this pleasant interlude there followed a succession of those smaller exploits which seem so slight in any chronicle, and yet collectively do so much to sustain the spirit of the Army. Now this dashing officer, now that, attempted some deed upon the German line, and never failed to find men to follow him to death. On November 24 it was Lieutenant Impey, with a handful of 2nd Lincolns; on November 25, Lieutenants Ford and Maurice with a few Welsh Fusiliers and sappers; on November 26, Sir Edward Hulse with some Scots Guards; on the same day, Lieutenant Durham with men of the 2nd Rifle Brigade—in each case trenches were temporarily won, the enemy was damaged, and a spirit of adventure encouraged in the trenches. Sometimes such a venture ended in the death of the leader, as in the case of Captain the Honourable H. L. Bruce of the Royal Scots. Such men died as the old knights did who rode out betwixt the

324   THE BRITISH CAMPAIGN, 1914

CHAPTER XI.

The winter lull of 1914.

lines of marshalled armies, loved by their friends and admired by their foes.

December 9 was the date of two small actions. In the first the 1st Lincolns of the 9th Brigade, which had been commanded by Douglas Smith since the wounding of General Shaw, made an attack upon the wood at Wytschaete which is called Le Petit Bois. The advance was not successful, the three officers who led it being all wounded, and forty-four men being hit. The attempt was renewed upon a larger scale five days later. The other action was an attack by the enemy upon some of the trenches of the Third Corps. This Corps, though it had not come in for the more dramatic scenes of the campaign, had done splendid and essential work in covering a line of fourteen miles or so against incessant attacks of the Germans, who never were able to gain any solid advantage. On this occasion the impact fell upon Gordon's 19th Brigade, especially upon the 2nd Argyll and Sutherland Highlanders and the 1st Middlesex. It was driven back with heavy loss.

Third Division at Petit Bois.

On December 14 the second and more sustained effort was made to get possession of the Petit Bois at Wytschaete, which had been attacked by the Lincolns upon the 9th. D'Urbal's Eighth French Army was co-operating upon the left. The British attack was conducted by Haldane's Third Division, and the actual advance was carried out, after a considerable artillery preparation from the batteries of two Corps, by Bowes' 8th Brigade, with the 2nd Royal Scots and the 1st Gordons in the lead. At 7.45 the guns were turned upon the big wood beyond Petit Bois, through which the supports might be advancing, and at the same hour the two regiments named swarmed forward, the Lowlanders on the left and the Highlanders on the right. The Royal Scots, under Major Duncan, carried Petit Bois with a rush, taking fifty prisoners and two machine-guns, while the Germans fled out at the other end of the wood. The Scots at once entrenched themselves and got their own machine-guns into position. The Gordons, under Major Baird, advanced with splendid dash and gained some ground, but found the position such that they could not entrench upon it, so they were forced to fall back eventually to their original position. Both they and the 4th Middlesex, who supported them, lost considerably in the affair. The total casualties in the Petit Bois action came to over four hundred, with seventeen officers, figures which were considerably swollen by the losses of the Suffolks and Irish Rifles, who continued to hold the captured position in the face of continued bombing. The French in the north had no particular success and lost 600 men. The importance of such operations is not to be measured, however, by the amount of ground won, but by the necessity of beating up the enemies' quarters, keeping them pinned to their positions, and preventing them from feeling that they could at their own sweet wills detach any reinforcements they chose to thicken their line upon the Eastern frontier, where our Russian Allies were so insistently pressing.

On the morning of December 19 an attack was made upon the German lines in the Festubert region by Willcocks' Indian Corps, the Meerut Division, under General Anderson, attacking upon the left, and the Lahore, under General Watkis, upon the right. The object of the movement was to co-operate with the French in an advance which they had planned. The Meerut attack was successful at first, but was driven back by a counter-attack, and some hundreds of Indian infantry were killed, wounded, or taken. In the case of the Lahore attack the storming party consisted of the 1st Highland Light Infantry and the 4th Ghurkas. Both of these units belong to the Sirhind Brigade, but they were joined in the enterprise by the 59th Scinde Rifles of the Jullundur Brigade. These latter troops had a long night march before reaching the scene of the operations, when they found themselves upon the right of the attack and within two hundred and fifty yards of the German trenches. Judging the operations from the standard reached at a later date, the whole arrangement seems to have been extraordinarily primitive. The artillery preparation for a frontal attack upon a strong German line of trenches lasted exactly four minutes, being rather a call to arms than a bombardment. The troops rushed most gallantly forward into the dark of a cold wet winter morning, with no guide save the rippling flashes of the rifles and machine-guns in front of them. Many were so sore-footed and weary that they could not break into the double. Some of the Indians were overtaken from behind by a line of British supports, which caused considerable confusion. An officer of Indians has left it on record that twice running he had a revolver clapped to his head by a British officer. All of the battalions advanced with a frontage of two companies in columns of platoons. Both the Ghurkas and Highlanders reached the trench in the face of a murderous fire. The left of the 59th, consisting of Punjabi Mahomedans, also reached the trench. The right, who were Sikhs, made an

THE WINTER LULL OF 1914

equally gallant advance, but were knee-deep in a wet beetroot field and under terrific machine-gun fire. Their gallant leader, Captain Scale, was struck down, as was every Indian officer, but a handful of the survivors, under a Sikh Jemadar, got into a German sap, which they held for twenty-four hours, taking a number of prisoners.

Day had dawned, and though the British and Indians were in the enemy trenches, it was absolutely impossible to send them up reinforcements across the bullet-swept plain. The 59th discovered a sap running from their left to the German line, and along this they pushed. They could not get through, however, to where their comrades were being terribly bombed on either flank by the counter-attack. It was an heroic resistance. Colonel Ronaldson, who led the party, held on all day, but was very lucky in being able to withdraw most of the survivors after nightfall. Of the hundred Punjabis who held one flank, only three returned, while thirteen wounded were reported later from Germany. The others all refused to surrender, declaring that those were the last orders of their British officers, and so they met their honoured end. It had been a long and weary day with a barren ending, for all that had been won was abandoned. The losses were over a thousand, and were especially heavy in the case of officers.

The Germans, elated by the failure of the attack, were in the mood for a return visit. In the early dawn of the next day, December 20, they began a heavy bombardment of the Indian trenches, followed by an infantry attack extending over a line of six miles from south of the Bethune Canal to Festubert in the north. The attack began by the explosion of

CHAPTER XI.

The winter lull of 1914.

Heavy losses of the Indians.

a succession of mines which inflicted very heavy losses upon the survivors of the Ghurkas and Highland Light Infantry. The weight of the attack at the village of Givenchy fell upon the exhausted Sirhind Brigade, who were driven back, and the greater part of Givenchy was occupied by the enemy. General Brunker fell back with his Brigade, but his line was stiffened by the arrival of the 47th Sikhs of the 8th Jullundur Brigade, who were in divisional reserve. These troops prevented any further advance of the Germans, while preparations were made for an effective counter-stroke.

Little help could be given from the north, where the line was already engaged, but to the south there were considerable bodies of troops available. The situation was serious, and a great effort was called for, since it was impossible to abandon into the hands of the enemy a village which was an essential bastion upon the line of defence. The German attack had flooded down south of Givenchy to the Bethune Canal, and a subsidiary attack had come along the south of the Canal with the object of holding the troops in their places and preventing the reinforcement of the defenders of Givenchy. But these advances south of the village made no progress, being held up by the 9th Bhopals and Wilde's 57th Rifles of the 7th Ferozepore Brigade between Givenchy and the Canal, while the 1st Connaught Rangers of the same brigade stopped it on the southern side of the Canal. Matters were for a moment in equilibrium. To the south of the Canal energetic measures were taken to get together a force which could come across it by the Pont Fixe or road bridge, and re-establish matters in the north.

THE WINTER LULL OF 1914   329

The struggle had broken out close to the point of junction between the British forces and those of General Foch of the Tenth French Army, so that our Allies were able to co-operate with us in the counter-attack. It was directed by General Carnegy, and the assault was made by the 1st Manchesters, the 4th Suffolk Territorials, and some French territorials. The Manchesters, under the leadership of Colonel Strickland, made a most notable attack, aided by two companies of the Suffolks, the other companies remaining in reserve on the north bank of the Canal. So critical was the position that the 3rd Indian Sappers and Miners were set the dangerous task, under very heavy shell-fire, of mining the bridge over the Canal. The situation was saved, however, by Colonel Strickland's fine advance. His infantry, with very inadequate artillery support, pushed its way into Givenchy and cleared the village from end to end. Three hundred of the Manchesters fell in this deed of arms. Not only did they win the village, but they also regained some of the lost trenches to the north-east of Givenchy. This was the real turning-point of the action. There was at the time only the one very wet, very weary, and rather cut-up Jullundur Brigade between the Germans and Bethune —with all that Bethune stood for strategically. To the east the 9th Bhopals and 57th Rifles still held on to their position. It was only to the north that the enemy retained his lodgment.

But the fight to the north had been a bitter one all day, and had gone none too well for the British forces. The Indians were fighting at an enormous disadvantage. As well turn a tiger loose upon an ice-floe and expect that he will show all his wonted fierceness and activity. There are inexorable axioms of Nature which no human valour nor constancy can change. The bravest of the brave, our Indian troops were none the less the children of the sun, dependent upon warmth for their vitality and numbed by the cold wet life of the trenches. That they still in the main maintained a brave, uncomplaining, soldierly demeanour, and that they made head against the fierce German assaults, is a wonderful proof of their adaptability.

About ten o'clock on the morning of the 20th the German attack, driving back the Sirhind Brigade from Givenchy, who were the left advanced flank of the Lahore Division, came with a rush against the Dehra-Dun Brigade, who were the extreme right of the Meerut Division. This Brigade had the 1st Seaforth Highlanders upon its flank, with the 2nd Ghurkas upon its left. The Ghurkas were forced to retire, and the almost simultaneous retirement of the defenders of Givenchy left the Highlanders in a desperate position with both flanks in the air. Fortunately the next Brigade of the Meerut Division, the Garhwal Brigade, stood fast and kept in touch with the 6th Jats, who formed the left of the Dehra-Dun Brigade, and so prevented the pressure upon that side from becoming intolerable. The 9th Ghurkas came up to support the 2nd Ghurkas, who had not gone far from their abandoned trenches, and the 58th Indian Rifles also came to the front. These battalions upon the left rear of the Highlanders gave them some support. None the less the position of the battalion was dangerous and its losses heavy, but it faced the Germans with splendid firmness, and nothing could budge it. Machine-guns are stronger

THE WINTER LULL OF 1914

than flesh and blood, but the human spirit can be stronger than either. You might kill the Highlanders, but you could not shift them. The 2nd Black Watch, who had been in reserve, established touch towards nightfall with the right of the Seaforths, and also with the left of the Sirhind Brigade, so that a continuous line was assured.

In the meantime a small force had assembled under General MacBean with the intention of making a counter-attack and recovering the ground which had been lost on the north side of Givenchy. With the 8th Ghurkas and the 47th Sikhs, together with the 7th British Dragoon Guards, an attack was made in the early hours of the 21st. Colonel Lempriere of the Dragoon Guards was killed, and the attack failed. It was renewed in the early hours of the morning, but it again failed to dislodge the Germans from the captured trenches.

December 21 dawned upon a situation which was not particularly rosy from a British point of view. It is true that Givenchy had been recovered, but a considerable stretch of trenches were still in the hands of the Germans, their artillery was exceedingly masterful, and the British line was weakened by heavy losses and indented in several places. The one bright spot was the advance of the First Division of Haig's Corps, who had come up in the night-time. The three brigades of this Division were at once thrown into the fight, the first being sent to Givenchy, the second given as a support to the Meerut Division, and the third directed upon the trenches which had been evacuated the day before by the Sirhind Brigade. All of these brigades won their way forward, and by the morning of the 22nd much of the ground which had been taken by the Germans was reoccupied by the British. The 1st Brigade, led by the Cameron Highlanders, had made good all the ground between Givenchy and the Canal. Meanwhile the 3rd Brigade had re-established the Festubert position, where the 2nd Welsh and 1st South Wales Borderers had won their way into the lost trenches of the Ghurkas.

This was not done without very stark fighting, in which of all the regiments engaged none suffered so heavily as the 2nd Munsters (now attached to the 3rd Brigade). This regiment, only just built up again after its practical extermination at Etreux in August, made a grand advance and fought without cessation for nearly forty-eight hours. Their losses were dreadful, including their gallant Colonel Bent, both Majors Day and Thomson, five other officers, and several hundreds of the rank and file. So far forward did they get that it was with great difficulty that the survivors, through the exertions of Major Ryan, were got back into a place of safety. It was the second of three occasions upon which this gallant Celtic battalion gave itself for King and Country. Let this soften the asperity of politics if unhappily we must come back to them after the war.

Meanwhile the lines upon the flank of the Seaforths which had been lost by the Dehra-Dun Brigade were carried by the 2nd Brigade (Westmacott), the 1st North Lancashire and 1st Northamptons leading the attack with the 2nd Rifles in support. Though driven back by a violent counter-attack in which both leading regiments, and especially the Lancashire men, lost heavily, the Brigade came again, and ended by making good the gap in the line. Thus the situation on the morning of the 22nd looked very

THE WINTER LULL OF 1914

much better than upon the day before. On this morning, as so many of the 1st Corps were in the advanced line, Sir Douglas Haig took over the command from Sir James Willcocks. The line had been to some extent re-established and the firing died away, but there were some trenches which were not retaken till a later date.

Such was the scrambling and unsatisfactory fight of Givenchy, a violent interlude in the drab records of trench warfare. It began with a considerable inroad of Germans into our territory and heavy losses of our Indian Contingent. It ended by a general return of the Germans to their former lines, and the resumption by the veteran troops of the First Division of the main positions which we had lost. Neither side had gained any ground of material value, but the balance of profit in captures was upon the side of the Germans, who may fairly claim that the action was a minor success for their arms, since they assert that they captured some hundreds of prisoners and several machine-guns. The Anglo-Indian Corps had 2600 casualties, and the First Corps 1400, or 4000 in all. The Indian troops were now withdrawn for a rest, which they had well earned by their long and difficult service in the trenches. To stand day after day up to his knees in ice-cold water is no light ordeal for a European, but it is difficult to imagine all that it must have been to a Southern Asiatic. The First Corps took over the La Bassée lines.

About the same date as the Battle of Givenchy there was some fighting farther north at Rouge Banc, where the Fourth Corps was engaged and some German trenches were taken. The chief losses in this affair

334   THE BRITISH CAMPAIGN, 1914

CHAPTER XI.
The winter lull of 1914.
Singular scenes at Christmas.

fell upon those war-worn units, the 2nd Scots Guards and 2nd Borderers of the 20th Brigade. Henceforward peace reigned along the lines for several weeks—indeed Christmas brought about something like fraternisation between British and Germans, who found a sudden and extraordinary link in that ancient tree worship, long anterior to Christianity, which Saxon tribes had practised in the depths of Germanic forests and still commemorated by their candle-lit firs. For a single day the opposing forces mingled in friendly conversation and even in games. It was an amazing spectacle, and must arouse bitter thoughts concerning those high-born conspirators against the peace of the world, who in their mad ambition had hounded such men on to take each other by the throat rather than by the hand. For a day there was comradeship. But the case had been referred to the God of Battles, and the doom had not yet been spoken. It must go to the end. On the morning of the 26th dark figures vanished reluctantly into the earth, and the rifles cracked once more. It remains one human episode amid all the atrocities which have stained the memory of the war.

So ended 1914, the year of resistance. During it the Western Allies had been grievously oppressed by their well-prepared enemy. They had been overweighted by numbers and even more so by munitions. For a space it had seemed as if the odds were too much for them. Then with a splendid rally they had pushed the enemy back. But his reserves had come up and had proved to be as superior as his first line had been. But even so he had reached his limit. He could get no further. The danger hour was past. There was now coming the long, anxious year of equilibrium, the narrative of which will be given in the succeeding volume of 1915. Finally will come the year of restoration which will at least begin, though it will not finish, the victory of the champions of freedom.

Chapter XI. The winter lull of 1914.

INDEX

Abell, Major, 70
Abercrombie, Colonel, 94
Agadir, 7
Aisne, battle of the, 162-199
Alexander, Major, 82
Algeciras, 7
Allen, Major, 209
Allenby, General, 56, 80, 88, 96, 97, 126, 155, 204, 226, 279, 287
Alleyne, Captain, 294
Allfrey, Captain, 149
Alsace, 43, 57
Anderson, General, 322, 325
Anley, Colonel, 105
Anley, General, 229
Annesley, Colonel, 284
Ansell, Colonel, 132
Antwerp, fall of, 193; Naval Division at siege of, 195
Ardee, Lord, 288
Army, the Russian, 138; at battle of Gumbinnen, 138; at battle of Lemberg, 139; at battle of Tannenberg, 139
Ashburner, Captain, 70
Asquith, Right Hon. H. H., 18
Austin, Dr., 93
Australia, offer of service, 34, 37; Bismarck Archipelago captured by, 312; German colony of New Guinea captured by, 312; 317
Austria, Archduke Francis Ferdinand of, assassinated at Sarajevo, 12
Austria-Hungary, annexes Bosnia and Herzegovina, 1908, 2; presents ultimatum to Serbia, 14; declares war against Serbia, 15

Baird, Major, 325
Balfour, Lieutenant, 167
Bannatyne, Colonel, 255
Barnes, Colonel, 241
Battenberg, Prince Louis of, 40
Battenberg, Prince Maurice of, 256

Bavaria, Crown Prince of, 145
Beatty, Admiral Sir David, 313
Belgians, King of the, 198
Belgium, infraction of neutrality, 12
Below-Saleske, von, 19
Benson, Captain, 73
Bent, Colonel, 332
Berners, Captain, 172
Bernhardi, General von, 1, 8, 159
Bethmann-Hollweg, von, 17, 21, 23, 28
Bidon, General, 247
Bingham, General, 283
Bismarck Archipelago, German colony, captured by Australian forces, 312
Blewitt, Lieutenant, 268
Boger, Colonel, 83
Bols, Colonel, 207
Bolton, Colonel, 244
Botha, Right Hon. Louis, 34, 313
Bottomley, Major, 259
Bowes, General, 218, 295, 324
Boyd, Lieutenant, 266
Bradbury, Captain, V.C., 130, 131
Brett, Colonel, 102
Bridges, Major Tom, 118
Briggs, General, 128, 130, 174, 282, 283
British Expeditionary Force: departure from England, 50; its composition, 52, 86; its arrival in France, 53; its reception by the French people, 54; advance into Belgium, 57
Brooke, Captain, 260
Bruce, Captain the Hon. H. L., 323
Brunker, General, 328
Buckle, Major, 222
Bulbe, Lieutenant, 78
Bulfin, General, 154, 156, 166, 167, 169, 170, 171, 179, 186, 265, 273, 287, 288, 320
Bulow, General von, 84, 144, 154
Bülow, Prince von, 3

338   THE BRITISH CAMPAIGN, 1914

Burrows, Major, 168
Butler, Colonel, 229
Butler, Major Leslie, 116
Byng, Captain, 70
Byng, General, 210, 233

Cadogan, Colonel, 237, 264
Campbell, Captain, 73
Campbell, Colonel (5th Dragoon Guards), 281
Campbell, Colonel (9th Lancers), 80, 149
Campbell, Lieutenant, 130
Campbell, Major, 227
Canada, offer of service, 34, 37; 317
Canneau, General, 144, 204, 212, 221
Capper, General, 232, 244, 265, 269, 295
Carey, Captain, 70
Carnegy, General, 329
Carr, Lieutenant Laurence, 259
Carter, Major, 253
Cary, General Langlé de, 144
Cary-Barnard, Captain, 306
Castelnau, General, 44, 145, 193
Cathcart, Captain, 168
Cavan, Lord, 289, 293, 300, 306
Cawley, Major, 132
Ceylon, offer of service, 34
Chapman, Corporal, 227
Charleroi, battle of, 141
Charrier, Major, 119, 120, 121
Chetwode, General, 58, 121
Christie, Major, 112
Churchill, Right Hon. Winston S., 5, 31, 40, 196
Chute, Lieutenant, 121
Clive, Hon. Windsor, 92
Clutterbuck, Captain, 111
Cobb, Irvin, American correspondent with German Army, 64
Cobbold, Colonel, 214
Coke, Major, 282
Coleman, American volunteer, quoted, 119, 149, 303
Coles, Colonel, 266
Congreve, General, V.C., 187, 229
Cookson, Colonel, 167
Cornish-Bowden, Major, 151
Coronel, naval battle off, 315
Craddock, Admiral, 315
Cramb, Professor, 30
Creek, Captain, 253
Crichton, Major, 241

Crossley, Sergeant-Major, 222
Cutbill, Captain, 102
Cuthbert, General, 71, 79, 98

Dalrymple, Lord, 244
D'Amade, General, 123
Daniell, Major, 212
Danks, Lieutenant, 93
Dashwood, Lieutenant, 167
Davey, Major, 70
Davies, Colonel, 301
Davies, General, 90, 93, 132, 153, 173
Davis, Harding, American correspondent with German Army, 62, 64
Dawnay, Colonel, 293
Day, Major, 332
Dease, Lieutenant Maurice, V.C., 70
De Crespigny, Captain, 128
Deimling, General von, 269
De Lisle, General, 80, 148, 156, 157, 174, 204, 226, 281
De Mitry, General, 247, 255
Derbyshire, Gunner, 130
D'Espercy, General, 144, 146
Dillon, Captain H. M., 302
Dimmer, Lieutenant, V.C., 181, 305
Doran, General Beauchamp, 60, 69, 113, 150, 174, 218
Dorell, Sergeant, V.C., 130, 131
Doughty, Major, 102
Dour, action at, 79
Drummond, General, 84, 103
Dubail, General, 145
Duff, Colonel Grant, 171
D'Urbal, General, 296, 324
Durham, Lieutenant, 323
Dykes, Colonel, 105

Earle, Colonel, 259
East Africa, German colony of, attack on, fails, 312
East Coast, raid on, by German cruisers, 315
Edmunds, Captain, 93
Edward VII., 6
Elliott, Dr., 93
Ellison, Captain, 152
Emden, exploits of the, 314
Emmich, General von, 44

Fairlie, Captain, 241
Falkland Islands, naval battle off, 315

INDEX 339

Ferguson, General, 80, 177, 190, 211
Findlay, General, 153
Fisher, Lord, 5
FitzClarence, General, 258, 270, 303
Flint, Lieutenant, 175
Foch, General, 144, 148, 150, 154, 202, 329
Foljambe, Captain, 168
Forbes, Major Ian, 241
Ford, Lieutenant, 323
Forrester, Major, 259
Frameries, action at, 77
Fraser, Major, 244
French, General Sir John, 54, 58, 62, 74, 75, 76, 77, 84, 87, 96, 97, 116, 119, 126, 135, 145, 156, 164, 183, 186, 198, 202, 220, 234, 236, 245, 246, 247, 251, 275, 276, 282, 285

Geddes, Lieutenant-Colonel, 169
George V. visits the Army in France, 323
Germany, Heligoland ceded to, 2; agitation in, against Great Britain during Boer War, 3; navy bill of 1900, 4; anti-British agitations in, 9; root causes of hatred of Great Britain in, 10; and world-power, 10; preparations for war by, 11; declares war against Russia, 15; against France, 15; proposes that Great Britain should remain neutral, 17; and Belgian neutrality, 19; character of her diplomacy, 19, 20; invades Belgium, 21; Great Britain declares war on, 21; treatment of the departing Embassies, 22; the claim for culture in, 29
Germany and the Next War, 9
Gheluvelt, battle of, 265
Gibbs, Colonel, 79
Giffard, Lieutenant, 269
Gifford, Lieutenant, 130
Givenchy, fight at, 327
Glasgow, Sergeant, 227
Gleichen, General Count, 61, 79, 82, 83, 98, 157, 207
Gloster, Colonel, 224
Godley, Private, V.C., 70
Gordon, Captain B. G. R., 259

Gordon, Colonel, 114
Gordon, General, 215, 230, 324
Gordon, Lieutenant, 181
Goschen, Sir Edward, ambassador at Berlin, 17, 21, 22, 23, 24
Gough, General, 126, 150, 155, 203, 204, 226, 279, 280, 282
Grant, Major, 168
Graves, Lieutenant, 114
Great Britain, cedes Heligoland to Germany, 2; sympathy and respect for German Empire in, 2; agreement with France, 1903, 6; agreement with Russia, 1907, 6; maritime power of, 10; efforts for peace by, 16; reply to German proposal of neutrality, 17; declares war against Germany, 21; preparations for possible naval war in, 31; effect of German war policy in, 32
Green, Major, 168
Grenfell, Captain the Hon. F., 82
Grey, Sir Edward (now Viscount), proposes a conference of Ambassadors, 16; replies to German proposal of neutrality, 17; suggests limitation of the conflict, 19; 20, 33
Grierson, General, 55
Griffin, Colonel, 105, 158
Guernsey, Lord, 172

Haig, General Sir Douglas, 55, 56, 72, 77, 84, 88, 89, 90, 126, 133, 157, 173, 183, 190, 236, 239, 241, 246, 247, 249, 250, 251, 256, 260, 265, 270, 275, 276, 282, 286, 287, 295, 306, 331, 333
Haking, General, 72, 94, 157, 173, 176, 302
Haldane, General, 104, 106, 112, 206, 324
Haldane, Lord, 36
Hamilton, Adjutant Rowan, 171
Hamilton, Captain, 93
Hamilton, General Sir Hubert, 77, 157, 177, 208
Hankey, Major, 270
Harter, Staff-Captain, 176
Hasted, Colonel, 177
Haussen, General von, 139, 144
Hautvesnes, action at, 153

Hawarden, Lord, 92
Hawkins, Lieutenant Hope, 285
Hay, Lord Arthur, 172
Headlam, General, 110
Heeringen, General von, 145
Heligoland Bight, battle in, 313
Heligoland ceded to Germany, 1890, 2
Herbert, Captain, 208
Hindenburg, General von, 139, 316
Hogan, Sergeant, V.C., 224
Holt, Lieutenant, 71
Hoskyns, Captain, 152
Huggan, Dr., 180
Hull, Colonel, 70
Hulse, Sir Edward, 323
Hunter-Weston, General, 104, 106, 107, 229, 230

Impey, Lieutenant, 323
India, offer of service, 34; 317
Ingham, Major, 69
Italy secedes from the Central Powers, 311

Jagow, von, Secretary for Foreign Affairs at Berlin, 21, 23, 25
Japan declares war, 312; captures German colony of Tsingtau, 312
Jarvis, Corporal, V.C., 71
Jelf, Major, 168
Joffre, General, 44, 57, 62, 74, 76, 126, 127, 144, 178, 198, 202, 251, 255, 282, 287
Johnston, Captain, 175
Johnstone, Major, 169

Kavanagh, General, 262, 279, 293
Kerr, Colonel, 269
Kitchener, Lord, becomes Secretary of State for War, 34; his estimate of duration of war, 38; appeals for volunteers, 38; 54, 56
Kluck, General von, 83, 84, 88, 95, 143, 144, 145, 146, 148, 154
Knight, Colonel, 154
Kruseik cross-roads, fight for, 256

Lamb, Lieutenant, 131
Lambert, Major, 292
Landon, General, 172, 248, 254 260, 265, 269, 276, 290
Landrecies, engagement at, 90
Lansdowne, Lord, 33
Law, Right Hon. A. Bonar, 33

Lawford, General, 273, 291, 294, 295
Lawrence, Colonel, 229
Leach, Lieutenant, V.C., 224
Le Cateau, battle of, 96-137, 141
Leckie, Captain Malcolm, 82
Legard, Captain, 222
Le Gheir, action of, 229
Leman, General, 45, 46, 47
Lemberg, battle of, 139, 316
Lempriere, Colonel, 331
Lichnowsky, Prince, German ambassador to Great Britain, 19, 20, 25
Liége, 45, 46, 47, 141
Lister, Captain, 71
Lloyd, Major, 167, 168
Lomax, General, 269
Longley, Colonel, 99
Longwy, battle of, 141
Loring, Colonel, 243
Lorraine, 43, 57
Lushington, Lieutenant-Colonel, 132
Luxemburg, duchy of, 44

MacBean, General, 331
McCracken, General, 69, 78, 88, 104, 190, 208, 215, 219, 291, 306
McKenna, Right Hon. Reginald, 5, 31
Mackenzie, General Colin, 209
MacLachlan, Lieutenant-Colonel, 171
MacMahon, Colonel, 70, 221, 299
M'Nab, Captain, 284
Maistre, General, 220
Maitland, Major, 171
Malcolm, Colonel, 283, 284
Manoury, General, 144, 146, 148
Marne, battle of the, 138-161
Martyn, Colonel, 304
Maubeuge, fortress of, 85, 141, 163, 184
Maude, General, 295
Maud'huy, General, 296
Maurice, Lieutenant, 323
Maxse, General, 169, 179
Messines, fight at, 280
Michel, General, 49
Michell, Captain, 122
Milne, General, 110
Milward, Major, 292
Mitford, Major, 241
Monck, Captain, 91
Mons, battle of, 50-95, 141
Mons, retreat from, chronology of events, 136-137

INDEX 341

Montresor, Colonel, 167
Morland, Colonel, 268
Morland, General, 211, 224, 286, 296
Morris, Colonel, 133
Morritt, Lieutenant, 73
Moussy, General, 288
Mülhausen, battle of, 141
Mullens, General, 80, 221, 283
Mundy, Lieutenant, 130
Munro, General, 269

Namur, 48, 49, 76, 141
Navy, the, mobilisation of, 40
Neeld, Admiral, 25
Nelson, Gunner, V.C., 130, 131
Nery, combat of, 127
Neuve Chapelle, first fight of, 219
Newfoundland, offer of service, 34
New Guinea, German colony of, captured by Australian forces, 312
New Zealand, offer of service, 34, 37; captures German colony of Samoa, 312; 317
Nicholson, Lieutenant, 121
Nicholson, Major, 171
Nietzsche, 8
Nimy, defence of the bridges of, 68

Oliver, Captain, 169
Ommany, Captain, 269
Orford, Captain, 102
Osborne, Driver, 130
Ourcq, battle of the, 145
Ovens, Colonel, 244

Pack-Beresford, Major, 79
Paley, Major, 269
Paris, General, 195
Parker, Major, 112
Pau, General, 44
Paynter, Captain, 243
Peel, Major, 268
Pell, Colonel, 266
Pennecuick, Lieutenant, 156
Penny, Sergeant-Major, 222
Perceval, Colonel, 269
Petit Bois, fight at, 324
Phillips, Major, 168
Pilken Inn, fight of, 252
Plumer, General, 320
Pollard, Lieutenant, 82
Ponsonby, Colonel, 168
Pont-sur-Sambre, action near, 94

Poole, Major, 111
Popham, Captain, 188
Powell, American journalist, quoted, 63, 198
Powell, Major, 250
Prichard, Major, 268
Prowse, Major, 231
Prussia, Crown Prince of, 145, 163
Prussia, Prince Henry of, 25
Prussian Guards, attack of, at Ypres, 297; Kaiser's order to, 297
Pulteney, General, 56, 126, 152, 157, 175, 178, 190, 206, 214, 215, 218, 227

Rawlinson, General Sir Henry, 224, 232, 236, 237, 241, 251, 256, 308
Rees, Captain, 268
Regiments:
Artillery—
Royal Field Artillery, 69, 70, 71, 78, 82, 88, 89, 92, 100, 105, 110, 120, 153, 169, 192, 249, 268, 271, 272, 273, 300, 301
Royal Horse Artillery, 263; E Battery, 285; J Battery, 122, 150; K Battery, 236; L Battery, 80, 128, 130, 131, 133
Heavy, 109, 110, 301
Howitzer, 88, 105
Honourable Artillery Company, 321
Cavalry—
1st Life Guards, 263, 293
2nd Life Guards, 263, 293
Royal Horse Guards (Blues), 263, 293
2nd Dragoon Guards (Queen's Bays), 85, 128, 131, 132, 155, 280, 282
3rd Dragoon Guards, 272, 306
4th (Royal Irish) Dragoon Guards, 58, 80, 118, 187, 188, 282, 283
5th Dragoon Guards, 280, 281, 282
6th Dragoon Guards (Carabineers), 283, 284, 285
7th Dragoon Guards, 331
1st Dragoons (Royals), 263, 272
2nd Dragoons (Scots Greys), 122, 263
3rd Hussars, 263
4th Hussars, 263
10th Hussars, 241, 272

Regiments:
Cavalry—
11th Hussars, 131, 282, 283, 285
15th Hussars, 93, 120, 121
18th Hussars, 149
20th Hussars, 58
5th (Royal Irish) Lancers, 227, 279
9th Lancers, 80, 82, 149, 281, 283, 285
12th Lancers, 122, 227
16th Lancers, 226, 279
Essex Yeomanry, 322
Irish Horse, 242, 322
Leicestershire Yeomanry, 306
North Somerset Yeomanry, 306, 322
Northumberland Hussars, 242, 322
Oxfordshire Hussars, 281, 282, 322
Guards—
Coldstream, 90, 91, 92, 119, 120, 132, 168, 169, 171, 172, 191, 248, 259, 265
Grenadier, 90, 92, 150, 237, 244, 258, 259, 265, 289, 293, 306
Irish, 90, 92, 132, 150, 172, 255, 265, 288, 289, 293
Scots, 119, 169, 171, 242, 243, 244, 252, 253, 259, 260, 271, 297, 323, 334
Infantry—
Argyll and Sutherland Highlanders, 84, 100, 102, 216, 230, 324
Artists' Rifles (28th London), 321
Bedford, 174, 207, 236, 264, 266, 297
Berkshire, 93, 153, 255, 272
Black Watch, 119, 150, 169, 170, 171, 252, 258, 259, 331
Border, 243, 260
Buffs (East Kent), 214
Cameron Highlanders, 169, 171, 248, 252, 253, 332
Cameronians (Scottish Rifles), 84, 100, 131
Cheshire, 82, 83, 154, 174, 216, 321
Connaught Rangers, 94, 157, 301, 302, 328
Devon, 210, 219, 224
Dorset, 207, 208, 210, 216
Dublin Fusiliers, 106, 112
Duke of Cornwall's, 62, 72, 73, 99, 150, 151, 174, 215, 216, 224
Durham Light Infantry, 187, 188, 229

Regiments:
Infantry—
East Lancashire, 106, 229, 292
East Surrey, 72, 73, 99, 103, 150, 151, 174, 190, 215
East Yorkshire, 187, 188
Essex, 105, 106
Gloucester, 171, 182, 248, 250, 254, 260, 290, 291, 302
Gordon Highlanders, 60, 69, 72, 78, 113, 114, 219, 259, 273, 289, 324, 325
Hampshire, 106, 231
Herts, 321
Highland Light Infantry, 188, 242, 296, 301, 302, 326
Inniskilling Fusiliers, 105, 158, 229, 281
Irish Fusiliers, 106, 206
King's Liverpool, 90, 153, 255, 300, 301
King's Own Scottish Borderers, 61, 71, 72, 103, 209, 211, 278, 282, 284, 285, 334
King's Royal Rifles, 93, 153, 166, 167, 168, 169, 182, 188, 253, 256, 265, 268, 290, 305, 332
Lancashire Fusiliers, 105, 158, 229
Leinster, 229, 230
Lincoln, 60, 151, 174, 210, 279, 280, 296, 323, 324
Liverpool Scottish, 321
London (Kensingtons), 309
London Rifle Brigade, 321
London Scottish, 280, 283, 284, 285, 296, 321
Manchester, 99, 100, 102, 216, 218, 220, 224, 329
Middlesex, 60, 68, 69, 70, 72, 78, 84, 100, 103, 131, 207, 209, 216, 219, 230, 324, 325
Monmouthshire, 321
Munster Fusiliers, 119, 120, 154, 169, 242, 331
Norfolk, 82, 109, 174, 219
Northampton, 154, 166, 167, 176, 180, 181, 252, 273, 289, 302, 332
North Lancashire, 154, 166, 167, 168, 170, 250, 253, 265, 268, 297, 332
Northumberland Fusiliers, 68, 72, 78, 208, 209, 210, 279, 280
Oxford and Bucks, 289, 301, 302
Queen Victoria Rifles, 321
Queen's Westminsters, 321

INDEX 343

Regiments:
Infantry—
Queen's (West Surrey), 168, 170, 176, 181, 182, 191, 240, 248, 253, 259, 260, 261, 266, 271
Rifle Brigade, 106, 323
Royal Fusiliers, 60, 68, 70, 71, 72, 209, 210, 212, 220, 221, 299
Royal Irish, 60, 210, 212
Royal Irish Fusiliers, 112
Royal Irish Rifles, 69, 78, 89, 219, 220, 221, 235
Royal Lancaster, 105, 111, 229
Royal Scots, 60, 77, 114, 207, 209, 210, 323, 324, 325
Royal Scots Fusiliers, 60, 68, 71, 72, 103, 210, 211, 237, 241, 242, 264, 266, 299
Seaforth Highlanders, 106, 112, 206, 304, 330, 332
Sherwood Foresters, 187, 188, 227, 228, 229
Somerset Light Infantry, 106, 229, 231
South Lancashire, 79, 88, 148, 215, 220
South Staffordshire, 153, 240, 244, 253
South Wales Borderers, 172, 191, 192, 248, 249, 261, 270, 332
Suffolk, 99, 100, 102, 108, 224, 321, 325, 329
Sussex, 153, 166, 167, 169, 187, 249, 273, 289
Warwick, 106, 111, 112, 206, 240, 243
Welsh, 172, 191, 254, 261, 266, 268, 332
Welsh Borderers, 260, 271
Welsh Fusiliers, 84, 100, 237, 240, 264, 323
West Kent, 61, 62, 71, 72, 79, 103, 215, 221, 222, 304
West Riding, 61, 71, 79, 103, 296
West Yorkshire, 187, 188, 190
Wiltshire, 88, 177, 190, 219, 221, 237, 241, 242, 306
Worcester, 150, 188, 215, 216, 242, 243, 270, 271, 292
York and Lancaster, 214
Yorkshire, 240, 264
Yorkshire Light Infantry, 61, 71, 103, 215, 221, 278, 282, 284, 285

Regiments:
Royal Engineers, 70, 100, 127, 164, 175, 289, 300, 301, 302, 323
Indian Army—
129th Baluchis, 279
9th Bhopal Infantry, 220, 328, 329
2nd Gurkhas, 330
4th Gurkhas, 326, 328
8th Gurkhas, 225, 331
9th Gurkhas, 330
58th Indian Rifles, 330
3rd Indian Sappers and Miners, 329
6th Jats, 330
59th (Scinde) Rifles, 218, 326, 327
15th Sikhs, 218, 219
47th Sikhs, 218, 220, 221, 328, 331
Vaughan's Indian Rifles, 225
Wilde's 57th Rifles, 281, 328, 329

Reynolds, Captain (R.F.A.), V.C., 110
Reynolds, Captain (9th Lancers), 149
Rheims Cathedral, bombarded by Germans, 189
Rickman, Major, 106
Rising, Captain, 250
Robb, Major, 188
Roberts, Lord, death of, while visiting the Army in France, 308
Robertson, Sir William, 134
Rolt, General, 61, 72, 98, 100
Ronaldson, Colonel, 327
Roper, Major, 207
Rose, Captain (Northumberland Fusiliers), 78
Rose, Captain (Royal Scots Fusiliers), 71
Ruggles-Brise, General, 245, 295
Russell, Second Lieutenant, 222
Ryan, Major, 332

Salisbury, late Lord, 2
Saltoun, Master of, 115
Samoa, German colony, captured by New Zealand, 312
Sandilands, Captain, 78
Sandilands, Colonel, 89
Sarajevo, 13
Sarrail, General, 145
Savage, Captain, 181
Scale, Captain, 327
Sclater-Booth, Major, 80, 130
Scott, Admiral Sir Percy, 42
Scott-Kerr, General, 90, 132
Seaton, Lance-Corporal, 281

Seely, Colonel, 158
Serbia, reply to Austrian ultimatum, 15; King of, appeals to the Czar, 15
Serocold, Colonel, 167
Shaw, General, 60, 78, 174, 186, 190, 210, 211, 279, 280, 303, 324
Shore, Captain, 83
Smith, Captain Bowden, 70
Smith, Colonel (Lincoln), 280
Smith, Colonel Baird (R.S.F.), 266
Smith, Colonel Osborne (Northampton), 181
Smith, General Douglas, 324
Smith, Lieutenant, 70
Smith-Dorrien, General Sir Horace, 55, 56, 60, 72, 83, 84, 88, 95, 96, 97, 108, 109, 116, 119, 217, 218, 220, 221, 222, 286, 295, 307
Snow, General, 89, 104, 106, 108, 126, 320
Solesmes, action at, 88
South Africa, offer of service, 34; insurrection in, 313
Spee, Admiral von, 315
Spread, Lieutenant, 168
Stephen, Captain, 260
Stewart, Captain, 9, 155
Strickland, Colonel, 329
Stucley, Major, 259
Sturdee, Admiral, 315
Swettenham, Major, 122

Tannenberg, battle of, 139, 141, 316
Teck, Prince Alexander of, 226
Tew, Major, 99, 103
Thomson, Major, 332
Thruston, Lieutenant, 152
Togoland, German colony, captured by British forces, 312
Tower, Lieutenant, 70
Treitschke, 8
Trench, Captain, 269
Trevor, Major, 103
Triple Alliance and Triple Entente, 6
Tsingtau, German colony, captured by Japanese, 312
Tulloch, Colonel, 127
Turner, Colonel, 151

Uniacke, Colonel, 259

Vallentin, Captain, 294
Vandeleur, Captain, 102
Vandeleur, Major, 208
Venner, Colonel, 225
Vereker, Lieutenant, 92
Vidal, General, 290
Villars-Cotteret, action of, 132

Ward, Colonel, 103, 126
Ward, Lieutenant, 73
War Loan, success of the, 40
Warre, Major, 168
Wasme, action at, 79
Watkis, General, 217, 325
Watson, Lieutenant Graham, 114
Watson, Major, 168, 253, 266
Watts, General, 295
Welchmann, Lieutenant, 78
Wellesley, Lord Richard, 259
Westmacott, General, 332
White, Second Lieutenant, 222
Willcocks, General Sir James, 224, 225, 286, 325, 333
William II., Emperor of Germany, telegram to Kruger, 3; visits England, 3; 20; his message to Sir Edward Goschen, 24; 28, 48; special appeal to his troops at Ypres, 261
Williams, Captain, 271
Williams, General, 230
Wilson, Colonel (Blues), 293
Wilson, Colonel (R.E.), 127
Wilson, General, 86, 104, 106, 281
Wing, General, 110, 224
Wormald. Colonel, 122
Worsley, Lord, 263
Wright, Captain Theodore, 70, 175
Würtemberg, Duke of, 141, 144
Wyatt, Corporal, 92

Yate, Major, V.C., 103
Ypres, first battle of, 232-310

Zandvoorde, fight of, 262
Zillebeke, action of, 292

www.ingramcontent.com/pod-product-compliance
Lightning Source LLC
Chambersburg PA
CBHW030816190426
43197CB00036B/499